Anonymous

Rights And Wrongs of the North And the South

Oil on the Waters

Anonymous

Rights And Wrongs of the North And the South
Oil on the Waters

ISBN/EAN: 9783744753913

Printed in Europe, USA, Canada, Australia, Japan

Cover: Foto ©Andreas Hilbeck / pixelio.de

More available books at **www.hansebooks.com**

RIGHTS AND WRONGS

OF THE

NORTH AND THE SOUTH:

OIL ON THE WATERS.

"The North and South, Thou hast created them." — *The Bible.*

BOSTON:
J. E. TILTON AND COMPANY.
1867.

TO THE MEMORY OF HIM,

NOW NO MORE,

TO WHOM THE "LETTERS" OF THIS WORK WERE ORIGINALLY
ADDRESSED; WHO, BORN OF EQUAL NORTHERN AND
SOUTHERN PARENTAGE, PASSED THE EQUAL
HALF OF HIS SHORT LIFE

AT THE SOUTH AND AT THE NORTH;

AND BEING WARMLY ATTACHED TO THE SUNNY REGIONS OF THE
FORMER, WHILE EQUALLY ENJOYING THE PRIVILEGES AND
ENTERPRISE OF THE LATTER, AND COMBINING IN
HIMSELF WARM, GENIAL, AND WINNING
QUALITIES,
WITH INDUSTRY AND TALENT OF A HIGH ORDER OF CULTIVATION,
MADE HIS CHARACTER BUT AN EPITOME OF WHAT
SHOULD BE OUR NOBLE UNION;

THIS VOLUME

IS AFFECTIONATELY INSCRIBED.

ERRATA.

On page 83, a comma after "people at large."
" 90, for "position" read "portion."
" 126, for "life" read "light."
" 133, the passage commencing, "This patriotic ardor," and ending — "on this continent," should be included in parentheses.
On pages 164, 166, 171, 209, 211, for "doctrine of State rights," read "doctrine of State-Rights."
On page 196, eighth line from the top, the word "constitutionally" should be in Italics.
On page 268, a comma for the semicolon between "sands" and "stranded."
On page 294, for "fortified" read "forfeited."
" 374, eighth line from the top, for "And" read "and."
" 375, for "*O tempores!*" read "*O tempora!*"
On page 382, for "they believe to be right" read "they believed to be right."
On page 405, for "his Excellency" read "the Executive."
" 434, for "cynosure" read "sinecure."

TO THE PUBLIC.

It would hardly be necessary to prefix these few lines, were it not, that, in the undoubted quiet which will immediately succeed the result and decision of the late great annual elections, the title for the present volume ("Oil on the Waters") might be considered a misnomer, a gratuitous and superfluous effort to allay the party-*strife* which no longer exists.

But this title was selected, the work prepared (mainly), and the publication designed, during the highest political excitement of the season; and it has only been by circumstances beyond the control of the author that the latter has been delayed. This is not regretted, however, as it has afforded an opportunity to follow up the discussions instituted to their latest and most important features; and with its original purpose, as a work of *conciliation* as far as might be, it will still, no doubt, come gratefully to the great political minority, and others of the country who may seem to have been politically defeated in the results of the late contest.

To the Republican party this volume is offered, as being in itself historical evidence of the original position of that party during the war, — the first half having been then written, — and contains, it is believed, but a reflection of the true state and opinions of the loyal sections at that time. The remainder of the work but follows logically from that commencement; and it is trusted that this exposition will clear up, to many minds, much that was misapprehended or but dimly seen. Thus to the whole country — to every section and to all parties — it is designed to appeal.

The "Introduction" also should, properly, have been remodelled, or might have been dispensed with, in the more recent circumstances: but, as the volume was already in type, it would have been difficult to alter the arrangement; and it has, therefore, been allowed to remain as originally written.

That this work may assist in developing and bringing to light the true principles and theory of our Government, especially in this now critical period, and that it may help to warm, sustain, and encourage the hearts and minds of many who have been laboring, as they believed, for the true welfare and interests of their country, is the highest hope and ambition of

THE AUTHOR.

NOVEMBER, 1866.

CONTENTS.

	PAGE
INTRODUCTION	9

SECTION I.
LETTERS TO A NATIVE SOUTHERNER.

A General View of the Causes and Principles of the War against Secession 15

SECTION II.
REVIEW OF NORTHERN ARGUMENTS FOR SECESSION.

FIRST ARGUMENT. — Examination of the Declaration of Independence and the Constitution of the United States 63
SECOND ARGUMENT. — Powers reserved to the People 79
THIRD ARGUMENT. — Who are the " People "? 82
FOURTH ARGUMENT. — Italy and the Italians 89
FIFTH ARGUMENT. — Difference between Revolution and Secession. The American Revolution, or Separation from Great Britain 95
SIXTH ARGUMENT. — Question of "Conquest" and Military Force.. 104
SEVENTH ARGUMENT. — The Right, and not the Right 107
EIGHTH ARGUMENT. — Civil and Religious Liberty. Our Fathers. The Work of To-day 122

SECTION III.
STATE RIGHTS.

Mr. Davis's Theory 135

SECTION IV.

Re-organization. The Present Congress 155
Arbitrary Arrests 174

	PAGE
Martial Law	181
Emancipation	188
Re-admission of the States	195
Treason and its Penalty	207
Reconstruction	213

SECTION V.

The Great Issues of the Country	231
Platform of Congress	233
Radical Republicanism	251
The Three Rebellions	265
The Good resulting	271
Conservatism and Progress	277
A Vision of the Future	280

SECTION VI.

The Present Aspect of Political Parties. The Radical Convention	285
Points of Agreement between the President and Congress	291
The Difference between the Executive and Congressional Party	298
The Massacre at New Orleans	311
Northern and Southern Radicalism	313
The Constitutional Amendment	318
Impartial Suffrage	325
The Civil-rights and Freedmen's-bureau Bills	337
In or Out of the Union	341
Origin of the Congressional Party	354
The Will of the People	379
The Issue before the People	384
"Peace" Proposals	389
Powers of the Government	399
Our Republican Faith and Principles	406
The Perils of the Hour	412
The Citizen-President	431

INTRODUCTION.

THE great throb and thrill, of national as well as individual life frequently goes on so vigorously and energetically, that one is apt, in youth at least, to feel that such life is in itself a guaranty of its own existence and perpetuity; forgetting, oftentimes, that the outward prosperity is not the real power and impulse, but that these lie embedded in the elements and principles of life within; and, what is more, that we must continue to recognize the principles underlying, maintain them sound and healthy at their core, and then regard them as the chart and compass by which we must be guided.

An individual without principle is like the driftwood brought down in our large mountain-streams, and cast hither and thither, becoming finally stranded wherever by chance it may have been carried.

So with a nation: without a strong and permanent constitution, it must be drifted wherever events, or the shocks and wear of time, may carry it, to be left at last to ruin and decay. On the contrary, with such constitution, *its* principle — if high, steady, earnest — it has a perennial growth, and may look, in a healthy old age, still to send forth new and vigorous shoots of life.

In order that such may be our destiny, we certainly ought to tread carefully through this period of transition, — our passage from youth to early but fast-ripening manhood.

We had grown hitherto with the principles instilled into our childhood, which were taken in by instinct, as it were, with our earliest breath, without — youth-like — discriminating, or investigating very closely, what these were; our knowledge of them, rather, being general and indefinite. But, buoyant, healthful, and elastic, we felt no further need. In the mean time, as is natural with all rapid development and prosperity, there came to be latitude on all sides, and venturesome daring more or less, until we have found by experience the necessity of recurring to the real foundation elements of our existence; and henceforth, in our maturer age, these should, undoubtedly, be more thoroughly understood and applied.

It is with a view to this necessity that the following pages are offered to the public, believing that their simple treatment of these subjects will come home to all classes of readers.

The work had its origin in the "Letters" of the first section, which were actually written at the commencement of our civil war to a young friend who was deeply interested in the course of events; and these, or extracts from them, are here introduced as comprising a general view of the state of affairs at that time, and as recalling to us the simple, precise platform on which we then stood. The writing was then further continued for the author's own more perfect information on these great topics, believing, also, that the intelligence thus elicited might be useful to others; and it will be so at this time especially, it is trusted, when a multiplicity of ideas has obscured, in some respects, the simple points at issue.

Being exempt, by position, from party bias, the author has written with no view to party feeling or party purposes; being impelled by a simple love and duty to our country,—our whole country, as such, — and by the sense that every citizen should do what in him lies for its true welfare and prosperity. Now is the time, it is believed, when many of the former bonds seem loose and broken, that we ought to endeavor to establish and make permanent in this our favored country that happy period of republics, as it was in ancient Rome, —

> "Then none was for a party
> Then all were for the State," —

by forming one great party of the nation, that would rally around its true and simple principles; regarding these, in our birth and history, as the providentially-given guides to our peculiar place among the nations of the earth.

The writer does not presume to imply, by the title chosen for this work, that there is to be found in it a panacea for all the evils to which our country has been and still is subject: on the contrary, it being one of argument mainly, there will be those, undoubtedly, who might produce opposing arguments. The name is designed simply to express the calm, fraternal, and impartial mode and feeling in which it has been the aim to treat these important subjects; believing that the work will thus commend itself to all sections of our country, notwithstanding that there has been no "compromise" offered on any of the great questions of the day, any further than would seem to be warranted by strict propriety; and no hesitation in using strong and decided expressions wherever they seemed called for. Only such treatment would be manly and honorable, and acceptable to manly and honorable readers, — those who desire sincerely to seek and to know the *truth*.

On this ground, too, the author has not hesitated to speak of the *wrong* wherever it has appeared to exist, and to acknowledge the *right* wherever it has seemed to be manifested. So only, it is believed, can we become reconciled and harmonious one with another; readily acknowledging errors, even if they are our own, and willingly recognizing the truth wherever it may be found.

RIGHTS AND WRONGS.

SECTION I.

LETTERS TO A NATIVE SOUTHERNER; BEING A GENERAL VIEW OF AFFAIRS AT THE COMMENCEMENT OF THE WAR.

. . . NATURALLY, you are warmly attached to the land of your birth, and will ever, perhaps, experience a sentiment in regard to it that you may not possess for any other portion of our country. We have dear relatives living there; and so have innumerable Northern families friends or relations in the Southern States. For myself, I have no other personal feeling than that of tender affection and interest for every part of the South equally with the North; and I think I may speak for the thousands who are thus situated, certainly for those with whom I am here acquainted.

I cannot call up in myself a single feeling of partiality for one State over another, as a State, — not even in favor of that of my birth; which, also, is to me now but one of the great whole, since my greatest privileges and interests have been elsewhere. The only exception in regard to peculiar attachment is that in which I now live as *my home*, not as a State. But naturally, where one's home and personal interests are, one's affections must be closely centred. You yourself undoubtedly prefer ——, because there is your home, and your particular interests are there; and, wherever this is the case, — yours, mine, or any one's, in one State or another, — *there* must be an individual, private feeling, predominating over that for any other place.

But in regard to the country *as* a country, our whole country, I can truly say that I know no difference or any partiality for one portion of it more than another. My heart never throbs for one particular section, North or South. I never think of looking upon these with sectional interest. It never occurred to me, until these late differences brought it so palpably to light, that there was a division. I had thought of the United States but as our one, united country; and it seemed to me a noble thing, our embracing under one government so vast a diversity of climate, soil, and resources. I have ever looked with pride upon the South, as the blooming, luxuriant garden of our land, never feeling for a moment that I, or any one, had not a claim and interest there as well as the Southerners themselves; and I was disappointed that the English prince,* during his visit here, should not have seen that rich and glorious portion of our country, — glorious in the exuberance of its soil, and so rich in its natural productions. I have often, myself, looked forward to the time when I should enjoy this favored sunny clime; not as a *foreigner*, but as a *citizen;* not as a *privilege*, but as my *birthright*, — the birthright of any citizen of the United States.

It is this habit of looking upon our country as an inseparable whole, not being able to divest one part of it of the character and responsibilities of another portion, that has made so sensitive much of the Northern mind on the subject of slavery. And owing to this, too, it was, that to myself and to other travellers when abroad (being enabled by distance to view our

---

* The visit of the Prince of Wales occurred in the autumn preceding.

native land more distinctly as a unit, and as a unit only) the fact of slavery loomed up like a dark blot on our virgin territory, which *should* lie so fresh and fair in this New Western World, separated from all that had ever stained the history of the past in the Old.

It is common to say that Northerners do not understand the "institution of the South;" but if the South, from nearness to it, see it only on the more favorable side, the North, by being able to view it from a distance, is more qualified to behold the dark side of it. To say there was no dark side, would be simply ignorance; or, worse, falsity. The dark side is not only in regard to the Africans, but in the demoralizing effect that slavery must inevitably have upon the whites. It would be in vain to assert, in defiance of our knowledge of human nature, that the whites would not oftentimes be wrought up to the highest state of irritation by the provocations of dull and inefficient slaves, — as thousands of them must be, — even if this were the worst. I do not mean, nor does any one mean, to say that there have not been kind and excellent masters, and good and well-conducted slaves: there have been, no doubt, thousands of the one and the other. But, with all the good that might be brought forward, the counter-balancing evils are so many and so great, that it seems remarkable that any person could be found, removed from its immediate influences, and able to judge impartially, who should for a moment uphold slavery. Not that I consider the people of the South themselves so highly responsible in this great evil. It had descended to them, and it is not to be wondered at that they should not have found any means of ridding themselves of it. It is a difficult thing, often, to abandon even an old worn garment that we have become accustomed to; and we had rather a thousand times, for ease and comfort's sake, wear it, than put on a new one. It is a natural feeling of attachment which we acquire: how much more, then, must the people at the South dread to let go that with which they, and even their ancestors, have had all their lifetime living associations and a daily interest! I do not, thus, in the least wonder at the persistency with which they have clung to slavery, appalling as it must be in many of its features to some of the most reflective among them.

That we should not blame those who are thus born to evils that they know not how to avoid, or who, by custom, are so familiar with them, that they do not seem to them such, is natural; and every exculpation should be allowed as far as possible. But that those, as I have already said, who do not occupy the same standpoint by custom or necessity, and who must know all the political as well as moral evils and wrongs of slavery, should yet defend and advocate it in these States, or anywhere else, is, to say the least, a very different matter.

Nevertheless, this subject has been to our country, in every way, a great and perplexing question. Being so great, and affecting in its measure and in its influences the country as a whole, the North could not but be interested in it as well as the South, and sensitive with regard to it; although but very few, comparatively, would have made efforts to agitate the subject, feeling that it was one for the particular States themselves to deal with. And because it was so perplexing a question — as to what should be done with, or what would become of, the negroes, &c. — was one reason, no doubt, why the South was reluctant to do any thing about it. To my mind, no effectual movement with regard to slavery could have been made but by the Southern

States themselves, unless some *genius* or other, elsewhere, had been able to make some proposition that should have been to them feasible and acceptable; for the Constitution guaranteed to the South non-interference with the system, as with all other State institutions. Besides, it is in the order of things that they who possess any thing may renounce it or not, as they please, or as they honestly think proper. No one could compel them where the holding or the renouncing did not infringe upon that other's rights.* Therefore, undoubtedly, the GOVERNMENT, standing between the North and South, would still protect the latter in her own political rights a hundred years hence, as it had always done, *unless*, in the mean time, the Constitution were altered on that point; for we could have no executive magistracy, that, in the short space of four years, could violate that Constitution with impunity. The enlightened sense and the *sensitiveness* of the whole community on such a point would be too great: a *revolution* is in the hands of the people every four years to remove such a one from office, and put another in his stead. Therefore, as far

---

* Of course, allusion is here made simply to civil and political rights.

as the National Administration is concerned, the Constitution must and would be carried out; and it would be left to the States forever to manage their own system of slavery, *unless*, as was said before, the Constitution should be amended on that point. No change in slavery could have been effected, therefore, from that quarter (excepting always in the event of such change or "amendment" of the Constitution): and as the South never had made any movement towards that end; and as the difficulties in the way were continually becoming greater; and as, from the immense sacrifice of property it would involve, it was hardly to be looked for that the Southern States should take any steps towards emancipation; and as, in fact, their purpose seemed evident to try to invigorate the system rather than to diminish it,* — there appeared to be no prospect of any voluntary or peaceable discontinuance of it. Yet, at the same time, the sentiment of all civilization was but becoming stronger and stronger against it. Its inju-

---

* It was not only the effort of the South to extend slavery into the Territories, but also so to amend the Constitution as to allow of its passing into and establishing itself in any of the States. — See Debates in Congress of 1860, 1861.

rious effects, both moral and political, were constantly becoming more obvious; and any solution of the difficulty could only become, apparently, more and more hopeless.

At this juncture, while men's hands were tied, as it were, on every side, voluntarily or involuntarily, a new force suddenly came in, and that from the very South itself, to give a new phase to affairs, namely, that of absolute resistance to the National Government, and from this very cause, — slavery; which it (the Government) had ever protected to the very limits of the Constitution, because that Constitution gave to the States the *right* to be so protected. This state of affairs was wholly unexpected. No man dreamed of the present condition of the country, and certainly no one ever planned the events that have so dramatically succeeded one another.

This new current, new influence, brought in, must, undoubtedly, change the whole complexion of affairs; since they could hardly be supposed to remain the same after this upheaval as before. And, if a settlement *in the Union* be the end, some new legislation in regard to slavery must take place in order to put the subject at rest in one way or another; for, most assuredly, we could nevermore look for peace in respect of it on the same footing as formerly, since the issue that has now been made, *not* on the part of the Government, — which constitutionally had ever protected slavery, or, at least, had given to it its rights, — but on the part of the Southern States themselves, who chose to make this issue.

We cannot but believe that Providence is thus working out, unexpectedly to us, what no man or men have ever been able to do; and that, eventually, the whole South, as well as the North, will be thankful if they shall be disburdened in any practicable way of their "peculiar" institution; its *peculiarity* making it so difficult to harmonize the different portions of the nation, — such a difference of habits and institutions preventing assimilation.

I should indeed feel for the people of the South in their being stripped of what is to them *property*. Personally, I have attached no particle of blame to them for keeping their slaves, *if they did not see it their duty* to let them go; but when they attempted to extend their system over places as yet untainted, and over which they had no peculiar right, I did feel that every individual in the country, who, unswayed by custom, by attachment or interest, could see all that political and moral evil, should stand up in his utmost right and might to defend such Territories from that taint until they should have the power (in becoming States) to say whether or not they would adopt the system. And this was exactly the state of things; this was the one question at issue. And the same moral right — right of freedom of opinion — that the South had to advocate the extension of slavery, carrying it into the free Territories, the North had to resist such extension; and, if it felt that this was morally and politically wrong, it could only rise with every fibre of its being against the equal exertions of the South in its favor. This was but just, and the only justice, — *that those innocent Territories might be left to their own choice when they should be admitted to be States*, and not be fettered beforehand with a system under which they might groan ever after. For this the North had a right; not to " dictate," — that she could never do; she had no right to do so; and the instinctive sense of the community would be aroused against any portion of the country " dictating" to another portion, — but to contend by speech, by discussion, by any lawful means in her power.

She had a right also, on other grounds, to maintain, with all the energy possible and needful, that the South should not carry into the public Territories a peculiarity which the North had nothing to balance with; for free labor in this country has not been on a political level with slave labor. Slaves are both labor-machinery and votes in one: whereas the free man is a vote; but the machinery with which he works is separate. His mechanical labor is not represented as the slaveholder's is; and there could be no justice in the Southern emigrants or residents having their labor represented by a vote in Congress, and the Northerners not. This "right," however, the North had not much insisted upon, although it is certainly a very prominent one. Her view was more particularly to the future welfare of the Territories when they should become States; and in this we think the whole outside world would, in general, take part with her.

This was a question (whether slavery should be carried into the Territories) for the people at large to decide; and when put to the vote, as it was, in effect, by the Chicago Platform which nominated Mr. Lincoln, an overwhelming majority, in the election of that president, decided for the position taken by the Northern and Western States. In such a case, under our system, or under any representative government, there would be nothing left for the party which had failed in its choice but to acquiesce until another election should give it an opportunity, if possible, of reversing the decision. Was such the course of the Southern States? Did they calmly and dispassionately yield to the acknowledged principle of our institutions, of our National Government, to which the South was as much pledged as the North, — the principle that the majority must decide? On the contrary, did they not, even before the election took place, begin to repudiate that fundamental principle on which the very Government was formed, and declare, that, if such should be the vote of the majority, they would not submit? — which rebellion, if successful, must necessarily overturn the whole constitution of things.

The want of a "popular majority" in the election of Mr. Lincoln is spoken of. The majority by electoral votes, which alone is required by the Constitution, was overwhelming. The popular vote for his predecessor, Mr. Buchanan, was very much less than that for Mr.

Lincoln; and, in that contest, the opposing candidate (Gen. Frémont) was undoubtedly the choice of the Northern people. But did they dream of seceding because a Southern president was elected? or admit the thought that his administration was not binding upon them after he was constitutionally elected, because such election was not *pleasing* to them? They waited patiently until the presidential term was over; and then it was not unnatural that they should be pleased to have *their* turn in the national councils, which had remained in the hands of the South for so many years. They are not able now, however, it seems, to pass this term in peace, but are compelled to spend it in maintaining the very existence of our institutions.

Is there, then, no sacredness in governments? Should any government in the world, regularly organized by the will of the people, be thus lightly regarded, broken up, and destroyed, against the will of a constitutionally established majority, by any portion of the people, on such grounds, — that the minority could not carry their point? What the defeated party had resolved upon before the election they carried into effect immediately after, without pausing to see what course was to be pursued by the new administration. What should they have done but discuss the matter in full congress of the people? and, with the strong feeling at the South, who knows but that, possibly, a majority might have been obtained for a peaceable separation? But, in their precipitation, no opportunity was given for any such consideration of the subject; and thus, by *force*, was violated the sacred compact of government. It is well known that the Federal Government had in every way refrained from violence; that it was the seceding States that fired upon an unarmed vessel,* employed by the Government; which shot was not returned by the Government. It was the seceding States also, that, with seven thousand troops, assailed an almost ungarrisoned fortress.† It is well known, too, that the National Administration disavowed any intention of retaliation for this assault upon its property, but placed itself in an attitude of defence, and of legal, constitutional authority. The South maintains that it was provoked or incited to this by the Government persisting in retaining property situated within its borders.‡ Most truly: for in no pos-

---

* Star of the West. † Fort Sumter.
‡ The Constitution provides for the national property — forts, &c. — being dispersed among the several States.

sible way, on any principle of the Federal Government, could it give up, on demand of any State whatever, the national property, which belonged to the whole people; not even to sell it, unless that people by its united vote relinquished its claim to it. The opportunity to do this (by peaceful deliberation) had never been given; and there was nothing, therefore, for the President to do, but to remain firm to the Constitution, which he had sworn not to break or alter, but to support. . . .

That the Southerners themselves, many of them, believe that they are engaged in a "holy" war, there cannot be the least doubt: for, unquestionably, there is the same proportion of earnestness and sincerity among them as elsewhere; though *we* believe that attachment to their "peculiar institution" has often blinded them to many things. A war, then, for "freedom of opinion," or for "rights," on their side, as far as it was honestly believed in, would not be deemed by them "vile." Nor would the same war carried on by those at the North for equal rights and freedom of opinion be deemed "vile," it is to be trusted, by any soul within its borders: on the contrary, war, when it comes inevitably, and is waged to maintain law, order, and the rights of humanity, is not only *not vile*, it is "*glorious*," as every contest for the *right* is glorious, whenever needful. It certainly is to be deprecated, if it can be avoided; but, if forced upon a people, there is nought to do but for every individual to rise to the rescue.

Nor are we to suppose that this war would be deemed " vile " by any portion of the enlightened world abroad. We are not to imagine that England would declare herself on the side of slavery. Her foot has been broadly placed on the ground of freedom in her own history, never, we believe, to be taken back. Would it be possible for France, after what she has done for Italy in the face of the world, to retract by declaring for the principles now manifested by the South in their declaration? Even were not slavery concerned, France would not so readily acknowledge the right of subversion of an organized government by the forcible will of a minority of the people. And could we suppose that Russia, after her struggle to free her own serfs at an immense sacrifice of wealth, would now fraternize with a confederacy whose avowed strongest principle was African slavery? If the United States should eventually acknowledge such a confederacy, undoubtedly every one of those powers would do the same; but, should such an event necessarily take place, I fully believe it would be to the regret and disappointment of all the better part of Europe, which, although monarchical, is looking with interest and hope to see our Government prosperously carried out.*

. . . We have been accustomed freely to use the expressions, "North" and "South," as if the question were simply between these two sections; but assuredly this is an error, and conceals the true issues of the war. It is necessary to make a distinction of the National Government *per se;* for the question is between a *part* of the country and *it.* The other part happens to be for that Government; but it might have been the reverse. It might have been, from some cause, — as when, a few years ago, the spirit of disunion was so rife among a certain class at the North, — it might have been the Northern States that had rebelled. The South now secedes for

---

* Notwithstanding the seemingly opposite course taken, to a great extent, in Europe, during the American struggle, the author has no disposition to recall the above remarks, believing that they express but the real and better self of Europe in its truly great and good minds, who, for the benefit and improvement of the world and humanity, regarded with tender solicitude and hope the "experiment" which was being carried out upon these shores.

the sake of slavery, to have power over its own institution; but, had "disunion" prevailed, the North would have seceded to become rid of slavery. But the principles with regard to the Government remain the same in either case: the contest would have been against *it*. We should know, therefore, no "North" or "South." Such distinction in the conflict could only arise from their natural situation. There are secessionists, no doubt, in the Northern section, though loyal men predominate; and there are loyal men at the South, where secessionists predominate. The Administration, which is the representative of the Constitution, must act against these latter wherever they may be found; and the former, in whatever part of the country they may happen to be, will go for the National Administration. In such a contest, therefore, one should side with the "North" or the "South" but from principle. If, with a clear conscience, and an honest intelligence of all that has happened, and a just idea of the real question, he sides with secession, then only can he be justified in going for it, and not because he is a *native Southerner*. And so with the Northerner: he is not justified in going with the Administration merely because he lives at the North, where a majority of the people support it; because, as has been already said, the war is not one, rightly, of *rival sections*, but between a *portion* of the nation and the lawful and organized government of the land. To say that the South, or any other portion of the country, has an intrinsic right to secede, appears to me simply irrational; for such must be the very principle of disintegration of all government whatever. Either the idea itself of a fixed government must be given up, or, when regularly organized, it must be binding (else it is a solemn farce), unless by the general consent it be dissolved. No people, in deliberately forming a constitution, does so with other than a serious and an earnest intention, and with the design that it should be permanent unless specified to the contrary. The State of New York brought up this very point, wishing to join the Union with the privilege of leaving it if she desired; but this was not assented to, and she was obliged, like all the others, to come in unconditionally. In our very Constitution and original Union, therefore, is a distinct individuality and independence above any single State or States; and this individuality and *innate* independence (marked in many other relations also) constitute our "National Government," or the essential principle of it at least.

There can, therefore, be no *independent* right of secession; and, if Southern politicians and statesmen assume a "right," it can only be, consequently, a right of revolution, which, of course, any people, or part of a people, must possess with justifiable cause. Our form of government puts that peaceably and legally into the hands of the people every four years, as far as an administration is concerned (and there is ample provision for the amendment or re-forming of the Constitution itself when the nation may deem it necessary); so that an obnoxious administration may be removed, if the people so choose: and, unless such legal course were obstructed, it would seem that there could be no cause among us for so serious a resort as to arms.

This is why a civil war here, like the present, has a very different aspect from any that has taken place in any other country. The civil wars of Rome were not, in the time of the republic, between the government and its *constituents* the people, but between *rival factions*, of which one, in general, had just the same right to the supreme power as another.* The very element of the

---

* It is true, that, in the war between Pompey and Julius Cæsar, the cause of the former was ostensibly that of the government; but,

consular power — *two equal heads* — laid them open to this danger; and the authority, at the best, was never so defined but that any man might overstep it: consequently, there would be frequent struggle and re-action. And, when the government became consolidated by Augustus Cæsar, it could not remain permanently so, although it continued for a long time, because it was power assumed, and not delegated by the nation, and was beyond bounds, and which, in the succeeding rulers, finally led to a dissolution of the empire.

In England and France, the revolutions have been occasioned by the degeneracy, or want of integrity or of enlightenment, of the successive kings themselves at the head of those nations. These, in the long habit of reigning, forgot the rights of the people, and were faithless to them, while over-grasping for their own. The people succeeded in obtaining the mastery for a time in both cases: but, in each of those countries, events proved, and

unquestionably, personal rivalry had much to do with his efforts to obtain the ascendency. In that, too, between Mark Antony and Octavius on one side, and Brutus and Cassius on the other, — this being but a continuation of the struggle of Pompey and Cæsar, — Brutus and Cassius were on the side of the country, but were able to do scarcely more than defend themselves against the *personal* rivalry of their opponents.

the verdict of the nation was, that *that* also was a usurpation; and the original government was at length restored. At this day, no people in the world is more loyal than that of England to that same kingly government, with the succession even on the same old plan. The difficulty was, that neither the prerogatives of the monarch nor of the people were accurately defined, and the one was always encroaching upon the other. In the course of time and experience, they have found more and more, on either side, the necessity of precise limitations, and have gradually formed them; so that they now know better where they stand, both rulers and ruled: and there could not, probably, be a *rebellion*,* — the common sense of the people being against it, — unless there were really oppression and injustice, or an actual belief that there was.

In France, it has been the same. The people, after

---

* The case of Ireland may seem exceptional. Although by natural situation a sister island, which might be supposed destined to form with England but one kingdom, its population being of a different race, and having an essentially different system of religion, it may long remain antagonistic. And, whatever the truth of the case may be, it undoubtedly believes itself oppressed, and therefore endeavors to become independent; and, from having been originally a conquered province, it no doubt must have this right of revolution.

repeated trials of kings, &c., formed a constitution, and chose a president; but that people, by vote (although led, perhaps, by the powerful influence of the man), raised that president, at length, to the old sovereign power. But the Emperor Napoleon well knows, that, at this day, it would not be submitted to that the *whole* of *sovereign* power should be in the hands of the governor, or monarch. The same spirit that broke out in the revolution of '93 would again burst forth; and therefore gradually, step by step, he defines and makes obvious the prerogatives of the *people* also.

It is not that the *principle* of *government*, in either of those cases, was destroyed. It remained through all the successive changes, even through anarchy and confusion, and always, in the end, prominently triumphed; and in both of those instances it has come back to its original monarchical form, but with this improvement, — that the rights of the people are more known and acknowledged. Therefore those governments may probably be considered to-day stronger than they ever were, simply because that necessary counterpart of government, the people, is more recognized: that is, the power is more equalized, more fairly divided; the rights of both the governor and the governed being more understood and conceded.

In this country, our original position was different. All was made precise and definite at the beginning, on both sides; so that there can be no real encroachments that may not be readily and peaceably rectified; and where all are politicians, and alive to their rights, any usurpation must be quickly perceived. Hence we can have no tyrants here, nor any mal-administration, for any length of time, guarded and restricted as we are. *Our revolution is at the polls, and may be had every four years if necessary.* It is but a short time to wait, even should the whole country desire a change; thus making a necessary resort to arms impossible: for, whatever was really and essentially right, the general sense of the community would sooner or later guarantee to any portion of it, without the need of fighting for it.

A civil strife here, therefore, by force of arms, ought not to have been a *sine quâ non*, an experience which we "must necessarily have" as well as others. There is no doubt, however, that it will be of essential benefit, showing just what the National Government is, and where it needs amending, if at all; and putting to the test the genuine character of the people, whether we are one disciplined with law and loyalty in our breasts, or are swayed by impulse and capriciousness. It will try many men's souls; for in our almost complete freedom from all outward restraint heretofore, as far as government is concerned, because it has not often been obliged to *enforce* political law, the sentiment has no doubt gained ground with very many, that we were, practically, not to be "subjected" to any "government," as such; that "our government" is, as it were, *no* government. Not only "Young America," but a vast proportion of our people, has undoubtedly had the habit of making very practical use of the doctrine "free and equal;" overlooking in *our* highest officer, under the simple title of "President," any thing but the simply "equal" and private *man*. But we are to remember, that even our head of government is not merely "Mr. So-and-so," or "The President," acting in his individual, private responsibility, thereby making it lawful for us to give deference or not to what "he sees fit" according as *we* may see fit. He, as President, is but the representative of the authorized power of the land; and deference to him, in his official capacity, is but deference to that power; and insubordination to him — to what he, in his legal authority, sees fit — is insubordination to the organized law and order of the country.

This habit is very much to be deprecated, as encouraging lawlessness, and destroying all respect for authority or government, which is not only humanly, but divinely ordained in the natural constitution of things, and must be made as *strong* in this country, although simplified, as in any other.

It has, no doubt, blinded many minds to the truth of the actual weight and necessity of an authoritative power, and has brought them, practically, to indulge the false sentiment already alluded to, — that our Republican Government is, as it were, " no government," in the usual sense of the word.

This " independence " of spirit has been fostered from our very cradle * by all our habits and associations; and

---

* We were not a little astonished, we might say shocked, lately, in coming across a passage in a book of *nursery tales*, with these political allusions: —

" Mrs. Greenhorn's twins, poor afflicted toads! . . . James Boocannon Greenhorn, the eldest, . . . face turned the wrong way, and unfortunately no eyes in the back of his head to see what people were doing. And his other brother, . . . you'll cry harder when you hear about Stephen Doublus Greenhorn, — that's the other one, . . . has got what is called the . . . presidentum complaint. . . .

it is, no doubt, as erroneous a spirit as any that can be cherished. The instinct of the need of government is as obviously implanted in the original, unbiassed constitution of man, as any other of his instincts. All history, and the very existence of society, with its multifarious wants and passions, declare the need of a central, order-arranging power; and such cannot be disregarded with impunity. . . .

It is this power, then, in the legal right and capacity which are inherent in its very nature as the Central and Federal Government, to which alone we must look for moving constitutionally and responsibly in these public affairs. The people, individually, have no authority to move hand or foot: they are as much bound by systema-

"' How are you going to cure him?'"

"' Oh! cut his head off! It's the only way.'"

Is this the temper with which we are to imbue not only our now innocent children, but our future politicians and statesmen? May we not attribute much of the personal invective and abuse which so often disfigures even our national councils to this not only crude and irreverent, but harsh, disdainful, and unfeeling spirit which is thus taken in with our infant breath, and grows with all that fosters it in our maturer years? What parent would not shrink from instilling such germs of evil, such a spirit of sarcasm, and incitements to crime, even, in the infant hearts of his offspring? Verily, our juvenile literature needs reforming.

tized order and by *law* as if they were verily chained and fettered. Nevertheless, private and individual feeling will constantly break forth, manifesting itself so and so. It is human nature thus to follow its own quick impulses, instead of what is simply right and lawful; and in thousands of instances, undoubtedly, both at the North and the South, narrow-mindedness or ignorance will regard this as a personal conflict of animosity and hostility of one section against another. Were this the truth, it would be but a civil war of force, without principle on either side; and the one must conquer who can. One would have the same right as the other. But, amidst all this personal excitement, we must not forget the great fact underlying, — that it is a contest between the people, or a portion of the people, and the Government. This was the issue taken by the Southern States, — *withdrawing from the Government*, peaceably if they could, forcibly if necessary.

I have before admitted a lawful right of revolution with sufficient cause. Granted to the Southern States, therefore, the right of resorting to arms, had they in this case justifiable cause? This was not misgovernment, (which would seem to be the only thing to justify a nation, or part of a nation, in going to war); for they did not wait to ascertain what course the new administration would pursue, the movement commencing at the moment it was known that there would be a new administration, having been planned as soon as such administration had begun to be talked of. It was not, therefore, from any actual cause of tyranny or oppression, which would, undoubtedly, have dignified such movement with the name of "revolution," but without aggression on the part of the Government; and, being voluntarily engaged in, it could only be insurrection or rebellion. In such case, of course, the National Government, in its innate power over and above any portion of the country whatever, stands upon its dignity, its responsibility. It has its rights and functions to maintain; and these it must maintain, unless it allow the balance of power to be destroyed, and the inorganic populace to obtain more than its due; whence disorder and anarchy must necessarily prevail. And this would be the case if such rebellion were successful (the principle of authority of government being broken); and then the National Government must succumb. But as the principle of right must eventually, even in human affairs, be recognized, we cannot suppose that the usurpation of the "people," or populace, would remain permanent, any more than the usurpation of a tyrant, but that, sooner or later, a counter-revolution would take place to right things again; and then we might look to be brought back, as was the case both in England and France, to the very same form or system we had formerly had; namely, with the *equal* rights of both ruler and ruled: as all experience and philosophy make it more and more evident that such is the *juste. milieu*, the only true and wise relation between the governed and the governing, the people and the administrative power; rights, not the same, not identical, but *equalized*. . . .

That the true issue was this, — between a portion of the people as such and the Government, — and not as a "revolution of States," is obvious: otherwise, what would become of the Unionists at the South? Are they to be merged as "rebels" and "revolutionists"? This is very marked in the cases of Kentucky, Missouri, Maryland, and Tennessee,* where the Unionists are, in number, on a par, at least, with the Secessionists. Are *they*, although multitudes of their citizens are in arms,

---

* Tennessee had not then joined the Confederated States.

to be put down by *conquest*, as rebellious or revolutionary States?* (for, where it is a simple case of revolution and subjugation, of course the stronger and victorious power treats the other as conquered property.)

What is true in regard to those States must be true in regard to every State. We are all precisely in the same natural relation to the Federal Union; the only difference in the actual *status* of those border States and the other Southern States being, that, in the latter, the spirit of secession was more universal, and obtained more dominant sway for the time. . . .

As to the question of "subjugation" of the States, I maintain, that, with our present system of government, this is impossible. Were there the right of this, of course there would be an equal right, on the part of the State, to resist; for neither in nature or philosophy

---

* We, in our more undisturbed regions of the North and East, could scarcely imagine the death-throes with which some of these border States — as Kentucky and Missouri — were threatened; or the ardor with which they threw themselves into the contest, striving hand to hand and inch by inch for their own lawful *self-possession*. Theirs was the brunt of the battle. They were fighting literally for their firesides and their homes; their very political existence even. The conflict in these States shows the true nature of the insurrection, — that it was by a faction of the people.

is the right to *subjugate* granted, without the counterbalancing right on the other side to resist. The triumph in such a case could only be from the greater power of the one or the other, which is the principle of a foreign war, — that between two independent States, — the one holds who can. With what propriety could one be called a " rebel," if he had the right to resist, and defend himself?

As it is, the Government does not claim to go against the States, *as such*, to interfere with any private individual State right: Mr. Lincoln has always disclaimed any such intention. There is simply the right of *putting down the rebellion* in those States, leaving the structure of the States as before.

In this way, and in this way only, could it be that Mr. Davis and the other senators who withdrew from Congress, not by resigning their seats, and becoming discharged, as public functionaries, from the oath to support the National Constitution, which they took on entering, but to carry out their purpose of secession, with the oath still upon them, — in this way only could they be considered " traitors," and not simply revolutionists, with all the rights of such.

The South resents the idea of being conquered, subjugated: but it appears to me there are only these two alternatives, — either this is a rebellion of a portion of the country, and requires to be treated as such; or it is a revolution of *States*, and must therefore submit to the chances of war, to be " conquered," or not, as may happen. In the latter case, they could, of course, retain no "private, individual right" as States, but must be treated as the conquerors may see fit. Neither, in that case, could their sons be regarded as " rebels" or " traitors," having exercised simply the right of revolution; which, of course, as was said before, *States* must have with justifiable cause.

It is the same with regard to political parties. As to confounding the —— or any other party *as such* with the sentiments and course of the Administration, guarded and guided as this must or should be by the definite Constitution of the country and the deliberate legislation of the people, we ought as soon to think of any other impossible thing. We ought not, then, to apprehend, or have ground to suspect, any " dark, political plot" underlying any of its movements, or that it is governed by a " party," any more than it is governed by a "section." Both the Executive and Congress, in their integrity, stand for the whole, and not for a part, of the country. . . .

Thus far, the Federal Government has conducted itself in a Christian and an honorable manner. It has shown itself, on every point, calm, conciliating, and forbearing. Witness the proclamations after the taking possession of Baltimore and Alexandria: nothing could be more protective and re-assuring to peaceful inhabitants. Were the Government weak, and destitute of means for carrying on its own proper measures, very probably so many States congregated would be successful in accomplishing whatever they designed; and then, indeed, we might be broken into two separate communities (or as many more as we should choose to make of ourselves). But notwithstanding that strength of numbers might, for a time, give them success, the *principle* would remain the same as if one State alone had attempted to rebel or "nullify." We know that nullification has been tried heretofore, and has always been denounced as unconstitutional.

The great fact to prove the strength of our National Government, and which we cannot but expect will bring it in the end to perfect success, is the manner in which it has been rallied to as the popular force; and in this strength, if it sees it necessary, in order to maintain its authorities and responsibilities, it will not hesitate to go east, west, north, or south, into any and every corner of the Union, by its own inherent right, not for the purpose of "interfering" with the rights of any State, but in the right and necessity which belong to it from its very nature as the Central or Federal Government, and which right cannot be violently wrested from it by any one State or by several States. A majority alone could by right of force break up this central or federal authority; and that would be revolution, to which, of course, the *people* have a right, with any justifiable cause. But in this case, although the States were numerous, the attitude was not one of right revolution, since there could be shown no justifiable cause; and the ordinances of secession were not in general submitted to the *people*, even of the seceding States themselves. It was, therefore, an attitude of rebellion, which justifies the National Administration not only in acting on the defensive, and resisting the encroachments of the new force, but also in *attacking* and *invading* wherever and whenever it may be necessary.

In this same manner, too, standing in the midst in its own dignity, truth, and uprightness, it will, no doubt, put down whatever is "ultra" (in an opprobrious sense) that may appear on any side.

This war has brought out a very remarkable feature, (one nation as we have always been); namely, the emphatically placing an individual State above the whole country, — the lesser before the greater; requiring that the State, and not the nation, should demand our preference. This appears to me on the same parallel with the being loyal to one's town or city in preference to the State.

True, there are certain rights belonging to the States; but these do not conflict with those of the National Government; and the latter are to be equally regarded with the former, unless there were really injustice and oppression exercised by that government. The South, indeed, claims, theoretically, that there has been wrong and injustice; but she has not been able to point to it in reference to the Federal Government.* . . .

* An examination of the wrongs alleged, upon which the actual movement of secession took place, is contained in another volume of this work.

Our foundation of a glorious freedom, and the capability of one self-governing republic, though as large as, or larger than, any monarchy in the Old World, is yet to rest, it is to be trusted, on a firm and enduring basis. There will be much suffering, no doubt: but, in the end, we shall come out stronger and more prosperous than ever; for all will have been thoroughly tested and proved. And this is what was needed. Nations as well as individuals have to go through the furnace of affliction, difficulty, and trial, to know of "what stuff they are."

I do not in the least look upon the Union as broken. There are loyal citizens in all those States; and, when the insurrection is quelled, — "conquered," if one pleases, — the *States* will still remain as they were, part and parcel of one noble Government and Constitution.

SECTION II.

REVIEW OF NORTHERN ARGUMENTS FOR SECESSION.

THE attempt of the secessionists to withdraw from the Union has been considered in general, by non-secessionists, as treason to the National Government: but it is well known that the great mass of Southerners have not so regarded it; on the contrary, they have made it a matter of *conscience* and *duty* to fight for their "State Rights," as they call them, in opposition to the Federal Government. It is known, too, that the moral and religious element has been as strong and active among them as elsewhere, and that personal bravery, valor, and self-sacrifice, have been displayed equally with those qualities in any part of the country, even if they have not surpassed them; which, were it so, would not be surprising, inasmuch as they believed themselves fighting almost for their very existence. It is said that Gen. Stonewall Jackson spent a whole night in prayer before he came to a decision upon the subject; and is it to be presumed that such a man, and many others in the same position, decided otherwise than *conscientiously* when they went with the rest of their people in secession? Thus what is called treason by one part of the nation was considered patriotic duty by another.

Such facts manifest a great diversity of thought and feeling, which, on either side, has amounted to *conviction;* and, while such discrepancy of views exists, there can be no true union between the different sections.

The physical power of the Government, indeed, has been able to repress and regulate outward movements; and increasing communication between the different parts, and growing business and prosperity, will tend to produce external peace and harmony. But to conciliate the minds of our people, and bring them again into the fraternal bonds of mutual kindliness and respect, we need to know precisely what and where is the actual truth.

We need this discovery, too, for a further purpose. We believe that our great danger as a people is not yet over; that it may occur again and again; and that it lies in the want of a perfect apprehension of the true elements of our republican system. Other nations have had to grope their way through great and frequent convulsions, because their *outward* limitations were not well defined. We may, in a similar manner, be liable to continued shocks and convulsions, because the *inward* elements of our national existence are not closely apprehended or understood. These perils can only be avoided by a just apprehension of the great questions of the day. This of secession or non-secession comes first in the list, and thoroughly to sift and unravel it will be a step towards making clear all others.

This principle in the abstract has been a development not only of one portion of our country, but of all parts of it; arising, we believe, from that innate spirit of independence and freedom which is the very characteristic of the American people, — the rapid, luxuriant growth, as it were, of the American soil.

In the cooler North, this spirit reached its climax a few years since, with but a *show* of flower and fruit, in the threatening and exciting cry of disunion among a certain class; slavery, the withdrawing from slavery, being the impelling cause. It was then the part of the Southern States strongly to remonstrate, and to deprecate this voluntary severing of our national bonds.

It would, undoubtedly, have been difficult to induce the mass of the Northern people, with their more calm, reflective temperament, to yield to this demand of a small but vehement party; and probably that point (disunion) never would have been reached, *the fructifying stimulant, slavery, not being in the soil itself, but merely in the atmosphere.*

The efforts of that small party, however, were very great, and bore their fruit, undoubtedly, in another way, — in accustoming the mind of the people to the idea of separation, and tending to excite it, in the South, to that practical issue. There, in that almost tropical region, and with the nourishing stimulus, slavery, on *the very ground itself*, the spirit of secession (only another form of disunion) came to its full and outbursting growth. The seeds were the same in one and the other section; the warmer climate and greater fertility of the soil bringing them to fuller perfection in the one case than in the other.

So true is this, that, at the commencement of the secession movement, great numbers of the Northern people scarcely knew whether the Southerners might not be right in the abstract: their thought and expression on the subject were undecided. All that numerous class in the free States who have advocated *specific* rights of all kinds, — "Human Rights," "Woman's Rights," "Rights of Man," &c., — would, most likely, have merged themselves, in *theory*, on that side.* It is only the actual attempt to put this theory into execution that has revealed its difficulties, and allayed its advocacy, for the time. For the time, we say; as we cannot believe that a root of such magnitude is made extinct by outward repression or circumstances merely, but that it will be ready to spring up in some modified form, on any new occasion, at the North as well as at the South. On this account it is, that an examination of this whole

* "The New-York Tribune," in the first days of secession, gave utterance to the following:—

"We fear that Southern madness may precipitate a bloody collision that all must deplore. But if even seven or eight States send agents to Washington to say, 'We want to get out of the Union,' we shall feel constrained by our devotion to human liberty, to say, '*Let them go!*' And we do not see how we could take the other side, without coming in direct conflict with those *rights of man, which we hold paramount to all political arrangements, however convenient and advantageous.*"

question is so necessary, that the real truth may be laid plain before us.

For this, it is not necessary to search for arguments among the Southerners themselves, although they have produced them sufficiently for their own purposes; the Hon. John C. Calhoun of South Carolina being, it is well known, their first great apostle. We believe it is all-sufficient to examine some which have been brought forward at the North; and we prefer so to do, as they are undoubtedly the most favorable towards secession that may be found, being the arguments of a (religious) party which claims for itself the most liberal and advanced thought of the age.*

But, before we come to this discussion, we will revert to the exciting moment when this topic (in its Northern phase) was first introduced into the national councils, and will obtain from history some outlines of the subject.

* Notwithstanding these arguments for secession, it is but just to say, that, practically, there was no party, as such, more patriotic, and more loyal to the Government during the war, than this; and that probably but few of its members may have indorsed this theory, although the pamphlet which we are going to discuss was written by one of its leaders, reported to be a prominent Unitarian clergyman.

In the year 1842, some citizens of Haverhill, Mass., signed a petition, which they forwarded to the Hon. John Quincy Adams to present, praying Congress to "immediately take measures peaceably to dissolve the Union of these States." Mr. Adams, in his seat in the House of Representatives, presented the petition, and, at the same time, made a motion that it might be referred to a committee with instructions to report an answer, saying *why it should not be granted*. Nevertheless, the excitement was intense; and the Southern and Western members immediately took steps not only to denounce the petition, but to reprimand the representative for offering it. Resolutions were drawn up, and the next day they were presented by the member from Kentucky (Mr. Thomas F. Marshall). The preamble was in these words: —

"*Whereas*, The Federal Constitution is a permanent form of government, and of perpetual obligation, until altered or modified in the mode pointed out in that instrument; and the members of this House, deriving their political character and powers from the same, are sworn to support it; and the dissolution of the Union necessarily implies the destruction of that instrument, the overthrow of the American republic, and the extinction of our national existence: a proposition, therefore, to the representatives of the people, to dissolve the organic laws framed by their constituents, and to support which they are commanded by those constituents to be sworn, before they can enter into the execution of the political powers created by it and intrusted to them, is a high breach of privilege, a contempt offered to this House, a direct proposition to the Legislature, and each member of it, to commit perjury, and involving necessarily, in its execution and its consequences, the destruction of our country, and the crime of high treason."

They then " *Resolved therefore*, That the —— member from Massachusetts, in presenting —— a petition praying for the dissolution of the Union, has offered the deepest indignity to the House of which he is a member; an insult to the people of the United States, of which that House is the legislative organ; and will, if this outrage be permitted to pass unrebuked and unpunished, have disgraced his country, through their representatives, in the eyes of the whole world." And

" *Resolved further*, That ——, for this insult (the first of the kind ever offered to the Government), and for the wound which he has permitted to be aimed, through his instrumentality, at the Constitution and existence of his country, the peace, the security, and liberty of the people of these States, might well be held to merit expulsion from the national councils," &c. . . .

At the close, Mr. Adams rose with calm dignity; and, when replying to the charge of high treason, he said, "I call for the reading of the first paragraph of the Declaration of Independence. Read it! read it! and see what that says of the right of a people to reform, to change, and to dissolve their government."

The paragraph was read, and the excitement turned.*

No precise interpretation of those words of the Declaration were given, however, at that time; nor were they called for. It was simply a recognition of the idea, that a people, having the need, may remodel or change their government; and, in such a case as ours, the peaceable, legal way, undoubtedly, would be by that very form which was then introduced, — by petition, or by conventions, and so forth. But, to make this effective, there must be a majority of the people, of course, in such

* See Memoir of John Quincy Adams.

petitioning, or in meeting in convention. Mr. Adams, an ardent lover of his country, undoubtedly did not think it necessary or well to introduce this topic, and therefore, in presenting the petition, desired that the committee should be instructed to report *unfavorably* to it.

From this history, we see with what repugnance the idea of breaking up the Union was originally received by the South, and their strong expressions of its treasonable nature. The balance has swayed round, and the North has had its turn in making use of the same expressions against the Southern attempt. We may thus believe that the first instinct of the people in general has been for a permanent Union. Any plausible theory being once broached, however, the mind will continue to dwell upon it, and, if possible, work it out to a logical result. Such has been the case with this theory of the dissolution of the Union. We were long familiar with the growing arguments of the Southern States for it, and we will now (as we have said) proceed to examine some which culminated at the North in its favor.*

---

* Some of the following pages of these "arguments" were published in a few numbers of a weekly paper, — the only part of this work which has ever been in print.

FIRST ARGUMENT.

EXAMINATION OF THE DECLARATION OF INDEPENDENCE AND THE CONSTITUTION OF THE UNITED STATES.

From the pamphlet* referred to on a previous page we quote : —

Page 13. — " To us, it seems clear, that, according to the fundamental principles of our government, the secessionists are right in their main principle. If a State considers itself oppressed in the Union, it has a right to leave the Union peaceably. This is only affirming the principles of self-government, which are asserted in the Declaration of Independence, and in almost every State Constitution. The Declaration of Independence asserts in terms, that, whenever any form of government becomes destructive of the ends of government, ' it is the right of the people to alter or abolish it, and to institute a new government; laying its foundation on such principles, and organizing its powers in such form, as to them shall seem most likely to effect their safety and happiness.'

" So too," continues the writer, " declares the Constitution of Massachusetts; saying, that, ' when the objects of government are not obtained, the people have a right to alter the government.'

" The Constitution of Maine says, . . . ' All power is inherent in the people; all free governments are founded in their authority, and instituted for their bene-

---

* " Secession, Concession, or Self-possession: which? Boston: 1860."

fit: they have, therefore, an inalienable and indefeasible right to institute government, and to alter, reform, or totally change the same when their safety and happiness require it.'"

The writer then specifies the Constitutions of most of the States, all of which declare the same thing.

The correctness of this principle, — the power of the people to revise and remodel, or even wholly to alter or change, their government, with sufficient cause, — no one in a republican country will deny. But it is necessary in this argument to bear in mind, that although thus asserting, as they believed it, a general and universal principle, founded in natural rights of mankind, they were applying it (the Declaration) at that moment to the "people" of the *United States;* and the States, to their own particular selves *as* States. All of these, singly and in the mass, having been dependent colonies, but now feeling justified in holding themselves a free "people" and free "States," took to themselves the right of remodelling or creating anew *their particular Constitutions*, and also a federative or central form of government; each of the States, as colonies, having had a distinct and separate one before, and all of them together a general one, under one monarch.

But this general principle, although expressly applied to their peculiar condition *at the time*, as then stated, we cannot doubt would, thus recognized, become a provision (whether so designed at that moment or not) in the States for them to alter or modify their Constitutions in future if they should deem it requisite, and, in the *United States*, for it also to re-form or modify its government. Such an inherent "right" must, no doubt, be acknowledged in any rightly founded system. We cannot suppose, however, that any one of those new Constitutions meant to indicate in that principle, or in those "terms" laid down, that the inhabitants of any *single town* or any *county* in the State should thus revise and remodel, or alter and change, that Constitution, according to *its* own especial ideas or purposes; or that they were giving the right to any such town or county to abolish or throw off that government (of the State), independently of the rest of the State. Had such an idea been theirs, it would undoubtedly have manifested itself in more explicit terms. On the contrary, the State, in forming such Constitution, was in its people a *unit*, and its own author. It must undoubtedly, therefore, be *itself*, the same unit, the same *whole*

5

people, — or a majority at least, — to re-form or remodel it.

So, also, the Declaration of Independence, in the United Congress of the States, had reference only to the united people of those States; that is, to the nation at large. We could not suppose, any more than in the case of the State Constitutions, that the authors of the Declaration of Independence, and of the Constitution succeeding (for they are but the complement, one of the other, — what the one omits the other embraces, both together forming our political "system"), — we could not suppose that they had in their minds — as far as those "terms," those "assertions," were designed for a *future* provision as occasion might demand — any idea of the citizens of any single State, independently, on their own account, abolishing or overthrowing that which belonged to, and had been declared for, all the States in general. Without doubt, they meant to imply that the power to revise, remodel, or "institute a new government," belonged to that very people, and to that only and intrinsically, which had possessed the old or former one; and that was the *united* people. The Declaration and the Constitution belonged, not to one portion more than another, but to each and every part of the country equally. If, then, there were an implied principle that any one of the States (whose population forms but a *part* of the *people in general*) should undertake to do that of itself independently of the others, it would be giving it, to say the least, a tremendous power of detriment to the general well-being; endangering the stability of that central, undivided government to every other portion of the people, no matter how happy, satisfied, or prosperous they might be under it. We cannot conceive of such an element of discord and confusion — injustice even, any one State having the power thus to disturb the whole nation — having been intentionally introduced into the very formation of our system, and as a fundamental principle. It has been suggested that a State might " withdraw " *peaceably*, and so leave the others just as they were. The " withdrawing " is and can be only a rejection of the old government, and a forming of a new one, which is the very principle in question; and, whenever that once occurs as a precedent, any other of the States must be entitled to the same overthrow or rejection whenever its citizens shall deem there is " cause " for it: and henceforth the General

Constitution, or Government, would be only a thing to be cast off, shaken as a tottering pillar, by any who might choose to do it.*

Rejecting then, as impossible, the introduction of *such* a fundamental principle on the part of the framers of our system, who were men of intelligence and devoted patriotism, and were undeniably endeavoring to secure the good of the whole country, or of the country *as* a whole, to our apprehension the only simple and reasonable construction of those " terms," " assertions," or principles, laid down (if they were not limited to that particular occasion, but were to be carried over to the use of future times, — which, of course, they being a general principle, we must naturally infer), would be, that, as the people of the " United States " *in general* (in Congress assembled) had the right to form, originally, their own system of government, that *same* people, that is, the people of the " United States " *in general*, in a similar man-

* Experience has already shown how, from the very first suggestions of, to the final attempt at, " withdrawal," or " seceding," — " peaceably " or otherwise, — the whole nation was agitated to its foundations; which agitation and alarm, pervading every quarter of the country, was, no doubt, but a warning of the injury and danger that would accrue from the actual fact itself, and which, moreover, shows how intimately all are united in one general sympathy and interest.

ner (in Congress assembled), — not any single or partial portion of it, or in a subversive and inimical manner, — must continue to have the same right to form a new system or mode of government if they see fit.

This appears to us the natural, and only natural, deduction from the principle laid down in the Declaration of Independence; and they themselves — the actors at that time — initiated or made emphatic this simple deduction, by proceeding, ten years or so afterwards, to form a new Constitution, not finding from experience the old one to be sufficient; and they have given an example to the *nation in general* for similar future action, whenever it may be necessary. But, in the mean time, we are to remember the one fundamental principle of any constitution whatever, — that, as long as it exists unrepealed, its articles are of binding force and obligation (unless, by tacit or general consent, they become obsolete). If any statute be oppressive to even a considerable portion of the people, it must no doubt wait, in an orderly way, until a majority shall be obtained to effect the remodelling of that statute; for which, provision is made in the very Constitution itself. There is, therefore (as has been said in the "Letters" of the First Section), no opportunity or occasion under our system of government for a revolution of force, an appeal to arms, for the people to obtain the redress which they require, *unless* the minority really and obviously possessed the more legitimate cause, and a majority could not be found sufficiently disposed to do them justice. In no other way, it appears to us, could there be a justifiable revolution by arms in this country; and any thing less than a justifiable cause must assuredly class a resort to arms with " insurrection " or " rebellion."

Unless, then, our people became greatly demoralized, we had no reason to anticipate a revolution of force such as have characterized other countries, and which, indeed, was the beginning of our own national existence.

But we have wandered from our subject, and must return to the proposition of our author, — that any State has " a right to leave the Union peaceably," — that is, independently, — in accordance, as he infers, with that principle (the power of re-forming or re-modelling a government) laid down by the authors of the Declaration of Independence; or, as he afterwards says, that their " right to go is asserted by the Declaration of

Independence, and in nearly every State Constitution."

We maintain, as has been seen, the improbability, or we might say impossibility, of any such broad construction of that principle, as simply stated, either in the State Constitutions or in the Declaration; and that the framers of the latter were not thinking, at the moment, of applying it to any single State in distinction from the Union, is abundantly shown by the whole tenor of that instrument.

The thirteen original colonies were all under one ruler, — the crowned head of England. They were in one and the same condition, each being aware of and recognizing it; and, after long-repeated acts of oppression from the mother-country, these thirteen colonies, *as one*, rose to resist that oppression. No one can read the "declaration" signed by every one of those colonies, in which each had the same vital interest, and which was the spoken word for *all*, without perceiving that they were acting as one confederation, one band.

Feeling themselves entitled, from their condition and the oppressive power exercised over them, to independence, and a separation from the former government of England, they style themselves at once,— no longer colonies, but States. They had all been one assemblage, under one and the same authority; it was their normal condition: and now no change whatever was designed in their relations one with another, but the assumption of the name of "States" had reference only to their relations with England, as no longer "colonies." If there was any change in their natural condition and relation to each other as a family of sister colonies, or now States, it was only to strengthen and confirm their *union*. And this was indeed done in the establishing of the Continental Congress; showing thereby, not a design of relinquishing all centralizing government, but merely of taking it from the parent country into their own hands, — the hands of this family of sister States.

They allude to themselves, in the commencement of the Declaration of Independence, as "one people," to whom it had become necessary to "dissolve the political bands which had connected them with another, and to assume among the powers of the earth the separate and equal station" (using the word in the *singular*, as of "one people") "to which the laws of Nature and of Nature's God entitle them."

They then proceed, for "decency's sake," to justify themselves before the world; to enumerate the causes of complaint; and speak of the refusal of laws for the "public good;" invasions on the rights of "the people;" the endeavor to prevent the "population of these States" (again in the singular, as "one people"); sending swarms of officers to "harass *our* people;" keeping "among us" standing armies; subjecting "*us* to a jurisdiction foreign to *our* constitutions, and unacknowledged by *our* laws;" plundering "our seas;" ravaging "our coasts;" burning "our towns;" constraining "our fellow-citizens . . . to bear arms against their country" (again in the singular, as of one). "A prince whose character is thus marked . . . is unfit to be the ruler of a free people" (again as ONE).

They go on to say, not "the representatives of South Carolina, of Georgia, of Massachusetts, of New York, of New Jersey," and so on, as separated States, but "we, therefore, the representatives of the UNITED STATES of America, . . . in the name and by the authority of the good people of these colonies" (still in the singular, as of one aim, one object, one people), "solemnly publish and declare that these United Colonies are, and of right ought to be, FREE AND INDEPENDENT STATES;" not free and independent of *each other*, — they are saying nothing about that, — but " that they are absolved from all allegiance to the BRITISH CROWN, and that all political connection between them and the STATE OF GREAT BRITAIN is, and ought to be, totally dissolved; and that, as free and independent States" (in contradistinction from being dependent on England), " they have full power to levy war, conclude peace, contract alliances, establish commerce, and to do all other acts and things which independent States may of right do." *

Throughout the Declaration, there is not a single allusion to any individual State as such; which coincident testimony of itself must condemn the assertion of our author, that the " right" of any one " to go " (or secede) is asserted by the Declaration of Independence.

---

* It might be objected, that the continued use of the term " States " disproves the idea of a centralizing government. It merely shows, in our opinion, the fine instinct of republican institutions which existed in the very birth of our Government. As colonies, they had been independent in their domestic functions, one of another; and they were not thinking of altering those relations, but simply of forming a central authority to take the place of that which they had thrown off.

Neither in the Constitution, afterwards formed, is there the least allusion to any such secession principle, or independent State's right, — the liberty to go or not, at pleasure: on the contrary, we will take from it some passages that completely militate against the idea, even, of such principles being implied.

It commences speaking in the name of ALL, as did the Declaration: " We the people of the *United States, in order to form a more perfect union* " (for the express purpose of making themselves perfectly *one* people), . . . " do ordain and establish this Constitution " (one and singular, as for one people) " for the *United States* of America.

" The Congress " (one and general) " shall have power . . . to . . . provide for the *common* defence and *general* welfare of the United States; . . . to regulate commerce . . . *among the several States;* . . . to exercise *exclusive legislation*, in all cases whatsoever, . . . over all places purchased by the consent of the legislature of the State in which the same shall be, for the erection of forts, magazines, arsenals, dock-yards, &c.

" *No State* shall enter into any treaty, alliance, or confederation; grant letters of marque and reprisal; coin money, &c.

"*No State* shall, *without the consent of Congress*, . . . keep troops, or ships of war, in time of peace, enter into any agreement or compact with another State, . . . nor any State be formed by the junction of two or more States, or parts of States, without the consent of the legislatures of the States concerned, *as well as of the Congress.* . . .

" The United States shall guarantee to every State in this Union a republican form of government, and shall protect each of them against invasion, and, on application of the legislature, . . . against domestic violence.

" This Constitution, and the laws of the United States which shall be made in pursuance thereof, . . . shall be the *supreme law of the land*" (in general; and in the singular, as ONE land); and the judges in every State shall be bound thereby, *any thing in the Constitution or laws of any State to the contrary notwithstanding.* . . .

" The powers not delegated to the United States *by the Constitution*, nor *prohibited by it* to the States, are reserved to the States respectively, or to the people."

All the above, as well as the whole tenor of the Constitution, shows emphatically the paramount authority of the Constitution, of Congress, of the United States, over and above any independence of the individual States Had such government been arbitrarily imposed upon them, they would, no doubt, have the intrinsic right to rebel against it, and throw it off if they pleased, according to that fundamental principle of the Declaration of Independence which we have been examining. But that Constitution, and paramount authority, or Central Government, was voted for and confirmed by each one of those thirteen original States,* who were therefore a party to it, placing to it their hand and seal as their voluntary work. Thus consenting and pledged, they no longer have the right to reject it, unless law is no law, and government no government, of no force and stability, and word and promise have no vital and honorable significance. The only way in which they could become rid of this constituted authority would be by the right

* Every new State coming in, of course, gives the same allegiance; voting for and confirming the Constitution, and thereby becoming a party to it.

of revolution; and that, as we have seen, can only truly exist with a justifiable cause.*

We maintain therefore, after this review, that no argument for secession, or that any State "has a right to go," — as is asserted by the author of our pamphlet, — can be drawn from the "terms" or principles laid down in either of the documents of our constituted government, but that, on the contrary, the whole weight of evidence is directly the other way.

---

* That our system of government is a "national" one, and not a "confederation," or a compact between States, — besides being amply testified to, as we have seen, in the whole spirit and tenor, as well as precise expressions, of the Declaration and the Constitution, — is corroborated by the very pertinent paragraph (with which we were all made familiar by its going the rounds of the newspapers during the war) from a speech of Patrick Henry, showing the view taken of it by a contemporary statesman. He says, —

"Have they said, '*We the States*'? Have they made a proposal of a compact between *States?* If they *had*, this would be a confederation: it is, otherwise, most clearly a *consolidated government*. The whole question turns, sir, upon that poor little thing, the expression, '*We the people*,' instead of '*the States*' of America."

Again: on another occasion, he asked "whether the county of Charlotte would have any authority to dispute an obedience to the laws of Virginia; and he pronounced Virginia to be to the Union what the county of Charlotte was to her."

Such emphatic explanation during that period, the period of its organization, is sufficient to show the original meaning and intention of "the UNION."

SECOND ARGUMENT.

POWERS RESERVED TO THE PEOPLE.

We come now to another point taken up by our author, and which is involved in the last passage which we quoted from the Constitution; namely, —

"The powers not delegated to the United States by the Constitution, nor prohibited by it to the States, are reserved to the States respectively, or to the people."

On this our author remarks, " Now, one of the powers which the States and the people possessed before accepting the Constitution, was the power of deciding whether to be in the Union, or out of it; for, otherwise, they could not have come in. Now, this power is nowhere delegated to the United States, nor prohibited to the States: therefore it is still retained by them. This seems to me conclusive as regards the constitutional right of secession."

What power is " still retained "? Evidently the writer means the power of deciding whether to be in the Union, or out of it.

Assuredly, this power of decision had been their own; "otherwise," as the writer says, "they could not have come in." They could not, certainly, on any republican principle; for, if the Constitution had delegated to the United States the power of deciding for any State, or had prohibited it to the States themselves, these would truly have had the right of rebelling at any time, it not being their voluntarily chosen form of government. But this was not the position assumed by Congress: the States belonged to themselves, and owed no allegiance at that time but what they spontaneously gave. They had been a confederated Union indeed; but this was *instinctive*, as it were, for their common defence: no compact or permanent pledged Union had been formed and ratified. But, in the new organization, no one was compelled or bound one way or the other: each was its own master, — had the acknowledged right of making its own decision. But from the very moment that decision was made, and the pledge was given to join the Union, that *power of deciding* no longer existed. The deed was done; the "power" was employed to unite themselves; and, from that moment, there could be no further use of it one way or the other. The opportunity was improved as they thought best; and, in the fact of an affirmative decision, the "power" was, as it were, exhausted. There was no further call or occasion for the exercise of it: in short, it was finished, — swallowed up in the very act of deciding. In that *state of union* itself, there was nothing whatsoever of it left or remaining.* This, therefore, could not be one of the powers " reserved to the States respectively or to the people ;" nor can it be " still retained by them," after such positive use and exhaustion of it. It was a power of deciding in reference to that single point, — of being in the Union, or out of it; and, that settled, it died, or vanished absolutely.

This cannot be " conclusive," therefore, for the " constitutional right of secession," as our author seems to think : but, on the contrary, it is, to our mind, conclusive precisely in the opposite direction ; namely, for NON-SECESSION, — for the impossibility of " seceding," — unless yes means no, and the affirmatory pledge and decision were of no weight or significance whatever.

---

* So long as they hesitated, — were undecided, — the power, of course, remained; but it appears to us a solecism to say, that, after the actual decision was made and sealed, *they still possessed the power to decide.*

THIRD ARGUMENT.

THE "PEOPLE."

We extract again (page 17) : —

"Great stress has been laid by Judge Story, Mr. Webster, and others, on the fact, that the preamble to the Constitution commences with the words, 'We the people of the United States,' and not, 'We the States.' This, no doubt, shows that the people were then acting in their sovereign capacity; and this, I think, requires that they shall act in the same capacity if they secede. It must be the *people* who go out, as it was the people who came in. Secession cannot be accomplished by the act of a legislature, but must be accomplished by a convention of the whole people in any State. This, I think, we have not only a right to demand, but are bound to insist upon by the article of the Constitution (art. iv. sect. 4) which declares, 'The United States shall guarantee to every State in this Union a republican form of government.' Judge Story, commenting on this, says, 'The people of each State have a right to protection against the tyranny of a domestic faction.' For these two reasons, therefore, no State should be allowed to secede until a majority of the people of the State have distinctly voted for secession."

In this argument, there appears to us a remarkable oversight in the want of distinction between the "people of the United States" and that "of the States" individually. A recognition of the former is apparent (or, at least, it is not denied) in this sentence: "This, no doubt, shows that the people were then acting in their sovereign capacity; and this, I think, requires that they shall act in the same capacity if they secede. It must be the *people* who go out, as it was the people who came in."

What people? The people of the United States, certainly: it was they who were acting in their "sovereign capacity." And the "people of the United States," undoubtedly, have the right of "seceding," if you choose, although we consider it a false term in this case, — in a body, that is, the whole people, — from their constituted government. Although it be the best and most harmonizing of all political relations, yet the "people," having made it, have the right, according to the fundamental principle of our Declaration of Independence, to reject it, and form another. But, in the very next sentence, the pamphlet unwarrantably and illogically substitutes for this people at large the people in general, the "people of the United States," those of a single State only. "Secession cannot be accomplished by the act of a legislature, but must be accomplished by a convention of the whole *people in any State*." Again: "No State should be allowed to secede until a majority of the *people of the State*" have voted for it.

This confusion of two separate and distinct things is assuredly as unjustifiable as it would be to substitute the votes of even *all* the inhabitants of a town or village for that of the whole State.

There is also a singular oversight and inconsistency in the following out of this point in the next sentence of the paragraph: —

"This (a convention of the whole people in any State), I think, we have not only a right to demand, but are bound to insist upon by the article of the Constitution . . . which declares, 'The United States shall guarantee to every State in this Union a republican form of government.'"

Why, then, are we not " bound to insist " that it shall not secede, since it is impossible to guarantee such form of government to a seceded State? What possible authority or right could the United States have to " guarantee " any form of government at all to a State that had the " right " to secede, and was separate? If that State were " independent," and had an inherent right to be " out of the Union," not even the faintest shadow of authority could the United States have over her to *require* any kind of government whatever. This single article of the Constitution, therefore, that the United States *shall* guarantee to every State . . . a . . . form of government, nullifies even the possibility of secession.

So, too, "the people of each State have a right to protection against the tyranny of a domestic faction." *

In some of the States where the secession movement took place, — as in Virginia, Missouri, Kentucky, and Tennessee (and, were the truth known, it would probably have been found so in all the States), — there was, originally, a strong party for the Union. In these, therefore, secession could only be called a " domestic faction," — the " tyranny " of one portion of the people over another, sometimes even to compelling that other

---

* The whole article in the Constitution is this: " The United States shall guarantee to every State in this Union a republican form of government, and shall protect each of them against invasion, and, on application of the legislature or of the executive (when the legislature cannot be convened), against domestic violence."

by force of arms. Such a condition of affairs required, in accordance with the statutes, that the National Government should interfere with, put down, that "domestic violence." It was its bounden duty so to do, and a neglect of this would be unfaithfulness to the laws. If any party or majority in such State, however, had a "right" to proceed on the principle of secession, the National and State rights would inevitably and plainly thus be brought into collision. But so guarded were the framers of the Constitution against the rights of one conflicting with those of the other, that it is impossible to suppose, that, either designedly or carelessly, they would leave any such palpable point as this, where it would be impossible to avoid the conflict if each carried out its appropriate rights and powers; and this in itself is an argument against secession. But, moreover, being required to proceed against *any* cause of domestic violence (for, as no one in particular is specified, there can be no exception), the National Government is given a right over the secession or any other principle (of domestic faction) to put it down; which again, of course, nullifies the power of secession. But, if this were an inherent and constitutional privilege in the

State, the Federal Government, in the required necessity of such proceeding, would have been invested with an arbitrary rule, unjustifiable, anti-republican, and inconsistent with every other principle of our Constitution.

"For these two reasons, therefore," — the necessity of guaranteeing to every State a republican form of government, and of protecting a State against domestic violence, — we argue, in opposition to our pamphlet, that no State should be allowed, or can be allowed, to secede, *whether* or not a "majority of the people" (its people) have "distinctly voted for secession."

This confounding of two things — the people of the United States in general, and those of a single State as such — has vitiated many an argument on this topic. The abolitionist orator, Mr. Phillips, plunged into the same illogical error in a speech made at the commencement of the war. He said, —

"How did South Carolina and Massachusetts come into the Union? They came into it by a convention representing the people. South Carolina alleges that she has gone out by convention. So far, right. She says, that, when the *people* take the States rightly out of the Union, the right to forts and national property goes with it. Granted. . . . Yes, the South has a right to secede; the South has a right to model her government; and, the moment she shows us four millions of black voters even against it, I will acknowledge the Declaration of Independence is complied with; that the PEOPLE south of Mason and Dixon's Line have remodelled their government to suit themselves, and our function is only to recognize it."

Mr. Phillips brings forward a similar opinion of John Quincy Adams, in the following passage. He says, " Recognizing the right of the *people* of a State, . . . Mr. Adams says, 'The PEOPLE of each State in the Union have a right to secede from the Confederate Union itself.' "

All this, to our mind, is but trifling with the simple facts, and is as inconsistent and mischievous an error as can be maintained. We have already acknowledged a revolutionary right, where there is no other mode of redress; but this is wholly distinct from the political doctrine of secession, as we shall hereafter see.

To say that a single State, on the ground of *its* people alone voting, can defeat, and thus break up, the National Government, is, to our mind, no more plausible than to aver the same of any single town in regard to its State government. In its own municipal affairs, it is perfect independent, and can remodel them; but, when it comes to State legislation, it cannot, of itself, lay one finger upon it.

FOURTH ARGUMENT.

ITALY AND THE ITALIANS.

We cite again from the pamphlet: —

"Acting on this principle, which is the foundation of all republics, that sovereign power resides in the people, and that they have a right to change, abolish, or renew their form of government at pleasure, we have seen this very year several States in Europe vote themselves out of one union, and into another."

Here we must query what was the principle on which those provinces of Italy voted themselves "out of one union into another." For foundation, it will be necessary to know what had been the actual state of Italy.

It was a country, which in geographical position, in unity of climate, productions, &c. (or with little diversity), is naturally one, and also from the characteristics and language of its inhabitants: but still more was it intrinsically one by sentiment, and the spark, the fire of *union*, which for centuries had been smouldering in the veins, in every part — in the north, south, east, and west — of that beautiful but unhappy land; unhappy, because in every position, from the remotest times, it had been torn in pieces, the victim and the prey of whoever should be successful enough to seize upon the spoils. But, notwithstanding such repressing and covering up of the native instinct of the people, — of unity and of patriotism, — that instinct, that sentiment, that fire, was only smothered, never extinguished, but ever ready to burst out the more vividly whenever there was the least opening, the least lifting-up of that bondage from a people who had the same inalienable right to be *free* and prosperous as we in our more fortunate condition.

This burning, imperishable desire for *unity* of nation and purpose, had, from time immemorial, caused the ever-struggling attempt of the Italian people. It was but claiming the right to that, which, from the undue dominion or interference of others, they never had possessed. In such a case, they, and every other nation on the face of the earth (we ourselves were once of that number), had the right of *revolution* until they could right themselves; until they could obtain the place to which they had a *natural* right by every law, human and divine, — the right of *self-possession;* to be themselves, their own masters; an independent people, free of any *foreign* power, — power outside of their own peninsula, their own domain. On this right of revolution, — the right to *right themselves,* — the Italian States separated themselves from one condition (because it did not meet their *rightful* needs and desires), and joined themselves to others. It was REVOLUTION (there being a justifiable cause), although effected by quiet vote. Who shall say that it was not *lawfully* " revolution," although peaceably done?

In no way that we can see, could they, a subjected and an oppressed people, groping instinctively, with a God-given right *to be themselves,* to possess themselves, to have the privileges of nations, — in no manner, it appears to us, could their condition be regarded as on a level with that of our Southern States. The former were emphatically justified on the principle which we as republicans profess, in endeavoring to attain the position which they never yet had reached, — that of being " free," and " equal " with any other nation. Our Southern States, on the contrary, were already free, and equal with every other State in the Union, and, *in* that Union, with every other nation on the globe; and in their course they were violating the natural principles of *fraternity* and unity, which the Italian States, in their endeavor, were seeking but to strengthen and to cherish.

Further: "The people of Savoy and Nice have voted to secede from Sardinia, and join themselves to France. True, this movement was not initiated by the people, but originated with their government; yet, when the governments called upon them to vote on the question, they distinctly recognized this right in the people. We have also seen Parma, Modena, Tuscany, Naples, and Sicily, and most of the provinces of the Pontifical States, annex themselves by a popular vote to the kingdom of Sardinia. Europe recognizes, at least by acquiescence, their right to do so."

What possible parallel has this secession, or, more properly, *cession* to France of the provinces of Savoy and Nice, instituted by the government, — the people being simply called upon to vote, to express whether they preferred to go or remain, — what parallel has this with or what likeness to the armed designs initiated by our people, in the name of "secession," *against their own* organized government, to which they were legally bound? The recognition of those European "governments" of that "right in the people," was simply, in our opinion, that the latter should have a voice in a matter which concerned so closely their attachments or their interests; and that the governments would not take upon themselves the responsibility of an arbitrary transfer, but one according to the voluntarily-expressed wish of the people; and was not, by any means, acknowledging an " independent right" in the people to leave, whether or no. On the contrary, we cannot but be aware, from all history and experience, that every nation in Europe would rouse to arms on the mere annunciation of such a principle in any part of their dominions; and that they have never dreamed of recognizing such, even by " acquiescence."

The voluntary annexation of the other States to Sardinia was but the exercise, although by peaceable vote, as was before said, of their lawful right of revolution, inasmuch as they *had not hitherto attained* to the condition to which they were entitled by Nature and by God, — that of choosing their own government; and now, as they had the opportunity, were but justly using this privilege.

Again : —

" The most striking case, however, is that of . . .

(those) . . . which have seceded from the Pontifical States, and annexed themselves to a foreign power. The Papal Court complains, and endeavors to retain them by force; but even the Catholic powers of Europe refuse to aid it. Thus even the despotic powers of Europe acquiesce in the exercise of this right of secession. We also approve of it when it is exercised by an Italian State. Shall we deny the right only to the people of our own States?"

Who does not know that here comes in another principle, — that of separating the spiritual and temporal powers? What State of Europe, under its political or State leaders, although Papal in religion, would not rejoice and be thankful that the people of the Pontifical States themselves had taken this point, which had been so much desired, into their own hands? and they would not — long hoping and desiring this just separation — raise one finger to obstruct or hinder it. Thus, indeed, even the despotic governments of Europe, as well as all republican governments, would and do gladly "acquiesce" in the exercise of *this* right of secession, — the separation of the temporal from the spiritual authority: yes, we also approve it, be the right exercised in an Italian or any other State. Every Protestant nation knows by instinct that it is a proper, lawful, and

needful separation. But is such what the " people of
our States" were seeking? Were they, in declaring
the principle of secession from the Union, struggling for
their existence, — for an equal, just, and honorable existence? Were they endeavoring to free themselves from a
difficult and baleful politico-religious combination?

When the premises are the same, we will not indeed
deny to the " people of our own States " the rights which
we " approve " when exercised by an " Italian State."

●

FIFTH ARGUMENT.

THE DIFFERENCE BETWEEN REVOLUTION AND SECESSION. — THE AMERICAN REVOLUTION, OR SEPARATION FROM GREAT BRITAIN.

We quote again (page 18) : —

" What is the difference between revolution and secession, but this, — that revolution is secession accomplished
forcibly, secession is revolution accomplished peaceably?
If the British Government had agreed to our independence, our Revolution would have been peaceable secession. Who was to blame for its not being so? The
power which refused to let us go peaceably ; for, if we
had a right to go, Great Britain had no right to prevent
us from going. If, therefore, you grant the right of

revolution, you grant with it the right of secession. The greater includes the less. If a State has a right to obtain its independence by force, it certainly has a right to obtain its independence peaceably. I do not see how those who grant the right of revolution can deny the right of secession."

Here, as it appears to us, is revealed the grand error underlying almost all arguments in favor of secession, — the confounding of two things essentially distinct. Revolution (as has been several times repeated) is a natural and God-given right, and will ever be continued and lawfully exercised so long as peoples, nations, states, or provinces, are not in a just position, and have force enough to try to obtain such for themselves. There can be, therefore, no limit to revolutions, as regards the *principle:* there may and probably will be modifications; and, as civilization or enlightenment advances, they will become, it is presumed, more and more peaceable, — less violent, — as has been so eminently shown in the late Italian revolutions being effected, in some places, by the *ballot*.

This principle of revolution has existed ever since the world began, and will probably last as long as it shall endure.

The principle of secession, on the contrary, is a political assumption, and has come into existence (the especial form of it with which we have contended) now, in this era, for the first time. It is *sui generis*; a principle raised for the special occasion. Never before in the history of the world has there been one announced with such premise; namely, abandoning, violating, breaking up, a national government, which had led hitherto to greatness and unexampled prosperity; all whose machinery had worked in a marvellously and unprecedentedly happy manner; in the midst of such favorable public conditions, *assuming the right* to throw to the winds all this national, governmental machinery, in so full and successful operation, to *experiment* in making some other. Did ever, in the whole experience of mankind, the magistrates, the representatives, the senators, of a people, thus recklessly trample on the peaceful happiness of that people, flinging suddenly away all their usual privileges and facilities, depriving them of their accustomed course, and substituting for this a made-up system of their own, to which neither Providence nor necessity had impelled them; a new government, requiring limitless means to put it in operation, thereby burdening and impoverishing the populations by new and extraordinary taxes laid upon them; in one word, checking, stopping, all their habitual modes and channels, and requiring them to turn into new ones? A revolution in the wrong way, we should say, was this. Revolution is to improve, make better: *this* was revolutionizing from prosperous to adverse fortune, from plenty and peace to restriction and instability (for we cannot presume that a new government of so sudden, superficial a formation, and driven to by no inevitable, providentially-guided circumstances, could ever have proved a firm and solid one); all this in the name of a principle newly, and only politically (not naturally), developed, — *manufactured*, we might say, with pains and labor.

There is no resemblance in this assumed idea of politicians, — the leaders of the people; for we will venture to pronounce it an impossibility that such could ever have originated with the *masses* of a population pursuing their quiet avocations unoppressed and uninjured. There is no resemblance, we say, in such "political assumption," to the inalienable privilege of "revolution," — seeking to improve one's condition, — and which is given by Nature and by God to even the poorest and humblest of mankind; and, indeed, is most often put in motion by them.

Right revolution, then, is the using a lawful power of change, either by force or by vote, as need may be, as was done in the Italian States. "Secession" is a political theory carried out for political purposes and ends. True revolution originates, perhaps always, with the masses. Secession was a movement of the rulers, or office-holders. It is no argument against this, that a large or even immense proportion of the people of the Southern States went at first with their rulers. Men of any capacity or talent can always succeed in carrying the people with them, for a time at least, until the good sense or intelligence of that people may discover a want of base to their plausible representations. Then, if that time should come, the *people* would of themselves initiate a counter-movement to repel that false one of their leaders; which, thus originating, and thus well founded, would be true, right "revolution." This is but an illustration of the simple republican principle of our institutions,— that it is THE PEOPLE who move and plan: the officers are but the index, the exponent, of their will. It was the PEOPLE who framed the Constitution: the magistrates but carry it out.

And this, again, puts secession on the wrong ground; as, in general, it was not submitted to the people of even those States themselves. The officers were acting their own will, not the will expressed of the people. In other words, the *head* was trying to do the work which did not belong to it, — the work of the body; and we must believe that it would necessarily and inevitably, in the end, therefore, fall through.

It must be plainly seen, then, that our separation from Great Britain can by no means be classed with the attempt of the Southern States at secession. The former was instinct in the community: it was the "body" emphatically moving, instead of the "head." The magistrates or rulers, the highest officers[*] at least, distinctly opposed it. It was the reverse of the Southern movement; and with all its grounds, its "Bill of Rights," and of defence, we can but consider it,—and all society has hitherto considered it,—rightly, truly, lawfully, REVOLUTION, in the broadest, grandest, and most vital sense of the word. It might, indeed,

---

[*] The king and the royal governors.

have been a "peaceable" separation, could Great Britain have been wise and far-seeing enough (which was hardly to be expected of those times) to let her grown and matured colonies go peacefully from under her bosom with her blessing, as a daughter or a son from their father's and mother's house. With three thousand miles of ocean between, with a new home already formed, distinct in its wants and purposes, it was not possible for the far-absent parent to oversee and care for it as it required. A branch, laden and weighed down with its own growth, breaks off of itself, or inevitably tends to; and it is in vain to endeavor, by propping it up, to render it vital again on its native stem. Better to lop it off, and set it out, a shoot by itself, to send forth its own branches and roots, — a separate tree. Similar is the natural growth of prosperous nations, or like a spreading family, — each member becoming the parent of a new one. It was scarcely singular, perhaps, that the natural and inevitable necessity of such a separation should have come ungratefully to Great Britain: it was but the pain which every mother feels in her child's rending itself from her, never more to be under her especial sway; which, however, gives place at length to cheerful acquiescence in one case and the other.*

Such necessities, such separations, may occur again. England, in her far-distant province of India, has another growing daughter, which now, we may believe, needs her fostering care to train, to educate, and prepare for an equal and just position in the world; to which, perhaps, she may come in time. That daughter, impatient of those restrictions, sought, in her wildness, to break away; but the "crushing" of that "rebellion" in India we can only believe to have been providential, for her own good. She had not the capability of going alone in any enlightened way. But, when that period shall come, — as by analogy we presume it one day may, though perhaps not for centuries, — will England be wise enough to *let her depart if she so desire*, with her natural and inalienable right of being free? And shall we, should our distant States and Territories, — separated from

---

* A happy illustration of this is the frank, courteous way in which the first minister from the United States, Mr. John Adams, was received at the court of St. James "I was the last," said the king, " to acknowledge their independence, but will be the first to welcome their minister."

us by that great natural barrier, the Rocky Mountains, — should they one day have the desire to go free, shall *we* have the wisdom to let them depart in peace? It may not be so: they may never wish to leave us. Our form of government may prove itself of such perfection, and all facilities overcoming natural difficulties may bind us so closely, that we may still continue an extended nation. But should they desire it otherwise, feeling it necessary in their growth and progress, and should the principle of *natural* separation not be well understood or allowed, there might be, some time hence, a revolution of force initiated by them, similar to ours with England, for the purpose of setting up an independence of their own. In such a case, where there is every natural (geographical) and reasonable necessity for such separation, a State has a " right " to obtain its independence " peaceably," otherwise by force.

But the present case forms no parallel with either of these until it can be shown that there were plausible and just foundations for a revolution by force in our Southern States. When this is proved, we can no longer call their course " secession," but " revolution," and we must allow them the full privilege of that "right;" in the mean time, however, "denying" the right of secession on the grounds they claim, as a distinct principle from the other, and opposite to it. Secession, in its movements, was subversive: the essential idea of revolution, on the contrary, is *progression.*

SIXTH ARGUMENT.

THE QUESTION OF CONQUEST AND MILITARY FORCE.

"It is idle to hope to keep States in the Union against their will. . . . Suppose that, by using the whole military and naval power of the United States, we should conquer South Carolina: what should we do with it after it was conquered? How hold it as a conquered State? How guarantee to it republican institutions, when we are occupying it with a military force? Such questions show how impossible it is to attempt to prevent secession by exercising the force of the Government."

Here, again, we blame the little penetration, or the "oversight," when such great questions as these are at stake. Who ever dreamed of "conquering" "South Carolina," or any other State? * Who expected to

---

* The "arguments" of this section, as well as the first and third sections, were written during the war, before the theory of "conquest of States," as such, was broached.

hold it when peace should be settled, occupying it with a "military force"? The object, the call of the war on the part of the Government, was to quell, subdue, put down "rebellion," not a "State." Had it (the Government) set about so anti-constitutional a thing as the conquering a State, would it have carried out all its measures so "constitutionally"? Would it not at once, and as the very first necessity, have gone to work and thrown overboard the Constitution, and every restriction pertaining to it? But more than this: who does not know that this Rebellion, although it professed to be a State movement indeed, was not, in its commencement, universal in those States themselves, but was initiated by partisan leaders? (as was alluded to in the last paragraph.) The legislative officers alone do not form the State: it must be the *people* who originate vital changes; the people, *personated* by the legislative body, who act according to its expressed will. But the ordinances of secession were not, in general, submitted to the people; and it is well known that in several States, in the beginning of the movement, there was a large minority at least, and in some States there were actual majorities, against those ordinances. Were those loyal citizens to be confounded with the disloyal? and, in "conquering the State," were they to be conquered also as "rebels"? Were the faithful men in Kentucky, Missouri, Eastern Tennessee, Western Virginia, and wherever else they might be scattered, — were they to be stigmatized and subjugated and conquered as traitors and insurgents? (for "the State" includes all its members, right or wrong, of loyal or disloyal mood.) Heaven forbid! On the contrary, the Federal Government, proceeding in its simple right against the Rebellion as such, would affect only those concerned in it: the remainder of the inhabitants would be eventually free to carry on their State affairs as before. Its republican institutions were untouched, and were still guaranteed to it by the very fact of a force putting down that Rebellion, in order that things might go on in their usual republican channels; and just as long, indeed, as there should be a symptom of rebellion (in arms) remaining, so long, for guaranty and safety, there must and should be even a "military force" sustained, not for holding it as a conquered province, but for the express purpose of preserving and "guaranteeing to it its republican institutions," that they might not be violated or broken by any rebellion or insurrection whatever. All of which is but in consonance with the requisitions of the Constitution in that respect; and also with that other provision, that any State shall be protected against the " tyranny " of a " domestic faction," and from " invasion " by any other State.

This was eminently the condition of some of the States, as Kentucky, &c.; thus demanding a constitutional interference of the National Government by its military and naval force. We need not fear, therefore, that even " military " force, when thus necessarily employed, is unconstitutional or anti-republican.

" Such questions," then, do not, to our mind, show " how impossible it is to attempt to prevent secession by exercising the force of the Government," but simply show, that, *when secession employs force, it must be met by force.*

SEVENTH ARGUMENT.

THE RIGHT, AND NOT THE RIGHT.

(Pages 21, 45, 46): " The result, therefore, of our argument, is this: States *have a right to secede*; but secession must be the work of the whole people. The people must vote distinctly on that issue; and the separation must be accomplished regularly and deliberately, not by violence, but by an orderly method.

"South Carolina has put herself in the wrong by her rebellious acts and her revolutionary measures. She has seemed to choose armed revolution rather than peaceable secession. While we believe a State has a right to secede, we also believe that it must be done peaceably, and by agreement with the other States. This she must try first; and, failing this, she may resort to revolution. But South Carolina has not tried this. Instead of asking leave to secede, and treating on the terms of secession, she has rent herself away by violence, and seized the property of the Union. This ought not to be allowed. She must be compelled to keep the peace, first; and then we may proceed to treat with her. . . . We cannot coerce a State to remain in the Union against its will: we must not attempt to do this. But we will not allow any State to go out in a violent and revolutionary way. The laws must be obeyed by all parts of the country till any part is formally released from that obedience by the common consent. The public property seized by South Carolina must be restored: then we can treat with her about seceding. . . .

"When peace is restored, when the laws are enforced, when the country is quiet, then, if the Southern States, or any of them, desire to leave the Union, in my opinion they should be allowed to do so."

Contrary to the conclusion of our author, as the result

of his argument, that the "States *have* a right to secede," we believe it has been shown conclusively, that the arguments made use of are null and void, and must lead to the acknowledgment of no such right whatever, but to exactly the reverse, — that they have *no* right to secede.

Throughout these last quotations, there is an almost inextricable confusion of ideas; which ideas, if true, would show the same inextricable confusion in our system of government. We will attempt to unravel or examine them, in a measure.

If, in the first paragraph, is meant by the *whole people* the people of the " United States," we entirely agree with the writer, that it must be they to vote upon the issue, as it was by the whole people, in such a sense, that the Government was formed: and, as we have said before, the United States, *in a body*, assuredly have a right to secede (if one chooses to employ that term; although, as was formerly said, we consider it an erroneous and inappropriate one in this case) from their constituted government, and to form another; that is, they have the right to remodel it, as is implied in the foundation principle of our Declaration. But, in order to be consistent with or to be interpreted by a former paragraph of the pamphlet (which was extracted under the Third Argument), the expression, the "whole people," was undoubtedly intended by the writer, in this instance, to be limited to the whole people *of a State;* as he said, "Secession . . . must be accomplished by a convention of the whole people in any State. . . . No State should be allowed to secede until a majority of the people of the State have distinctly voted for secession."

If, then, a State is given distinctly the right of itself to secede, and we "cannot coerce it against its will to remain in the Union," what have we, what has any one, a right to say about its *mode* of doing it?

There might be some civility, some etiquette, in "standing upon the order of its going;" but there could be nothing essential in the manner of it, one way or another. What have we to say, if she "rends herself away by violence," instead of politely asking "leave" to secede? What are we, that we are "not to allow" her, if she has the right, her own course? How can we "compel her to keep the peace first"? how demand that she shall be only "formally" released? If she has a right, it must undoubtedly be emphatically a "right;" otherwise it is of no value or avail whatever.

But that the "people" of the United States should be made to mean the "people of a State," singly, we have already discovered (in the Third Argument) to be a wholly unwarranted and illogical construction; and our pamphlet itself, practically, although not formally, recedes from that position (as we perceive in these last extracts), and adopts the other, as follows,—that if the individual States do act "regularly and deliberately" by their own vote, yet this must be also combined with the vote or voice of *all* the States; or, in the author's words, "it must be done . . . by agreement with the other States, . . . treating on the terms of secession. . . . The laws must be obeyed by all parts of the country till any part is formally released from that obedience by the *common consent*. . . . When the laws are enforced, . . . then, if . . . any of them desire to leave the Union, . . . they should be *allowed* to do so."

If, then, the "allowance," consent, agreement, of the whole is required, where is the right, the "independent" right, of secession? (and, if it is not "independent," it is no available right whatever.) If it is courtesy only which requires the whole to be consulted, and our dignity only which claims it, we surely might waive it in a case, a point, which the secessionists had taken so seriously to heart, especially where an intrinsic "right" was concerned; and, if they choose to omit such courtesy or ceremony, not even saying, "By your leave," we cannot be justified in enforcing it at the point of the bayonet, any more than they can be in going out in a "violent and revolutionary" way. It would be much more to our "dignity," on the contrary, silently to let them proceed as they pleased. We must remember also, in this case, that that violent and revolutionary way, on their part, was in consequence of the attitude of resistance on ours; which would give us the double responsibility of their wrong and our own, in a want of dignified propriety.

We perceive then, by this "unravelling," an inconsistency of ideas from the beginning to the end. If a State has a right to secede by its own vote, and we must "not attempt" to "coerce" it to remain in the Union, how can there be the requisition of a consultation and an agreement, or any propriety in our insisting that it shall and must keep the laws of the Union, from which it is, *per se*, at liberty to recede? The two appear to us simply incompatible, and a confused medley, without harmony or basis; and, were our organic Constitution of the same incompatible mixture, it could only be to us " confusion worse confounded." The inconsistency of these two propositions, deeming them both essential, as the pamphlet argues, — granting the right, and yet not the right, — to our mind, therefore, knocks the argument of secession in the very head.

" But the Union," continues the pamphlet, " will remain the same glorious Union without them (the seceding States) as with them. The disturbing elements eliminated, it will rise to a greater height of prosperity and power. . . .
" To admit the right of secession will not tend to break up the Union, or make it unstable, because the majority of the States are contented and prosperous in the Union. As long as they find the Union a benefit and blessing, and for a good while longer, they will continue in it: when they cease to find it so, they cannot be retained."

By " the Union," it is presumed, is to be understood our country, as it always has been since it came into national existence by solemn league and compact, pledge and promise; in other words, that it is but a synonyme with our "country." To say, therefore, that it can be divided, separated, destroyed, and broken, by taking back this league, compact, pledge, and promise, — leaving each constituent part to go free, — and yet remain one country as before, is simple contradiction, and an impossibility. That the Northern or any other congregation of States, in a separated condition, — if faithful to right ideas, — might still possess a "glorious" government, is not to be denied; but this is an entirely different question, and one with which we have now nothing to do. We are simply to look at our country — our Union — as it always has been, and to the one general Constitution of the Northern, Southern, Eastern, and Western States. To our mind, admitting into this country — this positive, hitherto undivided Union, this one and general Constitution — the right of secession, is but introducing, not "eliminating," "disturbing elements;" and should the united voice of our people, legitimately, in Congress assembled, take the issue of granting this right to any individual State, or to aggregated States, "allowing," "treating on," or "agreeing" to, "terms of secession," it is no longer a "glorious Union," — our "glorious" country, — but is dissolved, and vanishing. It can no more "guarantee" to any State republican institutions, nor even that we — thus separated — should have any national republican existence; since any other "confederated States," north or south, east or west, one after another, might leave on any day, or at any hour, on the same "admitted right," — by their own choice, on their own showing. And our National Government or Constitution will then have proved itself but a dream, a reed shaken by the wind, a feather wafted away by whoever might breathe upon it. "Unstable as water," it could not "excel," nor even remain: in short, *there would be nothing to remain*, — each or any part departing, one after another. It would but have shown itself, and passed away, the "baseless fabric of a vision."

The very act of secession, therefore, is a breaking-up of the Union; and it would but be laying a "flattering unction to our souls," to argue, on the ground of contentment and prosperity, that the majority of the States would still continue in stability. If the correctness of the principle be admitted, and they *have* the right, no contentment or prosperity whatsoever would be any guaranty. No enduring government in this age, certainly, could be built on such a basis simply, — with *rights* and *principles* ignored. Individuals and nations are incessantly and intuitively working to fathom their rights and privileges, — to know the principles, the foundations, on which they stand; and never are they at rest until these are understood and acted upon. Among any intelligent people, the mind must be informed and enlightened, as well as the body possessed in peace and comfort; and it would be, therefore, but vain and delusive to hope to keep in the background so forcible a principle underlying; or to expect that any of our nervous, mentally restless populations, always "seeking some new thing," would remain stable and conservative in the "Union," instead of living up to the "rights and privileges" which the rest of the nation had attained to, and going off, one division here, another there, in so many independent communities, and on any foundation they might choose.

Our author himself admits this uncertainty and instability when he says, "As long as they find the

Union a benefit and a blessing, . . . they will continue in it: when they cease to find it so, they cannot be retained."

If, then, we would perpetuate a " glorious Union," — as the pamphlet elsewhere says, — cherishing "faith in justice, humanity, and freedom," believing in the " principles of democracy and true republicanism," embodying those principles in "suitable institutions," let us not violate the great system of States, which now makes our Union, our Country, our Constitution, the vehicle and instrument for carrying out, in its progress, eventually, it is to be hoped, all of these. Let us not break this link or chain of our formed and pledged *nationality*, and in its place introduce that fabulous chimera (disunion or secession), which has no likeness in heaven or on earth; that hydra-headed monster, which would form of this one nation — so able, capable, and efficient a force among the powers of the earth — a hundred, perhaps a thousand, petty domains, irresponsible, except for their own private fantasies, and which might be pledged to any erroneous principle. Of this we have already had confirmation in the attempt of the confederated States to base a new government on the foundation of slavery.

Here we cannot forbear pausing to touch upon the argument of those who have formerly favored a disruption of the Union in order that *we*, the citizens of the free States, might be exempt from responsibility of the great wrongs of slavery; they not appearing to perceive that thereby those wrongs, unrestricted by the constitutional limits which had surrounded them,* would have been henceforth cast loose upon the world, to thrive and flourish in their own independent, unrestrained position. Surely, if to save a soul from death is to shine as the stars in the firmament of heaven, the converse must be equally true, that voluntarily to cast one out into the way of destruction would be but to fasten on our own souls the chains of the fathomless abyss;

---

* Mr. John Stuart Mill, in his "Contest in America," in reference to such an event, makes use of the following expressive language: —

"Suppose that the . . . Confederation . . . takes its place as an admitted member of the community of nations. . . . Are we (the English) to see with indifference its victorious army let loose to propagate their national faith at the rifle's mouth through Mexico and Central America? Shall we submit to see fire and sword carried over Cuba and Porto Rico, and Hayti and Liberia conquered, and brought back to slavery?"

we being verily guilty of that additional thriving, flourishing, sin, and wrong-doing. Thus casting it away from its confines, we should but have put oil on the burning waves, have added so much fuel to the flames.

Is it patient, forbearing, long-suffering, *Christian*, in short, to leave one to go on his own way, regardless of the consequences, because, forsooth, we wish to clear *our* skirts of his error? We may, and we must, indeed, clear ourselves of the error; we must not take of the accursed thing; no inducement whatever should bring us personally under the same. "Touch not, taste not, handle not;" and as we would cling to, and guard or watch, and entreat, a member of a family; so might we and should we, whenever opportunity offered, have endeavored faithfully to persuade and influence our sister States. But is it brave, manly, generous, upright, to cast one off on account of what we deem one's sin, and to say, "We will have nothing to do with you"? *

* How far this sentiment, which, it must be acknowledged, formerly prevailed to a considerable extent at the North, — though never, we believe, to the extent that the Southerners supposed, — how far this sentiment had a practical effect in alienating and exasperating

Not so would a parent turn from a child, not so should brother separate himself from brother. One might be wilful and persisting, and by main force depart from us; but then we should no longer be responsible: and, if our Southern States had succeeded in thus wilfully leaving the Union, the wrong would have been upon their own head: we were free. In this way only, *morally*, we cannot control, we cannot "coerce them against their will." As *members of a family*, we, individually, as *sister States*, are not given authority one over another; nor, if we were, should we have the power to produce *moral assent and obedi-*

the South, we shall probably never know. That influence is partially shown, however, in a late statement of Alexander H. Stephens, who, during the war, was Vice-President of the Confederate States. It occurs in a letter (July 23, 1866) in regard to the Philadelphia Convention. It is as follows: "I did, in 1860, exert my efforts to their utmost extent to avert the late most lamentable war, and to save the Union, on constitutional principles, without a conflict of arms. This I did, too, while many of those now so clamorous for what they call 'the Union cause' were giving encouragement, at least, to the extreme men at the South, by clearly and decidedly intimating, if not fully expressing, a perfect willingness on their part that 'the Union might slide' if the people of the South so willed it.

"I was even taunted with endeavoring to hold our people on to a Union that was no longer cared for by leading men of the dominant party at the North. I withstood these taunts, even when I knew," &c.

ence. It is only where governmental power is concerned that there can be control; and this can only be external, political. The parent, the Government, indeed, possesses authority to put down violence, insurrectionary insubordination; but it cannot *enforce moral conviction.*

This conflict, however, beside the external insurrectionary violence which the Government had to subdue (with the States as *aid*), was one of a principle or idea on one side; and, on the other, a *resistance* to it, *in which we all have a part* (*the people* or *States*, as well as the Government), — a resistance to the theory of secession; and also in maintaining the eternal truths that law is law, order is order, governments are governments, and constitutions, constitutions; and that none of these are to be violated with impunity. If, then, after all our efforts, the South had by main strength broken away, we should be guiltless. We had done what we could; we had denied the anomalous, self-destroying doctrine of secession or disunion, and should no longer be responsible for her doings, or what might flow from them. In such case, and in such only, — maintaining the principle, although overcome by force, — could we be lawfully separated; and we might hope to go on, although in a separated community, in integrity and strength. Indeed, we *know* that we should then, morally, flourish; not for having cast off our Southern brethren for their sin (as we considered it), but in ourselves maintaining uprightness, although they had wilfully or voluntarily separated themselves from us. Thus would it have been also with the South, had disunion prevailed with us, and had we thus voluntarily separated ourselves: *they*, according to whatever political integrity they might have retained, would still have thriven and flourished.

EIGHTH ARGUMENT.

CIVIL AND RELIGIOUS LIBERTY. — OUR FATHERS. — THE WORK OF TO-DAY.

We make one more citation: —

"Suppose the Union is dissolved. It is a great evil, no doubt; but is it irreparable? Is it impossible to do in 1860 that which was done in 1787? Were the people so much better and wiser in those days than they are now? or did the framers of the Constitution enjoy some special divine inspiration which *we* have not? Have we no longer trust in a Divine Providence which will guide us to-day as it guided our fathers then? . . .

"Men talk about the Union and our present Constitution as though they were arrived at by some happy accident, or some secular conjunction of the planets, which could happen only once in a thousand years."

It is not men, simply, who make governments, manufacturing them as they would a piece of cloth, according to some ingenious pattern or invention; it is, rather, *events* which form, *circumstances* which modify, *Providence* which guides. The events and circumstances which led to the formation of our Constitution, and which were but the forerunners and the foundation of it, — *it* not being itself an *independent* circumstance, but the sequel, the result, of those which were the basis underneath, — those events and circumstances, grand, marked, and peculiar, are as yet alone in the world's experience, and probably will ever remain different from all others. The founders of New England, at least, migrated hither for religion's sake; and a large proportion of the immigration to most of the thirteen States (or colonies then) was on account of religion, — for the sake of possessing their souls and consciences in religious freedom. Religious liberty was the first emphatic element in the permanent settlement of these shores. The principle was here developed and put in practice as it never before had been; and although at times tried, put to the test, and found wanting, as a principle it sank deep, ever gaining new strength, until at length, down to our day, it has come out triumphant. But, with our ancestors, religious freedom did not signify freedom *from* religion; liberty of conscience was not interpreted as liberty to be irreligious; it had not degenerated into scepticism or unbelief: it was merely expressive of the principle that religious faith must be voluntary, and not constrained by outward authority. And so religion still held its place, — was but confirmed and strengthened; and, with its balances and checks, it brought forth its fruits in a manly, substantial, God-fearing and God-respecting people.

Hand in hand with this, as a direct and necessary accompaniment (for religious principle enlarges and rectifies the whole mind), went the breathings, the aspirations, of civil liberty, faint indeed at first; for such ideas, in their full extent, were new in society. Those who had come from the Old World had not been accustomed to such: it was an experiment; new circumstances; a new state of things. Far away, thrown much upon their own resources, they were learning how to govern themselves, and were becoming more capable of this, and were feeling the right and need of it, not from any disrespect to lawful and appropriate authority, — the spirit of their religion preserved them from this, — but because Providence, in thus placing them, was bringing into prominent view and action the long-hidden rights and capabilities of a people to govern themselves, or to *regulate their government.*

These two elements — civil and religious liberty — formed a race of a manly simplicity and an intelligent integrity; free, and yet reverential; strong, and yet submissive to legitimate law and order; trained in substantial and practical wisdom by the discipline of the time and their critical circumstances. Such a race, long experiencing political or civil privations and wrongs, and feeling their needs, and glowing at the same time with the healthful and vigorous and truthful ideas which had expanded in this remote " wilderness," — such a race, when, in God's good providence, the moment came to embody this fresh and genuine life in new institutions that might continue to cherish and foster it, — such a race, at such a moment, after severest trials, and with the one need and necessity before them, and with their all at stake, were *capable* of, and providentially prepared for, forming that Union and that Constitution that thus immediately sprang from those pre-existing causes. They were the very offspring of them, necessarily and directly, and were not simply the result of man's effort and understanding, as certain philosophers had attempted to form a constitution for some of the States (or *colonies* as they then were).

The men of that time were driven, impelled, yea, compelled, thus to act. There was no escape for them. After a peace with Great Britain had been conquered, they found themselves drifting like sand upon the seashore, or like a vessel without rudder or mast. Self-preservation taught them the need; and may we not say that Providence, in and because of that need, gave them especially enlightenment?—enlightenment born out of that mistiness and darkness itself; the precursors of the needful life which is surely vouchsafed, when sought, wherever there is the need. Yes: we will say that in the pressing necessities of that period, with minds earnestly directed to what was necessary to be done, and to the best way of doing it,—we will say (for we believe it) that they had a special capacity, a knowledge, a wisdom, grown out of their long experiences, and from their innate character; a political "inspiration," in fact, which entirely and providentially fitted them for that special work, — God's own plan and designs for benefiting men and improving human affairs, now that the time was ripening for this improvement.

There may be men among us as pious, as religiously devoted, as the Pilgrim Fathers, who first, for religion's sake, came to occupy this soil; for such characteristics are not limited to time or place. There may be statesmen as wise for our day and generation as those who organized our Government. But, differently from our fathers, we, as a people, have been nursed in the lap of peace, prosperity, and luxury. The machinery of our Government has rolled on with smoothest wheels. We have neither been educated nor trained, nor constrained by necessity, to change it, or even to desire to substitute another. No providences have wrought upon us, by imperative circumstances, to attempt, or to exert ourselves towards, any such end; thereby creating within us the insight as to what and how to do. If we, then, with no outward or inward call,* throw away that which was thus providentially instituted, and instituted, we may believe, as the world has believed, for the benefit of humanity, or the nations at large; that which was arranged with such anxious and deliberate care and forethought, and was established on so wise, equable, and harmonious a basis, that it has moved with scarcely perceptible friction for more than three-quarters of a century,—if we throw away this, so wisely, and thus far so firmly, established by God in his superintendence of the world and of our country, have we any right to possess one iota of confidence that we, a generation so differently circumstanced, should be able to form a "better" one? that "Divine Providence," or God, whose work and plans we had thus cast aside, would do that for us, without preparation or call on our part, which he granted to our fathers only after paramount experience, pains, and labor? Shall we, a people bred on the easy lap of fortune, and accustomed (for pastime, perhaps) to the indulgence of all speculative and fanciful theories with which this nineteenth century is so rife,

* Even the secessionists made no charge against the Constitution, and took it as the model for their own.

particularly in our own quarter of the world (here all that is novel and specious has been greeted with an admiring welcome; aught of human philosophy that has been put forth with any *éclat*, or brilliancy of intellect, has often been eagerly sought and accepted in the place of God's simple realities and truth; with all this, it is not, perhaps, too much to say that we were verging, at least, upon a meretricious and superficial phase of character), — shall we, a generation thus conditioned and characterized, imagine ourselves to possess the profound, safe, and practical wisdom so essential for the forming of a theory or constitution of government; a wisdom which *can* come only from stern trial and experience, or which is the growth of these only, as we have seen it was in our fathers, — shall we, I say, for eighty years unaccustomed to any such labor, even to preparing ourselves for it by study (for it must be acknowledged that whatever intelligence there may be among the masses regarding local politics, or periodical elections, and whatever interest in them, yet, as a people, we have been profoundly ignorant of the deep principles and scientific bearings of the subject in general), — shall we, thus situated, flatter ourselves, that, without call, we could do that now as well in 1860 (or '66) which they were called upon to do in 1787?

On the contrary, we believe that "there *is* a tide in the affairs of men" and of nations; a period for a certain work, which is best done only in that period: and such time, or period, for our national organization, we believe to have been that of 1787; that Providence seized upon that time, that tide, to launch us upon the world of nations (for his own wise purposes); and that we can no more undo that work, or check or change that onward flow (*so* guided), but by a suicidal policy, which, by unriveting the planks, would leave our vessel to drift upon the stream, a wreck and a ruin.

If this our Constitution was not made perfect in the beginning (and that it should have been so would be expecting too much of any human work, however providentially guided; although we must say, that, in this case, imperfections have been rarely or scarcely detected), — if this was not made perfect in the beginning, we have the power and the privilege to "amend" it. If there be in it that which may not suit the present or the future condition of our people, we can thus modify it, step by step; each plank, as it requires it, being repaired, renewed, to keep pace with the changes and wear of time; and all this in a quiet, natural, provided-for manner, with no shattering, and no sudden shock to the structure. Thus in the end, and all the way along, though with a fixed Constitution, and a Government inviolable, we should come to that "improvement" and "progression" of things that many have so ardently desired, but who have seemed to think that these could only be attained by a "dissolution" of the Union, and a "new" Constitution.

In such a way, and such only, we believe, have we aught to do, in the way of altering or re-forming them, with that Union and that Constitution which have been given us; letting Providence only, and the requisitions of time, guide its changes and necessary modifications. If any of the States wilfully struggle, and separate themselves, that does not affect the principle of the Union, or the actual Constitution, to those who uphold them: it is only the granting the *right* to part, to one or many, which would pierce a hole in the very hull of our Ship of State, springing a leak that never could be stopped; and, from that moment, it could only founder, and fall to pieces.

Otherwise, those who will, by keeping fast their integrity, and believing in God, and in his designs for the government of the world, may indeed, on every occasion, have wisdom given them to guide their acts. And, in an emergency, we believe there will still be statesmen and a people endued with "inspiration" equal to that which guided our fathers; and, in such a case, we can and may trust as firmly in the Divine Providence of "to-day" as in that of any previous time. The work given us is not what theirs was, — to make anew, excepting gradually, as was said above, but to *preserve,* our Government; and the zeal and energy for this, this crisis (of the civil war) has proved us to be capable of.

Underneath all the individual tendencies so greatly fostered by our free institutions, of which we had taken such unworthy advantage as to throw off almost all restraint, feeling that there could be actually no "authority" over us, and that ours is, or should be, no "government" in the real sense of the word, — all which sentiment came at length to such bold issue in the movement of secession, — underneath all this, at the call, the touch, sprang up in the great majority of our nation an ardor and a fire of patriotism, that was ready to lay itself and all it possessed on the altar of our country, even to its last life-blood. This patriotic ardor, which was formerly the inheritance of our whole country, and in which the Southern States themselves were not surpassed, will hereafter, we believe, glow as fervently on that soil as elsewhere, according to the noble utterances of one [*] who was lately on the side of secession. He says, —

"Individually, my whole soul is enlisted in the cause of a speedy, full, and perfect restoration of the Government under the Constitution as it now stands. There is nothing within my power that I am not willing cheerfully to do to effect and accomplish that end. . . . I would be willing to offer up my life itself, if by so doing this great result could be attained, and peace and harmony, prosperity, happiness, and constitutional liberty, be thus secured to the millions now living, and the untold millions hereafter to live, on this continent."

This, then, was the CALL, the WORK, that was given to us of to-day; not to argue for the dissolution of the Union, supposing that thereby we might obtain a "better;" but, when this is threatened, to lay aside our

[*] Hon. A. H. Stephens. The extract is from the letter alluded to in the note on page 120.

ephemeral character and our speculative fancies, and to awaken and inure ourselves to the stern demands of DUTY, — to the realities of the time, and the dangers of our position. The work of rescuing the Constitution from being trampled upon, and of *preserving* our nationality, have required, and will still require, as profound wisdom (though in another direction) as was demanded for the original forming of them. Although these *are* but the " means to an end," let us not think more lightly of them on that account, but hold them as sacred *as* the end, inasmuch as the one is as essential as the other: for, without the ship, the cargo is not carried; without the " MEANS," THERE IS NO END.

We have now seen, in these arguments, the views of a calm, dispassionate observer at the North, who claims to be of the most advanced and liberal party in the country; therefore none more plausible, it is to be presumed, will ever be produced: and these appear to us sufficiently exhaustive of the subject of secession. The South, however, adopted still further ideas upon the topic of State rights, which we discuss in another section.

SECTION III.

STATE RIGHTS.

Mr. Davis's Theory.

SECESSION, in the South, was but the natural successor of the previous doctrines of Nullification and State Rights; a new form of the theory of an inherent and absolute independence of each State in the national organization.

That such inherent and absolute independence has no foundation in reality, has been sufficiently shown, it appears to us, even in the incidental examinations made of this theory in the preceding section; and thus whatever reasoning or philosophy may have been used in accordance with such theory, can only be, we apprehend, on a false basis. It seems to us that this is fully illustrated in Mr. Davis's first message * to the Confederate Congress, from

---

* Delivered at Montgomery, Ala., April 29, 1861. The Italics, wherever occurring, are in the original.

which we copy the following passages. (The numbers prefixed to the paragraphs are our own, for after-reference.)

" The occasion . . . justifies me in a brief review of the relations heretofore existing between us and the States which now unite in warfare against us. . . .

(1.) " During the war waged against Great Britain by her colonies on this continent, a common danger impelled them to a close alliance, and to the formation of a confederation, by the terms of which, the Colonies, styling themselves States, entered ' severally into a firm league of friendship with each other for their common defence, the security of their liberties, and their mutual and general welfare; binding themselves to assist each other against all force offered to or attack made upon them, or any of them, on account of religion, sovereignty, trade, or any other pretence whatever.'

(2.) " In order to guard against any misconstruction of their compact, the several States made explicit declaration, in distinct articles, that each State retains its sovereignty, freedom, and independence, and every power, jurisdiction, and right which is not by this confederation expressly delegated to the United States in Congress assembled.

(3.) " Under this contract of alliance, the war of the Revolution was successfully waged, and resulted in the treaty of peace with Great Britain in 1783, by the terms of which the several States were, each by name, recognized to be independent.

(4.) "The articles of confederation contained a clause whereby all alterations were prohibited, unless confirmed by the legislatures of every State, after being agreed to by the Congress; and in obedience to this provision, under the resolution of Congress of the 21st of February, 1787, the several States appointed delegates, who attended a convention 'for the sole and express purpose of revising the articles of confederation, and reporting to Congress and the several legislatures such alterations and provisions therein as shall, when agreed to in Congress and confirmed *by the States*, render the Federal Constitution adequate to the exigencies of government and the preservation of the Union.'

(5.) "It was by the delegates chosen by the several States, under the resolution just quoted, that the Constitution of the United States was framed in 1787, and submitted to the several States for ratification, as shown by the seventh article, which is in these words: —

"'The ratification of the *convention of nine States* shall be sufficient for the establishment of this Constitution between *the States* so ratifying the same.'

(6.) "I have italicized certain words in the quotations just made, for the purpose of attracting attention to the singular and marked caution with which the States endeavored, in every possible form, to exclude the idea that the separate and independent sovereignty of each State was merged into one common government and nation, and the earnest desire they evinced to impress on the Constitution its true character, — that of a compact between independent States.

(7.) "The Constitution of 1787 having, however,

omitted the clause, already recited, from the articles of confederation, which provided, in explicit terms, that each State retained its sovereignty and independence, some alarm was felt in the States, when invited to ratify the Constitution, lest this omission should be construed into an abandonment of their cherished principle; and they refused to be satisfied until amendments were added to the Constitution, placing beyond any pretence of doubt the reservation by the States of all their sovereign rights and powers not expressly delegated to the United States by the Constitution.

(8.) "Strange, indeed, must it appear to the impartial observer, but it is none the less true, that all these carefully-worded clauses proved unavailing to prevent the rise and growth in the Northern States of a political school which has persistently claimed that the Government thus formed was not a compact between States, but was, in effect, a National Government, set up above and over the States."

If the reader will reperuse the several paragraphs as the corresponding numbers are given, the remarks made on the above-quoted passages will be readily applied.

(1.) "The league of friendship" for "common" defence and security, was, as there was occasion to observe in the former review, an instinctively-formed one, as it were, as of members of one family, having one and the same cause. It was the recognized consciousness of this *natural* relationship: for, however separate were the different "charters," they were all settled under similar conditions, as colonies of a *single* empire, and may therefore be regarded, ostensibly, but as one great colony; so that, whatever "force" was "offered to or attack made upon them, or any of them," was vitally felt and resisted by the others. This increasingly warm feeling of attachment and mutual interest, pervading them at the outset of the Revolution, was the beginning — the birth, we might say — of their consciousness and individuality as an independent people, — a people separated from the mother-country. And it is a question, whether thus *born together*, as it were, by one and the same conscious impulse, — " a nation born in a day," — there would be likely to be thereafter, intentionally or otherwise, so absolute a disruption of that natural and providential tie as would make of them as many distinct *nations* as they had been colonies; or whether the more natural inference would not be, that in the full flush of their one and united success, and in the mutual growth of attachment arising from their former earliest interests, the balance would not have been greatly in favor of their remaining united as when that success was won. The presumption in our mind is strong, that the *instinct of union* (which was originally vital among them, they being all in the same condition, as colonies of one and the same power), now greatly confirmed through experiences of difficulty and danger, would have overruled or warded off the probabilities of any after, deliberate, permanent thought to the contrary.

(2.) Being conscious, however, from all their previous history as colonies, of an individuality and innate independence one of another (excepting that *natural* relationship, and what they had voluntarily merged for mutual aid and protection), they had an instinct here, too, born also, necessarily, of their previous situation, of *reserved* rights, of a certain * sovereignty, of a power to act for themselves, as being free and independent in their own internal relations; and all such as were not " expressly delegated to the United States in Congress assembled" they had a *right* jealously to keep and guard.

In this clause of the Constitution, there are two distinct principles, or powers, recognized: namely, their own special reserved rights, and *those which had been*

---

* We say " certain " sovereignty, because this was not then perfectly defined.

delegated to the Congress of all the States; in other words, State Governments and a Central Government.

(3.) From the very beginning, then, — from their birth, we may say, since it was the same from their very first origin as colonies, — having their separate charters, yet all amenable to one sovereign government, — from the very beginning, then, those two principles went side by side, State Constitutions and a General Constitution.

The treaty of peace with Great Britain was simply recognizing their "independence" in reference to that power; it had nothing to do with their relations to each other as States: and it was essential in this, that each State should be separately designated; that not one, by any flaw of procedure, should be left a "colony," or thereafter claimed as such.

(4.) All alterations of the "articles of confederation" being prohibited, unless confirmed by the legislatures of the States, after being agreed to by Congress, shows the complete *union* of the States; that all should have a part in the Government, and *that no one should make any change that was not agreed to by all;* and the action of the States in appointing delegates "for the sole and express purpose" of making alterations and provisions, which, being " agreed to in Congress," and confirmed " *by the States*" themselves, should " render the Federal Constitution adequate to the exigencies of government and the preservation of the Union," manifests, certainly, not that they were independent of the Union and Federal Government, but that they were, on the contrary, taking all possible measures to strengthen and make valid that Union and Government.

(5.) And those very delegates from the several States, coming to the conclusion to frame a general and revised Constitution on those very principles above stated, agreed, that, if but nine States (out of the thirteen) confirmed the same, it should be adopted, and *pass for law among those agreeing States:* so satisfied and decided were they that this centralizing Government was desirable; one to be ratified; that is, fulfilled, completed, carried out *by the States themselves as parties to it.* Any other State wishing to come in afterwards would necessarily accede to whatever had been there laid down: which was the case, among the original thirteen, of New York, which came in the year after; and of North Carolina and Rhode Island. They, as well as the others, accepted, and thus became parties to the new Constitution.

(6.) The expressions Italicized by Mr. Davis, — "by the States," "the conventions of nine States," "the States," — standing in the connection they do, cannot certainly, it appears to us, afford legitimate or even indirect proof of any attempt to set forth their separate and independent sovereignty. They obviously, more properly, go to show, in the first instance, that the *whole people*, that is, *all* the States (signifying, consequently, a very confirmed union), were to be united with the action of Congress: and in the other two instances it is implied that they had the liberty, certainly, to refuse to be in the Union; but, if they *did* ratify that Constitution, it should be *established* between them; of course, with all its restrictions and qualifications, thereby necessarily modifying whatever of State sovereignty there may previously have been; and this is distinctly recognized in the clause claiming the rights which are *not* "*expressly delegated to the United States in Congress assembled.*"

(7.) In the finally settled and permanent Constitution (of 1787), the clause mentioned in paragraph two of the former articles of confederation, naming explicitly State sovereignty and independence, truly has no place (as Mr. Davis states), nor was any similar one inserted in its stead; so that our actually established Constitution makes no such reference whatever. Of what was such omission significant? Certainly not of an acknowledged "separate and independent sovereignty," when not the smallest allusion, direct or indirect, is made to that principle. On the contrary, we see in the Constitution the powers of the Central or Federal Government branching into and pervading every State.

It was not until 1791 that amendments to the Constitution were ratified, in which alone direct allusion is made to "reserved rights;" but this was a happy, judicious, fortunate addition, because of placing things on an exact and equal basis, distinctly recognizing the powers of both the people, or States, and the Constitution, and precisely limiting each. The two articles (ninth and tenth) are in these simple words: —

"The enumeration, in the Constitution, of certain rights, shall not be construed to deny or disparage others retained by the people.

"The powers not delegated to the United States by the Constitution, nor prohibited by it to the States, are reserved to the States respectively, or to the people."

These are the only references to "reserved rights" in

all the Constitution. How, then, is it possible to conceive, with the qualifications in these very articles, and after the absolute and positive restrictions that had gone before, — as that " no State shall enter into any treaty, alliance, or confederation ; grant letters of marque and reprisal: coin money ; . . . no State shall, without the consent of the Congress, lay any imposts or duties on imports or exports, except what may be absolutely necessary for executing its inspection-laws, . . . and all such laws shall be subject to the revision and control of the Congress; no State shall, without the consent of the Congress, lay any duty of tonnage, keep troops, or ships of war, in time of peace, enter into any agreement or compact with another State or with a foreign power, or engage in war, unless actually invaded, or in such imminent danger as will not admit of delay," — how is it possible, we say, in the face of such restrictions, to conceive of those " reserved " powers as amounting to a separate and independent sovereignty?

The two conditions are absolutely incompatible: and it must be mere fallacy, the selecting of such a principle on so slight, or, as it appears to us, on *no* grounds, as the mainspring of our Constitution, or its fundamental element, and discarding the other; namely, that that separate, *original* sovereignty *was* merged in a national one, which is so clearly exhibited in every article of the Constitution.

Of the latter principle, although Mr. Davis has given the words, "not expressly delegated to the United States by the Constitution" (which words could not have been withheld by him without palpable misrepresentation), he makes no account, and takes no other notice of it whatever. But who can read our Constitution, and not perceive that *its* power, or *this other principle*, penetrates into the remotest section, charging itself with the weightiest burdens and necessities of each State and with its numberless ramifications, combining or weaving them all into one body politic, whose "supreme law"* shall be that same Constitution, "any thing in the constitution or laws of any State to the contrary notwithstanding"?

These characteristics, indicating a designedly strong and powerful Central Government, are patent in the Constitution, even to the unlearned; but it appears to us that one must search deep, and still search in vain, to

---

* Constitution, art. vi. [2].

find there the "**separate and independent sovereignty**," protected by "**singular and marked caution**," that one, reasoning, not from actual facts, but on an assumed basis, might attempt to draw from it.

(It must not be forgotten that the clause first quoted in Mr. Davis's message, containing the words "sovereignty, freedom, and independence," belonged only to the original articles of confederation, and have nothing to do with our established Constitution.)

But this strong and powerful Central Government is not all that is portrayed in our Constitution: this is but one part, one-half, of the system. Besides, it has truly left to each State a "freedom" and "independence," one of another, almost as if they were foreign States. "Full faith and credit shall be given in each State to the public acts, records, and judicial proceedings, of every other State." And yet "the citizens of each State shall be entitled to all the privileges and immunities of citizens in the several States;" thus granting them all a freedom, as of one great nation, one people. It *does* grant them also a "sovereignty," in the rights reserved to the States respectively; namely, in their internal, domestic affairs: there, each State, in all its essential and private wants and liberties, is of itself, as it were, a little independent, "sovereign" nation; that is, with all the privileges of one (and with more than the privileges and blessings of other nations, the greatest burdens and responsibilities being borne by the central power).

Just here, it appears to us, is the glory of our institutions, the even balance held. In the words of the Constitution, "Nothing in this Constitution shall be so construed as to prejudice any claims of the United States, or of any particular State;" which, though applied to another point (the public territory), we may expand to every point, and paraphrase thus: No principle or right is to be wrested, perverted, or made use of, to the prejudice of another: the claims of the National Government are to be fairly and justly interpreted, and so are those of the States.

Had this simple, rightful rule been followed, and other words been emphasized as well as those that were, namely, these, "Each State retains . . . every power and right *which is not by this confederation expressly delegated to the United States in Congress assembled*," — which occur in the original articles from which he quoted, — and these (in his seventh paragraph), " the reservation by the States of all their sovereign rights and powers *not expressly delegated to the United States by the Constitution*," — had Mr. Davis Italicized these also, he would have " attracted attention " to the true and exact nature, it seems to us, the secret, the genius, of our republican system; the two nicely-adjusted and balanced " sovereignties," so harmoniously and perfectly combined, that, without detriment to or conflicting with each other, they have stood the test of nearly a century, avoiding both despotism on the one hand, and the rivalries of petty nations on the other.

(8.) It would not then have appeared strange to him, or to any one else, that any " political school should persistently claim . . . that this was, in effect, a National Government, set up above and over the States;" in fact, that we are ONE great republic, with a single chief head and authority.

It is manifest that no interpretation or theory of the Government can be correct which is not grounded upon the actual facts, and which should overlook either one or the other of these elements. In such overlooking in regard to the Federal power, Mr. Davis and his coadjutors reasoned upon a thus "false basis;" and, in setting up this doctrine of independent State rights, they came to the principle of — secession: as he further says in his message, "They (the Southern States) consequently passed ordinances resuming all their rights as sovereign and independent States, and dissolved their connection with the other States of the Union:" which conclusion could never, by logical reasoning, have been arrived at, had they regarded the other actual fact and element; namely, the powers "prohibited" to the States, or given up and renounced by them in their solemn ratification, without a single condition of future resumption.

That ratification was the seal and completion of our national form and existence. It is in vain for us to look back to what had been held before (as in the clause quoted from the "Articles of Confederation") for present authority or precedent, all outside of our ratified Constitution being now as foreign to us as would be the articles of another nation, excepting as showing the steps of our history, and the *materials* out of which our Government has been matured; and in this instance they point most markedly to our present actual state as the antetype of it, recognizing distinctly the same *two* elements which have been actually incorporated in the Constitution; so that, if such a precedent were of any avail, it would be entirely in favor of the "National Government," and not of secession, or separate and independent sovereignty, for which Mr. Davis has claimed it.

But, as we have said, it is impossible to go outside of the Constitution, which alone forms our national existence, which has been the existence of these States for the last eighty years. We can argue of our rights and proprieties only from that, as a man can argue of the powers and capacities of his body only from its actual formation. The true way could only be in taking it exactly as it is, with its varied powers. If we set out to exalt one portion of it as vital only, and independent of all the rest, we immediately falsify its true character, in which *all* the parts are vitally intermingled. To say that one man is, in his constitution or corporeal form, independent of other men, is perfectly true; and that one nation or government should be independent and free of any other, is certainly a true, correct, and the only available principle. But that a constituent, component part of any one nation or people (as we have seen, by all the details of our Constitution, this Union must be held to be, in its fundamental principles) should set itself up as independent of the rest of the nation, is a wholly different thing, and as incongruous and suicidal as it would be for one limb of our body to be torn from the whole body on the ground that it was inherently or intrinsically independent.

A human body, with a limb thus violently wrested, might not indeed, in consequence, expire (though we should conceive that its duration might be shortened by such a calamity); and our Government, even after so violent a shock as the tearing-away or forcible seceding of some of its members, might still go on with a degree of healthfulness and vigor, if that action were without its own connivance, its moral assent; was but accidental, as it were. We will make no further comparisons; for a human limb thus abruptly torn and separated, although for a time it might quiver and palpitate with the red life that had always been coursing through its veins, must in a little while, having only physical life, wither and die: whereas members thus disrupted from the nation, although they, too, quiver and palpitate from the shock, having a moral and mental existence, cannot be absolutely extinguished, but must *live on*; what kind of a life, thus falsely and unnaturally instituted, we have no disposition to portray. We only know, that, proceeding from elements of dissolution and decay, we could expect them to go on only to dissolution and decay.

The design, intent, of such separation, was, however, the conceived idea of the Southern States, arising from the doctrine of State rights, which took palpable form, and reached its climax, in the movement of secession; which was truly but the initiation of the long civil war through which we have passed on account of that very doctrine.

This was a war in which our country bled at every pore, — laying, scattering its dead on every battle-field. It was particularly destructive to the Southern States, where it originated; and we believe they have paid the full penalty in the devastation of their once-beautiful country, — towns, fields, families, in ruin. But it touched not them alone. Their best blood and treasure was expended, and so was that of the North, as this agony of war passed through, and made to shake, tremble, and almost to totter, every part of our vast country.

The agitation which the war produced is thus an actual

illustration of the principles that we have endeavored to lay down, — that we are a nation not to be divided; that, if one member is attempted to be torn away, all must suffer.

We have no design to note here the varying phases of that four-years' strife. It is enough that it has settled for the people, outwardly, the fact of our *unity*, — that we are one and inseparable. It wants now only that the *mind* be firmly convinced of the truth of this theory, and that it is the only truth, and our country will probably be put at rest on this point forever. To assist towards this conviction, and to help to make clear the whole theory of our federal system of States, has been the design of the preceding pages. We go on to elucidate in the succeeding sections what appears to us to be the present state of affairs.

SECTION IV.

RE-ORGANIZATION. — THE PRESENT CONGRESS.

In the cities and towns, and along our borders, the din and tramp of war have now long ceased.* The recruiting-drum is no more heard, and the trumpet no longer shouts its call to battle. Peace, almost as suddenly and surprisingly as a vision from heaven, came nestling, with its infolding wings, over all. It is true, that, in one short week after the cessation of arms, a piercing, startling wail of sorrow went up over the land, — that our Chief Executive, who, under God, had led the country to its final issue, had been stricken down in the height of his triumph and hard-won success, and was no longer with us to rejoice in the happy labor and reward of his hands. This, for a time, caused renewed consternation. The bitter feelings of resentment awakened

---

* It was eighteen months from the time of the surrender of the Southern army to the publication of this volume.

against so foul a deed, and burning sentiments caused by the injury and outrage, seemed about to open afresh the wounds of hostility and civil strife.

The disastrous and aggravated death of Abraham Lincoln — honoring him with the meed of a martyr's crown, and enshrining his honest, noble heart and life within the living hearts of the world, as no man before ever was enshrined — was the last flaring-up of the misguided flame, which, unchecked, would have overwhelmed our nation in destruction. But, we believe, this very spirit, in thus

> "Vaulting . . . o'erleaping itself,"

and causing all to start in horror, made that mournful death but tend to facilitate and quicken the returning throb of national feeling; to bring us again into brotherly embrace as one people, with but "one Lord and one God:" for the "*chivalrous*" Southerner, though he had been engaged in the treasonable warfare, yet with "conscientious" honor, and still honest and high-toned at heart, no doubt, as instinctively recoiled at that sanguinary and uncalled-for deed, and as utterly denounced it in his heart, as any man of the loyal States; and thus a re-action would take place in favor of that one against whom and whose cause he had so persistently held himself, and sectional feeling would thus tend to merge into the national.

That such would be partially the effect of Mr. Lincoln's tragic death we might presume from our knowledge of human nature, which forgets or lays aside enmity whenever the grave has buried its object. Thus, what seemed at the first blow, and at the first moment, to rouse anew all the feelings of animosity and strife, tended perchance, under the good providence of God, to cement the more strongly the lately-conquered peace; conquered as much, perhaps, by the generosity and magnanimity, which, commencing with the then Chief Magistrate, seemed to pervade all grades of the military officers who received the surrender of the Southern arms, as by the triumph of the Federal army itself. On one side and the other, all was accomplished in a noble and praiseworthy manner. Victory was victory, — decided, but used with clemency. Surrender was surrender, — entire, unconditional, honorable.

What more was wanting, now that peace had come and warfare had ceased, but to get things which had been so long under the regulations of war upon a *peace* footing, — into their natural order as soon as might be, — and let the nation resume its quiet force, its energy and strength? It would take some little time, it is true, for the pulse and fever of high excitement, which had been so long predominant, to become subdued to the calmness of common routine, every-day life; but we could not but expect that so auspicious a beginning would, gradually but surely, lead to the accustomed healthy and vigorous tone of the body politic. Or, if any part were less disposed than another to return to this natural state, it was easy still to retain there the restrictions, checks, and balances so long as might be necessary. As, with the cause of disease removed, the human system quickly renews its vitality; so, with the great cause of the war (slavery) overthrown from the midst of our institutions, it seemed but natural to look for our former happy and prosperous life to begin immediately to renew itself. Has it not done so? External peace had stamped its seal over our whole broad country; the war-drum was heard no more; armies were withdrawn as fast and as far as possible; magistrates were appointed; and elections in the Southern States began to resume their course, filling the long-vacated offices. What more was wanted? Were we not *re*-constructed, — exactly in the same relations that we had been? — with the Rebellion put down, States resuming their functions, not one escaped, lost, gone out, on the nation's flag, but each remaining there, distinct in its integrity, according to the very principle for which we had fought, — that the States should not, could not, go out; that they were but parts and parcels of one great whole; that our Union must and should, if the power of the Government could effect it, be preserved unbroken; that our Constitution was inviolable; and that no State should ever sever itself, or be severed, from the Union. This was the principle of Mr. Lincoln's administration; and it was the principle on which the war was conducted, on the part of the Government, throughout. That this was the true principle, we think that a little reviewing will plainly show.

Had the Southern States, *as States in the Union*, proceeded to set up laws, regulations, institutions, in overt violation of the Federal Constitution, and persisted, in opposition to the Government, in carrying these into effect, with no thought of withdrawing themselves, but with the sole design of revolutionizing the Government, seizing upon it, and converting it to its own purposes, this would have been insurrectionary and revolutionary in the usual meaning of the words. And, in such case, the Government would undoubtedly have proceeded to " conquer " them, and hold them as " conquered provinces," as far as might be necessary, though this would undoubtedly be a painful infliction on our principles of *fraternal union;* and, had such in reality occurred, it would have been truly a revolutionizing, and must have produced a change in our whole system of government. But this was not what the seceding States did; this was not their ostensible purpose; or if it had ever been attempted, as indeed it was formerly, in an incipient degree in nullification, it was promptly put down. In the present instance, the constituted authorities of the States did not come in conflict with the Government *as such.* Up to the time of withdrawal, or attempted withdrawal, from the Union, there was no infraction of the United-States laws on their statutes. The States, as States, did not rebel *against the Constitution as such.* They simply separated, or designed to separate, on an assumed right to be independent — to be outside — of the Union. As this was an interpretation of the Constitution, an opinion, a political heresy, not possible to be allowed by the Federal Government, they therefore, on its refusal, proceeded by force to accomplish their wishes. This assumption, so falsely grounded (as we think has been made apparent in the preceding sections of this work), and the *forcible* action in order to carry it out, constituted the Rebellion in this case; and the Government, in order to arrest it, necessarily proceeded also to force; which state of things became war, or contest, *on that one issue.* The Government continued to have the same right — and no other — that it had in the beginning; and that was to re-claim those States, as *States of the Union,* by virtue of its own proper authority and supremacy; and the rebellious States had the same wrong — and no other* — in their persistency in that assumed right to depart or secede: the contest being *prolonged* made no difference. Therefore, when the conflict should cease (if with the triumph of the Federal power), each would return to the same relations as before, — the Federal Government to be the Federal Govern-

---

* We mean here merely to express that the PRIME ISSUE remained the same as at first; although, even in this species of rebellion, we believe that all usual and common kinds of rebellion were necessarily included.

ment, and the States to be States, as formerly, — with the exception of provisional governments so long as it might be necessary; and that would be until the States were able to get into order, and to resume their own functions. With the Rebellion crushed, the States remain, then, States, precisely as before. This was the very object for which the Government went to war: it was the one issue at stake.

That this is the true principle, notwithstanding what is said to the contrary, at present, by the prevailing party in the country, we have but to look at the converse. Let us suppose the Federal power, by its triumph, to have obtained complete control over the once-rebellious but now-subdued States, and that it could change, modify, reconstruct, their position in any manner to suit its views or desires. No provision having been made in the Constitution for this, it would be necessary to adopt some new mode, introduce some element not before a part of our Constitution; for we never before had had this power. This new element would, of course, be adopted and managed by that portion of the Union States that was still in the exercise of its functions, and by that only; for the other States, not having yet resumed their places, could have no voice or part in the matter. Here, then, would be a fundamental change in our system. Instead of its being an organization of equal States, coming voluntarily into the association, having the reserved power to decide whether they would come into it or not (which power was originally granted to all the States), it would be an organization in which a *part* decided for the others; those others being *compelled* to adopt a form of constitution which was not their own choice. Here, then, would be our Government changed at once from a republican to an anti-republican system; for republicanism consists in the people's freedom of choice in its form of government. With this power of choice taken away, there would be introduced, consequently, the element of revolution; for it is the established axiom of our Government, — and it is the vital principle of all republics, — that, when a people is not satisfied with its form of government, it has the *right* to revolutionize.

Thus, from a republic with a Constitution granting the same and equal rights to all the States, we should become an oligarchy, an aristocracy, a despotism, or whatever it might be called, where only a part had control; and, moreover, would be directly inserted the element, the seed, of revolution.

That such was not the form of our Constitution, that it contained no such principle of inequality, or seed of revolution, from such a source, our very instinct and understanding tell us; and it has also been proved by the very test of the four-years' war itself, which, on the part of the Government, was conducted on and for that very principle, — that the Union of these States is *indissoluble;* that they had come voluntarily into the Union, and that there they must and should remain; that no States had any *independent* rights over and above the others; that all were on precisely the same ground, one and indivisible. That is, they were not allowed to bring forward a new doctrine, — contrary to the received interpretation of the Constitution, — giving to single States, or to a number of States united, the power to act of themselves, without regard to the national system of organization.

This doctrine of State rights, which was the prime issue of the war, and which we have been accustomed to think belonged peculiarly to the secessionists, has not been wholly confined to the Southern States, but has insinuated itself very insidiously on various occasions elsewhere; for instance, on that of the "arbitrary" or military arrests made during the war. A governor of the Northern States said of these, in reference and in opposition to the national power, "It is a high crime to abduct a citizen of this State.* . . . Without consultation with its chief magistrate, a subordinate department at Washington insulted our people and invaded our rights. Against these wrongs and outrages," &c.

We might presume, indeed, that the National Executive (for the "subordinate departments" at the capital act, of course, but under the supervision of the Executive) would, in all cases, find it convenient and suitable, for greater facility and aid, to make known its determinations to the State officials, unless it goes upon the ground established by the Supreme Court (in connection with the Fugitive-slave Law of 1850, in the case of Briggs vs. Pennsylvania), that the United States must carry out its own laws by its own and not by the State

---

* Message of the Governor of New York to the Legislature of that State, Jan. 6, 1863.

officers ; and most probably this was the ground in all those cases of "arbitrary arrests." But that it should be *responsible* or amenable to the State where a *national* affair was concerned, was immediately to place the State authority above the national, and was so far setting up the doctrine of State rights. That those arrests were made on account of crime against the nation, open or suspected, was known to all: they were made only for known or supposed treason against the *National* and not the State Government. That the people are thus directly amenable to the national authorities, is plain from the first words of the Constitution, "We the people of the United States." It was they, at large, and not as people of *the States*, who formed it; and it is they, singly and individually, in whatever State or part of the country they may be, with whom the Government has to deal when a *national* question arises.

The jealous dignity of a State being thus easily touched, on these minor points,* shows how easily the doctrine insinuates itself, of the independent rights of States. (We allude further, elsewhere, to this subject of arbitrary arrests.)

* Other instances of this are noted in another volume of this work.

That a species or variety of this same doctrine now exists in a large number of the States, appears to us very clear in the views adopted by their delegates in the present Congress; namely, that a *portion* of the States may adopt acts and measures independently of the whole number of States. That is, we are entitled to consider those States as holding such views, through their delegates or representatives; though it is true that another election might reverse such representation. But we speak of this further.

We stand, then, on the simple ground, not of independent rights of one State over another, but on that of constitutional rights; of those which are inherent in our very form of Government, and which cannot be changed without essentially modifying that form. And these rights are undoubtedly the same for every State in the Union. All are on precisely equal ground, which is the very perfection and glory and strength of our republic, as it appears to us, in guaranteeing us against the hostility and ambition of rival States; in giving to each one freedom to develop itself in all internal resources and character, and in being thus generous and liberal in all that is desirable, so saving us from revolutionary aims and attempts; and in preserving us from disintegration by the impossibility of any State or States leaving independently of the others; which impossibility has now been tested and proved on that very issue by the civil war in which we have been engaged.

Such a Union, so glorious in its fraternal character, — enabling all these little *nations*, as it were (so extensive are they in territory and resources, and so independent in their domestic relations), to live in friendly and combined efforts for great and honorable purposes, — is glorious also in the prestige it confers on each one of these States; it being, in union with the others, of equal rank and power with any other nation on the globe.

Such is our Constitution; and it seems to us that its excellence has been supremely manifested by the tremendous ordeal through which it has passed, showing itself strong above ten millions of our people who were arrayed against it, or rather who attempted to interpolate a new element by giving it a new construction, which would have made it a wholly different code, in its influences and results, from what had been manifested in the previous eighty years of its existence. In short, it appears to us as perfect a political code, perhaps, as human means will ever be able to devise; granting all rightful and healthful freedom, with the just limitations of law and order; allowing all these numerous, separate, and, in a manner, independent States, to possess all the strength of a great, undivided one; each State, in private matters, being enabled to have its own idiosyncrasies, its individual tastes and characteristics, yet great questions, of interest to the whole world, perhaps, pronounced upon and secured by the united wisdom of all.

Happy the country with such noble privileges and opportunities! Shall we preserve it for ourselves and our posterity, with all its unmeasured blessings and advantages, unknown, in their full extent, to the whole world beside? Shall we retain the Constitution which our fathers left to us? so equal, so just, so unexceptionable, so harmonious in all its bearings, so perfectly adjusted in all its parts, that when put to the trial, even on points not before experienced, it has ever shown itself equal to the emergency, as has been well illustrated by the decease of a President in office: without conflict, without jar, without excitement, or a day's delay, his successor is already in his place, — the wheels of government undisturbed for a single moment. As in the case, also, of the late Rebellion: already foreign nations have been struck with admiration by our facilities for carrying out all our plans so *constitutionally* and prosperously.

Shall we keep this, we repeat, our Constitution, with all its checks and balances, its privileges, its just and equal rights and influences? which is the question of the present moment. It has stood us in good stead; it has not been wanting in the hour of trial and difficulty; it has borne us even through a period of national woe and anguish; in short, it has proved an ark of safety in many a time of anxiety and danger. Shall we retain it as it was formed, and as it has hitherto proved itself, worthy and efficient? or shall we change it for some new mode, and, in so changing, again break up or modify our whole system of government?

This one question is, to our mind, of vast and essential moment, not only to the present well-being, but to the future welfare, of these States, and of the world at large.

That which is done or conceived in each generation is but precedent and history for that which follows; as has been so painfully evident in the insidious doctrine on which we have so much commented, — State rights; introduced only a generation since, but which, in our day, had culminated, almost to the destruction of our country. *Opinion* is the commencement, the seed, of *action: thinking* is but the origin of *doing*. Therefore it essentially behooves the people, in whose hands to a great extent, in this country, is the power of *revolutionizing*, to guard with the utmost care and caution political opinions and theories; to be sure that they have a true and sound basis, and that all our ideas are founded only upon just and accurate grounds; remembering that we in our day, in all that we do and think, are but planting, step by step, that which must assuredly come to growth, be it true or false, of good or of evil.

With such cautious, truthful proceeding, our *revolutions*, be they in the way of opinion or amendment, or change of constitution or of government, will then be but safe, and probably those which were needed.

In reference to our present condition, it has been and

is still said that things were out of joint in consequence of the Rebellion; that we must be made over, reconstructed, before we could go on again in peace and safety. This was true in a measure. The war inevitably produced changes; and reconstruction, to some extent, was necessary. Our only care was to do this *constitutionally*: as the war had been carried on, through all its phases, constitutionally, so we should continue to finish and square off all matters connected with that and the Rebellion constitutionally; that is, *according to the Constitution*, as the *Constitution* may demand; in that, and in *no other* way. But what has the "Constitution" to do with this? one might say. Or we may be liable to be rebutted at the very outset by some such paragraph as the following: —

"I am at once met by a vast array of objections. 'It would be unconstitutional!' say some scrupulous patriots. Is it not a little surprising that the Constitution should be quoted most frequently and persistently in favor of those who threw that very Constitution overboard?" (Cheers.) *

---

* From the report of a speech at an emancipation-meeting at the Cooper Institute, New York, March 6, 1862. The author of this is now a prominent "radical Republican."

As if, forsooth, because the seceding States had violated their obligations, — and this was the very crime for which the Government proceeded against them, — we were to exempt ourselves from ours!

By what possible right or propriety was the war carried on, on our part, if we were no longer bound *constitutionally?* Then, indeed, would it have been " conquest," literally; we fighting, like them, to carry out simply our own wishes and desires; being in precisely the same category with them.

By all that is sacred and upright; by all that is honest, just, and true; by all our hopes of humanity, and desires for its redemption, — even of every slave from bondage, — let no man, woman, or child, in America, but repudiate forever such unholy sentiment! Let no sneer ever approach to violate the sacredness of these obligations! Morality and truth in politics, or affairs of State, are as essential a morality and truth as any other; and, as in religion, he that is here unfaithful in little will be unfaithful also in much. He who is sophistical and without conscience on these points will be likely to be so on all other points.

On the contrary, it is within the limits of the Constitution only that we can act: it is that alone which endues us with power to do aught. Without it we have no existence, either as States or as a nation, — are but a vast, agitated sea of irresponsible individual actors. Whatever, then, is done affecting the institutions and constitution of any of our States, can only be done "constitutionally."

"But," we may again be replied to, "this is a new state of things, such as has never occurred before; and we must now proceed to procure guaranties that it never occur again."

Here we leave this subject for the present, and return to that of "arbitrary arrests," wishing to expatiate a little further upon that topic, as it caused some excitement at the time, and as our discussion of it will lead to a view of the actual state of affairs and of the country during the Rebellion.

ARBITRARY ARRESTS.

With reference to "arbitrary" or "military" arrests, — which were arrests made during the war by the Federal Government, under the suspension of the *habeas corpus*, — we quote from the same document as before: "I deny that this Rebellion can suspend a single right of the citizens of loyal States. I denounce the doctrine, that civil war in the South takes away from the loyal North the benefits of one principle of civil liberty. . . . The abduction of citizens from this State for offences charged to have been done here, and carrying them many hundred miles to distant prisons in other States and Territories, is an outrage . . . upon every principle of right and justice. . . . This loyal State, whose laws, whose courts, and whose offices, have thus been treated with marked and public contempt, and whose social order and sacred rights have been violated, was at that very time sending forth great armies to protect the national capital, and to save the national officials from flight or capture."

It might now, perhaps, excite a smile of impatience or incredulity, that, in the height of the war, the occasional arrest of some suspected person, in whatever State, and his transportation to some one of the national fortresses used as prisons for State offences, should have created so much sensation as it did at the time in some places. But we admit that this was a grave charge, and that civil war, or secession, in the South, should not have taken away from any loyal citizen of the North "the benefits of one principle of civil liberty," excepting what were inevitably bound up in that state of civil war: for undoubtedly there were various ways in which the state of civil war, or secession in the South, did actually deprive every loyal State of certain benefits and privileges of the principles of civil liberty: namely, the restrictions of commercial intercourse, which the blockade of the Southern ports entailed; and also those of free speech or of the press, in the necessary prohibition to publish facts in regard to the army movements, *et cœtera*. These things were unavoidable, and what the simple sense of each individual would plainly tell him that he must yield to. But more than this did not seem clear. Military or summary arrests by the Federal Government, in the midst of these otherwise peaceful communities, were startling, and seemed to be despoiling us of the very blessings and privileges of the civil liberty we had inherited, and had hitherto long enjoyed. The *unusual* nature of the occurrence we apprehend to have been a great cause of the excitement. But, to discover the true grounds and bearings of this proceeding, it appears to us only necessary to take a cursory view of the whole state of the country during that period, by which we shall perceive how even the loyal States must have been affected in their dearest rights by the civil war, or secession in the South.

Before secession took place, the doctrine, or principle, appeared so plausible to some minds, that it found advocates or apologists among even our (so-called) most intelligent communities at the North. We have seen how it was theoretically indorsed by a leading member of the party of the most "advanced thought;" and a large proportion of the minds of the nation, as we all remember (and as was noticed in the second section of this work), really wavered, or were uncertain and doubtful whether the secessionists might not be, in the abstract, right. It was even thought that they might be allowed to go — on *experiment;* but, when the war actually commenced, the question soon settled itself for the majority of these. However doubtful they may have been as far as the theory went, they had no idea in actual fact of seeing their country broken into fragments. This feeling was not, however, universal. Some, perhaps many, at heart, continued to believe the secessionists to be right in theory; and, as the war went on, these became more open and sympathizing in speech and act. Of course, this was rebellion, of the same nature as and identical with that in the South. The being surrounded by the great masses of a loyal community could not exonerate these individuals from personal guilt in the matter. It was the more dangerous, if possible, this having the power to act as a corrosive poison, or a contagious disease, on those around. The question, then, must turn upon whether *it were necessary* for the Government to take notice of those instances of rebellion, and not upon the *lawfulness* or *right* of such notice, as, of course, this rebellion was no more justifiable or constitutional — although existing in individual cases only — in the otherwise loyal States than elsewhere; and if this crime *against the nation* should break out anywhere in a loyal Northern State, as in a Southern rebellious one, it was by the same duty and right that the national authorities would proceed to repress it in the former as in the latter case. This was the only impartial ground. We should have no right to proceed against the Southerners, and exonerate or screen any Northern secessionist. The Government proceeded against these in all places as its own people, its own constituents. They were citizens at large of the *United States.* Our whole form of government depends on this,—its general relation to all the populations of the States as *its* body politic; each individual having a general citizenship, and a direct amenability and responsibility to the General Government as well as to the States themselves. The document quoted from above admits that the General Government has power, through its courts established in all the States, to enforce authority; "to appoint officers to arrest, and commissioners to hear complaints, and to imprison upon reasonable grounds of suspicion." All this power it has in ordinary times; and in those times of general peace and order, when seditious cases would be of limited extent, there is no probability of the Government ever seeing any necessity, or having any temptation, to act otherwise than through those organized forms. But in a rebellion *out* of the usual order of things, and, to an extreme extent, absorbing nearly half of the country, with its sympathizers ramified throughout every section, it would seem that wherever detected, by open testimony, or on strong and "reasonable" grounds of suspicion, it must necessarily be treated also *out of a usual* way of proceeding; and there can certainly be no doubt that the Constitution gives, in these plain words, a summary mode of procedure in such cases (sect. 9 [2]) : " The privilege of the writ of *habeas corpus* shall not be suspended, *unless, when in cases of rebellion or invasion, the public safety may require it;* " the exception making, in this case, the rule.

Thus it appears to us that the National Government was on the strict ground of propriety in those arrests, and that it could not have done otherwise without partiality. It could not overlook secession in the Northern States, even if occurring only in individual instances, and at the same time, with the "iron heel of war," be putting it down in the Southern States. That the whole country, in parts, was affected and sore by the great upheaving, is not surprising; and, from all analogy, it could not be otherwise. A deep disease in the human body, although local, must infect more or less the whole system, appearing in spots here and there, and obstructing or checking the usual healthy circulations throughout. Instances of false imprisonment may have occurred among these arrests; but those were liabilities which the abnormal state of war must be expected to bring, — the accidents, and not the design.

MARTIAL LAW.

The above remarks need to be but a little extended, it appears to us, to embrace the whole topic of "martial law." The same document before quoted says, "Amidst all the horrors that have been enacted under martial law in the history of the world, and amidst all the justifications attempted of its usages, it was never before held that it could be extended over peaceful States. It was never before claimed that the power of a military commander was superior to the powers of government. . . . Eight of the twelve States which originally made up our Union explicitly declared that the military power should, in all cases and at all times, be held in exact subordination to the civil authority, and be governed by it: this was expressed in each constitution, in terms almost identical. It is incredible that a people who held these views, and who were jealous of their liberties, and who thus restrained State authorities under their immediate control, would give to the commander of the army of the United States this despotic power."

These remarks are admirably adapted to, and perfectly descriptive of, our normal state, — our natural state, as we may call it, — a state of order and peace; and, in that state, we believe that no one in this country ever presumed to elevate the military above the civil power. It never was a question: our regular army was always limited, and had always been subordinated to the civil government. Also the measure of power, both State and National, *is* "fixed by the Constitution;" and these powers are, in general, so clearly adjusted, that it would seem that neither one nor the other of them could, in a period of quiet and prosperity, go astray with impunity. If the General Government should exceed its bounds, the States would immediately utter their protest; and, if the States surpassed their limits, the General Government would as quickly check their encroachments. *It would seem that it should so be;* and, verily, for a long period it was so, — no other possibility being dreamed of: but the fact did not so remain. A tremendous rebellion showed an aggression of States upon the National Law and Constitution. We may say that this did not affect the loyal States; that they, peaceful, should go on the same as ever. But the truth is, it did affect them; and they could not go on the same as ever. This was not only a negation of the law of the Constitution in the rebellious States, but it was also the introduction of another positive condition of things in the "peaceful" States. Their trade, their commerce, in multifarious and essential ways, was upheaved; they were called upon to supply armies for the field; a constant draft upon their men and treasures was requisite; and the mourning, the loss of life and homes, desolated them as well as the most rebellious States. Truly, all was "out of joint." Thus rebellion is not simply a denial of a certain organized condition: it is the reign of a positive disorder, as palpable to the sense as (ah! in this instance, how much more palpable than!) any other condition. This condition is owing, indeed, to the withdrawal of or from law; but, while it lasts, it is as actual as any other state of things. It is, therefore, a great *power* of evil; and in this instance it shook our country to its extremest ends, thus showing the magnitude and the peril of the occasion.

That the usual civil and constitutional *quiet* routine could go on the same where the Rebellion had sway, it would be vain to assert. In no country in the world could the usual routine be carried out in such a condition of affairs. This great power of the Rebellion, going forth in aggression, rising "above the law," attempting an exactly opposite course to that which had been sanctioned and sworn to as the common law and order of the country, could not be competed with by that common law and order: *that* was established for *its* state of things. Rebellion can be met only by something commensurate with itself. If it rages with physical or military force, physical or military force alone can be adequate to contend with it. Therefore, in this country, as in every other, another order of things must be established to meet such emergency; and our fathers, recognizing the possible need, provided for this. They inserted in the Constitution — not as an accidental thing, but as belonging to it — the power to raise and support armies and a navy, *power to suppress insurrections*. This power must, of course, include *whatever will be necessary*, or it is no *power at all; and it is power separate and different from the common course, — from the usual, quiet routine,* — that formed for its own regular, ordinary state of affairs, being inadequate, and not expected to cope with an irregular, extraordinary state or condition. This authority, however, is not *above* the civil authorities: it is still held in the civil hands (the Executive himself is commander-in-chief, though not in the field) ; it is empowered by the Constitution, and is, therefore, equally constitutional with the other; it is, for the time being, but a substitute for the other, not for a permanency, but for the occasion.

This unusual, extraordinary exercise of power during war time, is martial law ; and this law, *out* of the usual exercise of power, is doubtless called for *wherever* the unusual state, insurrection, or rebellion, exists ; because it is precisely to meet such that it was created: and, *whenever* such arises, this also arises as the necessary consequence; that is, effect strictly following cause. It is just as unavoidable, therefore, for martial law to exist if the unusual state of things exists, and just as legal, because provided for in the form of government, as any other law or laws.

To our mind, then, it is plain that martial law does and must in force actually exist for the true integrity and security of the government and nation in times of extraordinary rebellion, extending even to " peaceful " States, in whatever form may be necessary. It exists there in its requisitions for men and means to carry on the war; and it appears to us that this authority might as well be disputed as any other branch of strictly martial law. No State, in a time of great excitement and upheaving, could answer for numbers of its own population not becoming infected with the same treasonable purposes; and therefore the ultimate security of each demanded that that extraordinary but not extra-constitutional power should be possessed by the Central Authority, and that it should hold that efficient hand — that martial law — ready for use, not only over the rebellious States, but, in that time of disorder, over the whole vast country, excited and sympathetic by natural ties in every part, liable to an occasional outbreak here and there, even in the most generally loyal portions. And, in denying that power, we should be cutting off from ourselves a necessary arm of protection, as might have been exemplified in the divided secession States, as Tennessee, Kentucky, Missouri, &c. Precisely with the same kind of authority — martial law, created expressly for that emergency — with which it put down rebellion in those semi-loyal States, we conceive that it should put it down in but a single individual, if it so be, in an otherwise wholly loyal State; and, if it had not the right to subdue precisely the same crime in the latter place by proceedings of martial or national law (formed expressly for that unusual state of things), we know not how it could possess the right in the former places; the two cases being precisely identical in nature, only unequal in extent. No: there must be requisite the same firm, impartial hand over every part, as need may be; and it appears to us, that, if this power were denied to the Government in the one case, it must be abandoned in the other; and that then we should have no Central or National Government, but would be resolved into wholly independent States.

We have only further to add, that this power may have been occasionally abused in all the subordinate offices of Government; that this would not be at all improbable in those new and untried circumstances; and that, therefore, the States themselves were not exempt from a vigilant care and protection of their own citizens, as far as would be warranted on their part; but that this did not supersede the necessity and the existence of the principle and the fact of martial law — the military power of the Government — being exercised in its proportionate measure, even, if needful, in the loyal portions of the country.

EMANCIPATION.

The address we have quoted from goes on to say, "There is little to fear in periods of peace and prosperity. If we are not protected when there are popular excitements and convulsions, our Government is a failure."

This remark was made in connection with the Proclamation of Emancipation of President Lincoln, and these sentences followed: —

"If presidential proclamations are above the decisions of the courts and the restraints of the Constitution, then that Constitution is a mockery. If it has not the authority to keep the Executive within its restraints, then it cannot retain States within the Union. Those who hold that there is no sanctity in the Constitution must equally hold that there is no guilt in the Rebellion."

What would have been an accorded right in the normal, regular, established routine, was no longer, for the *time*, a right: it actually *did not then exist*. That right (of slavery) was granted for a certain, recognized condition: it was abrogated, in itself, by the Rebellion having overturned and upheaved all things in the seceding

States. The whole relation of affairs, for the time being, was changed: usual laws were not in force; they could not have play. Those States declared themselves an enemy, in opposition to the Government; and thereby was created, or was required and brought into use, the new order of law, which was designed and marked out for exactly such emergencies; namely, military rule, the regular effect following cause. The very order (implied) to suppress insurrections must include power in the Government to avail itself of efficient means to break down such insurrection; and it would appear to the plainest sense a great dereliction of duty, and a want of earnestness on the part of the Government, should it leave untouched any thing that might check or stagger such overwhelming rebellion. Military law certainly gives the power of aught (within the pale of civilization) that would worst the enemy. It was never heard of in any region or army of the world, that an advantage would not be obtained over an opposing army by any (military) means available. It would be a farce and a cruel mockery for those employed to be attacking it, and yet to leave untouched its supply-trains by which it was fed and sustained day by day, if it were in their power to get possession of them. If the slaves were of essential aid and comfort to the insurgents by supplying the provisions at home, thus enabling the whole ablebodied force of white men to enter the army of Rebellion, thereby doubling its effective force, surely the military rule, the martial law, which alone can be executed in the case of insurrection, might be employed to weaken, paralyze, dispose of, that "aid and comfort," as well as any other, so far as it was able. The order of emancipation, therefore, from the Executive (being commander-in-chief), as a military measure, was not a mere "paper proclamation;" and although it might not have taken much effect, perhaps, any further than as the Federal armies advanced, wherever that was effected, little by little, the military advantage of the measure immediately accrued; for the negroes, diverted from aiding the Rebellion, were exactly in that proportion a gain to the Government.

The proclamation was issued on the ground of military necessity, and was the due mode of meeting the secessionists on their own grounds. They had by force defied the General Government, and with the "strength" of their institution. How was it possible, then, that they, by their persistency (Mr. Lincoln having previously offered them privileges in regard to it), should not forfeit it, and that the Government should not demolish that strength in the same manner that it would seek to demolish any other available force of the enemy, — by the use of the appropriate rule, martial law, which was co-extensive with the Rebellion itself, — the very power and rule which had been ordained for the suppressing of insurrections?

In the edict of emancipation, the letter of the Constitution was not touched. The statutes affecting slavery would remain the same, unless amended by Congress. No power less than that — the power of the people in their legislative capacity — could change the Constitution and laws of the country. The *immediate* status of slavery only was affected by the proclamation; and to that, according to the preceding views deduced, the secessionists exposed themselves in the same manner as they exposed their territory to become desolated, in having resorted to armed warfare, or by the fortunes of war.

This did not affect the vitality of the Constitution; the subject of slavery being an accessory, as it were, to be observed as rightfully and in as true integrity as any other of its provisions, while things were in their normal condition; but still liable to the incidents of war, as we have seen, in the same manner as were commerce, trade, postal arrangements, — on all which, in the Southern States, an embargo was necessarily laid, in consequence of hostilities. The *organic* relations, only, of the State and Federal Governments to each other, are the *essentially vital* ones, which, even in time of war, — *such* war, — are inviolable, so that we could not proceed to alter those relations. We could not proceed to change a State into any other form of relationship; into that of a colony, for instance, or a mere dependency, as such. Nor could we alter any function whatever of the Federal Government: the States were to remain States as they had been, and the Federal Government was to remain what it had been. This was the one issue of the war.

Thus the Constitution, through all those changes, remained intact. Any modifications from the usual state of the country — the state of peace — were for the time being only, and were those which are allowed by the very Constitution itself; as we have seen in respect of the *habeas corpus*, and of the use of the military power in putting down insurrections. This latter, of course, must include military rule or governorship of the rebelling States *until the insurrection should be effectually subdued;* until the States should be *restored,* — brought back in *good faith* to their former condition, simply and entirely as States of the Union. When this should be accomplished, the Union would be *as it was*, in every essential and vital feature unchanged, — the organic relations remaining the same *as they had previously been.*

The demolition of the former *status* of slavery may have been temporarily injurious or inconvenient, like the other desolations and incidents of the war; but, as we have seen, this in itself did not touch any vital feature of the Federal Union. The Constitution being untouched, and the protective clause with regard to slavery still remaining, we should still be amenable to it, if slavery should continue anywhere, until that clause should be expunged; and this could be only by general consent in "full congress" of the people. Had the Executive attempted to do this of itself, that indeed would have been laying violent hands upon the Constitution, which would have aroused the country to an indignant burst of remonstrance. Mr. Lincoln, in fact, did no such thing; nor can we dream that any man hereafter would dare thus to touch the sacred ark of our liberties, the charter of our rights. Any change or amendment there could be conducted only by the united voice of the nation through its constitutionally organized channels

Thus, in employing the military power, it was not a question of subjugating and destroying the South as an insurrectionary section, but only of subjugating and destroying *the rebellion within it;* so to bring the States back to their allegiance, into the *same Union* we had before, — the same relations of Federal and State governments, each with its own local laws and policy. The institution of slavery alone was incidentally changed; and war would probably have so shaken it, that it would never have been able to recover itself: but the Constitution on that point remained the same until legally modified by regular Congressional action.

These *constitutional* principles, then, are our political rock, and ark of safety; and, so long as the *virtue and intelligence* of our people continue, it will thus be an impossibility to " convert our Government into a military despotism." We need fear no such evil; and, with just faith in those principles, no such anomalous and "mischievous doctrine" could prevail, as that it would be necessary to "subjugate and destroy" any portion of the country in order to SAVE THE UNION. It would be a solecism thus to conduct; and it would be no "Union," not our true and genuine Union, unless the whole of it, every section and State, were preserved, and redeemed to its original integrity and position.

RE-ADMISSION OF THE STATES.

We have seen how admirably the Constitution carried us through all the perils of the Rebellion, as it had formerly carried us through our happy prosperity. No jar, no let, no hinderance, had ever occurred in all our experience: it had shown itself fully equal to every emergency; it had failed us on no point during the war, up to the very moment when the vision of white-winged Peace came hovering over us in the full and final surrender of the secession forces. *That* — the breaking-up of the Rebellion — had been the object of the whole war; and every mode and procedure in regard to it we had been able to carry out *constitutionally*, according to the right and power invested in the Constitution. Might we not, then, expect that the white-robed angel which approached at the laying-down of the rebel arms, and in consequence of this, and which was the very purpose for which the war had been conducted on the Federal side, would also be received, settled, and established again among us constitutionally? Would it be possible that the Constitution should allow us to go thus far, and not be equal to this emergency? (Such, we think, it might be named, as it seems to have proved a difficult thing to know what to do with this peace when it came!) How, when, where, should we receive or inaugurate it? How? We answer, To our mind, it should have been received with acclamations from one end of the country to the other; that we were no longer a disrupted nation; that the States had been recovered, their arms laid down, and that we were now an indivisible Union as we had been. When? We answer, From the moment that military power was no longer needed, and when trade, commerce, intercourse, could spring up mutually as before. Where? In every State that had been distracted by war, and which was now in good faith fulfilling its new-sworn allegiance.

Was not *this* the mode which the Constitution would devise for the settling of peace? Would not this be the natural, constitutional result of the previous constitutional measures, — the measures to bring about and produce this very result, — the state of peace, having warred upon those who would have destroyed it? There was no other object in the war than to re-claim the States about to depart, so to procure an abiding and everlasting peace. It was the usual effect following cause: this had been labored for, and it had come. We slipped into it naturally, so to say, by very force of *fact*. We could not have helped ourselves had we so wished; it had come; we *were in it:* just as much as we had been in a state of war, we were now in a state of peace. It was the *constitutional* result of the constitutional methods used. What other mode was needed? The Constitution had not permitted us to be parted; and now, that being settled, what more was there to be done? Had we not come back to precisely the same position as before? There was but one issue of the war; and, that settled in favor of the Constitution, why should we not go right on with the Constitution the same as formerly? The Constitution, in giving power to put down the Rebellion, implied that peace would be restored, and nothing else: it says nothing about any further change. When peace was restored, then, were we not exactly in the position the Constitution would have us? Thus, I think, we can discover by this logical reasoning what the Constitution meant by "peace," and what was the "constitutional" mode of proceeding after peace was first signed, sealed, and secured by the quelling of the insurrection. It was, in the first place, to get things in train as speedily as possible for the States to resume their long-obstructed or laid-aside functions. This was still the work of the Executive, as commander-in-chief, — *not* of the armies in the field: these had done their part; and now it was for the Chief Magistrate to continue his executive labors until all external things, at least, — civil and political relations, — should be completely restored. And here, *en passant*, we might say that this is all that the Government can do: it has no power to effect change of opinion or feeling, any further than external measures may have a natural influence. The Government may and must put down rebellion, insurrection, or any civil disturbance outwardly ; but it cannot compel *conviction*, or *change* the *sentiments*. These can be effected only by just, wise, and true measures, which in time have their effect.

The President, then, had only to go on in a just and true constitutional way, retaining supervision of the (internally) dislocated and out-of-joint States until they were able to go on of themselves. How effectually the provisional governorships were carried out, and with what prompt action, enabling each State, one after another, to get its affairs in train, may well be presumed from the known energetic character of our present Chief Magistrate. Neither was there undue haste, as may be seen from the long period which elapsed (sixteen months) after the military surrender of the States, before the last provisional government (that of Texas) was removed, and the State was re-instated in its own organic functions.

Such simple, natural proceeding was but in consonance with the general character of our constitutional provisions ; all which, as we have seen, have been so admirably adjusted, so equal to the occasion, that " *emergencies*," with us, have scarcely proved " emergencies:" and so this emergency, so to say, of peace, settled itself, as it were (or would have done so), as readily as all other events have done. All can see how consistent this was with the general character of our republican institutions, — that war did not change us into a military government; that we became nothing else, in fact, but our previous system of free and equal States, with each on the same ground that it was before. And have not the blessings of peace followed this condition of external peace, into which we so easily slid after our four years of the disturbance of war? Have not trade, commerce, intercourse, postal arrangements, all begun to revive again, and to become as healthful and vigorous as before? and, although it may take a long period to recover the devastated States to their former pitch of prosperity, under our munificent government this will come in time.

In the mean time, the legislative branch had had *its* work to do. Congress had not been all this time lying idle: it had, of course, gone on in its appropriate sphere. The whole country could not pause in its legislative functions because certain States had attempted to withdraw from the rest. No: those that were left must still continue in their legitimate work. The machinery of government was not to cease because some of the States had chosen to leave it. Congress must go on; the people, the country, must be taken care of, and legislated for the same as ever. Demands were made which must be supplied. Questions were constantly rising which must be met. One of these was in regard to that slave-clause of the Constitution: what should be done with it? Slavery had been overthrown from its pedestal by the upheaving of war, and the edict of emancipation had completely abolished it; at least, as a matter of present fact. Should it ever be revived? This was the question. Should Congress leave this so that it might be re-instated at any time in the States? or should it say that now it was done with, finished, settled forever; that that subject should never again bring the nation into peril? Was not this the time that the fathers had looked forward to, when future generations should do that in regard to slavery which *they* were not able to do, — to banish it forever and decisively from the Constitution? Was not this the very moment to seize upon — now that it was almost in its death-gasp — to give the final stroke which should settle the matter for us and for all posterity? Certainly: there were no two ways about it. Slavery had almost caused the overthrow of the nation: now it, in its turn, at this critical juncture, must receive *its* overthrow. Through the instrumentality of its own States, it had become loosened, broken up, despoiled of its prestige; it had attempted to make all these vast States *its* victim: now itself must become a prey and a victim. Therefore, " in full congress of the people," the slavery-clause was expunged from the Constitution; or an amendment of the Constitution was enacted, which forever prohibited slavery in the United States.

We say, "in full congress of the people;" for so it was, as far as the circumstances of the case would admit. It was the legal assemblage of the people, which had gone on uninterruptedly, as a matter of necessity, in its regular sessions. The Southern representatives were not present, because those States were not in a condition to be represented. They had voluntarily withdrawn from their seats in Congress, and they were still in a state of warfare against the Union.* It was by their own act that they were absent: they had not

---

* This amendment passed during the war.

been sent away or excluded; and therefore the Congress was the same *legal* Congress without them as with them. It was all that the country could have; and its acts, consequently, were as valid as at any former period of its history; and they became, as much as any former acts, the "supreme law" of the land. Thus Congress and the country, as we have before said, not being able to wait, — the "emergency" being upon them, — the opportune moment in the course of Providence having arrived, the Constitution was amended on this point.

When the formerly slave States were in a condition to be re-instated, this amendment was submitted to them for their adherence as a necessary preparation for or condition of their re-instatement; for, of course, the Constitution, as then legally amended, was to be the Constitution to which they must now give their allegiance. It had been through their own fault that their seats were vacant in Congress, and therefore they must receive whatever modifications had been pronounced in the mean time by the voice of the country beside.

Possibly some might say, "Why have been in such haste? Why not have waited until the States had been re-admitted into Congress, and so let all act upon amending the Constitution, instead of making assent to the amendment a condition of their re-instatement?"

In any other circumstances than those which existed, this would, undoubtedly, have been correct, since the whole country is to be united on any topic of change or reform; but, as we have said, the whole legislation of the country could not be waiting while those States should choose to be absent from their places. In the mean time, the *providential* moment had come for giving the decisive blow which would settle this troublesome matter for the future. All had been prepared and made easy by the providential course of the war, first loosing and freeing the slaves by thousands, and then by the constitutional (as necessary for putting down the Rebellion) and equally providential measure, we might say (because Providence itself presides over the issues of governments and events), the edict of emancipation. There was but one thing more to be done, — the amendment of the Constitution, or confirming this edict by legislation; and then that subject which had agitated us from generation to generation, and had been near destroying us as a people, would be finally laid at rest, being eliminated from our system. As far as slavery had been a "right," it was now truly forfeited by the course to which it had impelled the seceding States, and the peril to which it had brought the whole nation. It would have been but pusillanimity to have dallied with it longer, and the height of foolishness to presume that it must longer be "protected."

When this amendment was presented to each of the late secession States, under its provisional government, before it had resumed its State functions, one and all gave to it a full adherence and allegiance; so that this statute is now of the same force as any other part of the Constitution. Here, again, all was constitutional: every State, in giving its adherence and allegiance, had become a party to it, the same as to the original instrument.

With this subject, the cause of the war, thus acted upon and settled constitutionally; the secession ordinances of the States made null and void by their own action; the war-debt of the nation assumed by them (for, of course, being again in their usual functions in the nation, they must share its burdens as well as its privileges, especially burdens which had been brought about by their own course of action),—what more was wanting to restore them to their full and normal position of States in the Union, — which was the one object and issue of the four-years' war by the Government, and of its after necessary proceedings, — but that all the State machinery should be got into operation, the governor and officials chosen by the people, the senators and representatives to Congress elected? And then the peace, the refreshing peace, *internal* peace, that was to follow!

"Good heavens!" we might hear some one here exclaim, "are these people coming right in again to have all their rights and privileges in the Government, without any penalty, without any punishment, for their sins and misdeeds?"

We might answer in return, "Good heavens! have they not had punishment, deep and dire, in the almost total wreck of property and business; in the complete devastation of homes and firesides; in the desolation which the ravages of war have produced, far and near, in all their towns and borders; in the famine and destitution which have stared them in the face?" We see nothing of all this in our prosperous Northern towns and cities as the result of the war, and therefore we cannot realize that *they* have met with loss and destruction on every hand; and so, perchance, we still cry out for vengeance. "Vengeance is mine, I will repay, saith the Lord;" and we believe this has been amply repaid in the overthrow of all their expectations; in the disastrous effects and influences of the war, from which it may take a century to recover. A few words on this topic.

TREASON AND ITS PENALTY.

On this subject, much might be said; although, for the responsible political and military leaders in the movement, the country has not seemed to know what to say. We should presume that the words "treason" and "traitors," if they applied anywhere, would apply most appropriately to those members of Congress who had not *resigned* their seats, but *left* them avowedly to carry out their purpose of secession. If treason, in the *premeditated act*, occurred anywhere, assuredly it must have been then and there. Would not any other country have declared such cases "treason"? But, here, what was said? what was done? It was looked upon as a political movement. There was no outburst of alarm or indignation. Here, where freedom of opinion on all points has been extreme, the country did not really know how to regard this; considered it, perhaps, but as on a footing with other "freedom." It was only when the horrors of war actually came upon us that there was so deep objurgation of the movement, denouncing it as "treason." How difficult it has been to treat these cases, how unaccustomed our people are to the idea of treason, and how plainly it was

"Not to the manor born,"

is evident from the foreign, uncouth, old-time mode in which it has been endeavored to bring up these cases in the indictments of Mr. Davis and others. They are not of the nature or genius of our institutions, do not sit upon us with a native air. If we are to have treason among us (although it would seem to be a most rash, unnatural attempt deliberately to lift one's hand against the most beneficent government in the world), it would seem that we should have some mode for indicting it which would be appropriate to the crime and to our age and country. As it is, those cases appear likely to fall through from the simple uncertainty as to how and where to treat them. The Constitution makes treason with us to consist in levying war against the United

States. These would seem, therefore, to be plainly cases of treason; but still, that they are peculiar, and different in many respects from such simple definition of treason, must be acknowledged.

The ostensible purpose was, not an *assault upon* their government, but to *withdraw themselves* from it, peaceably if they could, forcibly if they must. It was a political sin and error, rather than a moral guilt; a want of true insight, arising from the pernicious and obscuring doctrine of State rights, which, however, had been introduced into and infused throughout the atmosphere of the South for a whole generation, with all the plausibility possible to one of the greatest intellects of our land.* How, then, might it not be expected that his particular countrymen or fellow-citizens should follow with pride and belief so specious and distinguished a leader?

Such treason appears to us to have been of the nature of a *disease*, rather than of a *conspiracy*. It was not an effort to destroy the Government for those who chose to remain under it; but presuming upon the *freedom of opinion and action* which had been uniformly cherished

---

* Hon. John C. Calhoun.

and fostered with pride among our whole people, and in a spirit of independence, as the inheritance of our country and the product of its institutions, they wrought out a theory of unlimited freedom, in those respects, for each State, and thereupon acted. This appears to us a profuse, wild, but not *unnatural* growth of our free soil. Not unnatural under the circumstances, until, by experience, it had been tested and proved that this was a rank, deleterious growth, that must be checked; and that our tree of freedom, like aught else, must be pruned and guarded in order to keep it of due size and shape. This (secession) seems to have been a disease, an excrescence, which sprung from our very state of freedom itself, — the wild oats of our youth and inexperience. Whether this species of treason was to be treated as treason elsewhere has been treated, or whether, being indigenous and peculiar to the soil, it should have some other peculiar treatment, might be an open question. In the mean time, it appears to us, that, inasmuch as penalty is for prevention of future evil, the questions might arise whether the repression of this disease itself of the body politic may not be its cure; whether our States, in any likelihood, will ever assert such a principle again as independence over and above the National Government; or whether it may be expedient, now, to give an example that may last for all time to come.

All this we leave to the legal opinion and arraignment of the country, and turn to consider rather the millions in the Southern States who were engaged in the same treasonable warfare. The doctrine of State rights, which was the head and front of their offending (politically), had, with all the plausibility of eloquence, oratory, and intellect, been ingrafted and embedded in the popular mind for a long period, — a whole generation, in fact. Now, were the great masses of those who toil for their daily bread, and the multitude of those unused to thought and investigation, and who are always the majority in any community, — were these to be able to resist those seductive influences, and to withstand the gradually penetrating, insidious, and almost unconscious working of years? In short, were they not to be affected by the very air which they breathed? It would be a miracle were human nature to escape such influences. It is impossible that the masses should be, politically, otherwise than what the public atmosphere, the public sentiment, makes them; or that we should expect those thus situated to think of stemming the current, backed by all the specious force that was setting in. The body of the people can only be what the head, the leaders, make it. Its very integrity requires it to yield, to be obedient, to the supposed superior intelligence.* They, in truth, it appears to us, have much the irresponsibility of a family, where the parents give guide and direction to all. That they, the children, the people, of the Southern States, clung with heart and soul to that guidance and direction, and believed it to be the true and right (however false it may have been seen to be by others), can, therefore, be no argument against them. And as the law, in criminal cases, should look always to the position and condition of the offender, in order to under-

* This sentiment may appear to be in contradiction to the idea generally advanced, and which is also contained in the second section of this work,—of the rulers being the servants of the people; that it is the masses, the *body*, and not the *head*, which is to inaugurate new or revolutionary movements, as in our revolutionary war with Great Britain.

Both are true in a sense. The heads, the leaders, of the people, are, in their acquired intelligence, the natural and appointed guide to direct, *when the people have undertaken or desired;* but no wise ruler, it is to be presumed, would attempt to initiate political changes among the masses, when these *had not of themselves* some emotions of discontent or uneasiness.

stand his real degree of guilt; so ought we, in this case, to understand the whole condition of the masses in the seceding States. They were, in their measure, irresponsible; and thus the same penalties — confiscation, expatriation, or whatever — awarded to them as would be awarded to the authors and directors, the real movers, would be but indiscriminate and unjust.

The only remedy could be to place over them a generous and genial government, alluring them back to their allegiance, and, under these different influences, giving to them a truer guidance and direction. Thus, with a more healthful atmosphere, they would eventually return to a more sound and healthful condition. But time and patience are needed for this.

RECONSTRUCTION.

We left, a few pages back, the late seceding States (with the preliminaries all gone through) standing at the door of the Union, waiting for the last ceremony that should again fully re-instate them and us in our happy normal condition of "free and equal" States, — the admission of the Southern members to their seats in Congress. This happy normal condition of our country is *the* " consummation most devoutly to be wished," which had cost us four years of the labor and struggles of war to attain, which was the very end for which the war had been waged by the Federal Government.

Where, then, are those States now, and their representatives? By the last advices, they were still waiting, with the exception of one (Tennessee), which, after standing, with its credentials in its hand, for eight long months, was at length admitted. And the peace so long looked for? It has not yet come.

A respectable journal of the Northern States * lately exclaimed, in allusion to this, " If Mr. Johnson could only have been content to let matters take their own course for a time, and subside into something like their old quiet ! "

It appears to us, as has been seen, that the President did his part very quietly and properly, and Congress did their part the same, up to the time when the States, one after another, were ready, by their representatives and senators duly elected, to be re-admitted. What, then, is the matter? Where is the obstruction? A

* Of July 26, 1866.

vague idea, which seems to have seized upon the minds of our people, that something more is necessary; that some "reconstruction" or other must take place before we can again be one. They have been afraid, as it were, to let things take their natural quiet course, — *how* quiet, in the simple constitutional mode, we have seen, — so admirably would the Constitution have met this emergency, as it had met every other.

The success of the war itself was reconstruction. Had secession triumphed, it must have been *sauve qui peut;* and we must all have got along as well as we could, subject to disunion, division, the rivalry and opposition of all separable sections. Then would strife of all kinds have been let loose; then would ambition, discord, anarchy, have place, where else might have been a peaceful sway, and the paths again of quiet prosperity and strength. But the war did not *so* succeed. The Constitution triumphed, and with it has come its mild, beneficent reign, putting an end to all discord, confusion, and strife. Or, rather, it ought so to have come, and would, we believe, have hushed all disturbances; but we have not allowed it so to do. We have wished to interpose or interpolate something else, — something that is not in the Constitution. We (that is, the Congress of the States which have been in their legislative functions through all the period of the war) are now acting according to our own views and opinions, instead of the letter and intent of the Constitution; and these views have not, as yet, been sufficiently wide and far-reaching to harmonize all things, and bring in the munificent reign of peace. In other words, we are acting outside of the Constitution, and therefore bring only confusion and disorder; for the tie of the Constitution is that alone which can unite all our people, and in that only it is that we have any political life or integrity.

We believe it must have been seen, from all the preceding views of this work, — which have been very fairly deduced, we think, from our whole previous history, and from the documentary charters of our Government, — that there can be no such thing as "reconstruction," in the comprehensive sense now politically given to that word. When peace should be fully established by the re-organization of all the States, — or as fast as they were ready to be re-organized, — the deliberative, constitutional assemblies could proceed to "amend" the

Constitution wherever it might be found to be needful and proper. We say, "as fast as the States were ready;" for the general legislation of the country could not stop, as we have seen, because some of the States, *through their own fault*, were not in their places. Whatever was so done, as was the case in the amendment of the slave-clause, is as valid as if it had been enacted by the whole Union. It is only when the States are constitutionally willing and ready, — that is, have fulfilled their constitutional conditions, but are excluded from participation, — that the proceedings of amendment, and so forth, would be illegal; for the Constitution distinctly says (Art. 5) "that no State, without its consent, shall be deprived of its equal suffrage in the Senate."

Our remarks have applied simply, of course, to the ordinary cases of "amendment." If any *organic* relation were to be touched, or if there were to be any general revision of the Constitution, affecting the State and Federal relations, most assuredly we must wait until *every* State should be able to have its proper vote. It must be the united voice of our people to revise or remodel our government, as it was by their united voice that it was originally formed. A *part* only of the

States could no more use this form of State rights than the secessionists could theirs.

We find in the Constitution no other doctrine whatever of reconstruction, any more than one of secession, excepting in this limited sense of "amendment;" and that reconstruction, as we have seen, had already taken place. The Constitution was amended, and submitted to the then absent States for their adherence when they should again become re-instated. All the other conditions, also, were fulfilled. Their secession ordinances had been denied, their share of the national war-debt was assumed, and whatever other qualifications were required — the test-oath, and so forth — were acquiesced in; and, in good faith, they proceeded to make their election of officers, both in the State and Federal relations. *This* was re-construction, re-organization, the getting things in operation in their usual mode. There was wanting but one thing to complete it, — the re-admission of the Congressional members to their seats, and thereby the States into the Union. They are not, of course, in the Union as free and equal States, until such admission, by their members, into Congress. Congress alone is the judge of these elections, and of the qualifications of its members, whether they are *duly* qualified and elected: their credentials must therefore be submitted to Congress to be properly pronounced upon. Has the present Congress performed this part, this duty of theirs, in regard to those re-constructed, re-organized States? It has not, excepting in the case of Tennessee, — and that not until eight months after it had applied for admission. What was Congress doing in the mean time? Was it proceeding to legislate for the country, with States all ready and desirous to come in, — to be in their seats, — but not admitted? Was it still making " amendments " to the Constitution, with States outside unable to participate, because it, the proper authority, had refused or delayed to examine their credentials? Of what force would be such amendments when made with members thus *excluded* from their seats, not voluntarily withdrawn? and what authority has it for legislating at all, with members not necessarily or willingly absent, but prohibited by *its* action from taking a part? In such case, it is not a " full congress " of the people, but a partial one; the members assuming to legislate by themselves alone, while other members were not only " ready " and "willing" to participate, but had presented themselves for that purpose, and were only deprived of so doing because the former members had not been willing to receive or admit them. It evidently is no true congress of the country, which assumes to act by a part of its members only, when the others *might* be present, and are absent, not from their own fault, but by the fault of that very part. In such a case, its acts can no longer be valid as they were during the Rebellion; some of the States then having *voluntarily* withdrawn. This makes the entire difference; and our present Congress appears to have forgotten that those States are no longer in rebellion, incapable of performing their functions, but have elected their Congressional members, who are only waiting at the door of Congress until their credentials shall be examined and approved, and waiting for this only. They are not waiting for Congress to make any further "amendments," or for "reconstruction;" since for this there is no constitutional mode or authority whatever, that which was necessary having already been done.

We have now come round to where we abruptly left off in the first article of this section, and recur to the proposition, which is, in substance, that of a large party in the country, and is partly the ground, doubtless, on which the present Congress justifies itself for its delay in admitting the re-organized States: namely, that "this is a new state of things, such as has never occurred before; and that we must now proceed to procure guaranties that it may never occur again."

This might be very well and right if we had the constitutional ability to do this; if, perchance, we were some other form of government than we are. But, as it is, the Constitution is our sole political charter; and in time of peace, as well as in war, we can be guided only by that. Any thing but faithfulness to that must be *our* real crime of "treason" in idea; the betrayal of our country, the *guilt* of treason peculiarly ours, as other countries have their guilt of treason in disloyalty to their king, &c. And, as has been stated above, the Constitution has made no provision whatever for any further reconstruction by a *part*, and not by the *whole*, *congress* of the people.

Whatever may be done, therefore, in this particular Congress, while other States *might and would be represented, but are not allowed to be*, can have no true validity, and can only be open to repeal if a succeeding "full" Congress should be disposed to repeal it. No "guaranty" can be obtained in this manner, because "the law," so called, would not be "law" in such a case, being of no constitutional force. It is authority outside of the Constitution, and can have, therefore, no inherent permanency.

To present this in another way. The "amendments" which Congress has been enacting since the cessation of the Rebellion are presented to the re-organized States for acceptance, as the condition of their elected members of Congress being admitted to their seats. Congress has been so persevering in this, that it has, perforce, made this acceptance *the* very condition of the States resuming their places, not in the Union (if a State can be said to be in its place in the Union that is not represented), for they had already given in, in good faith, their allegiance in all the requisite preliminaries, but their Congressional position, which, of course, each one of those "free and equal" States has a *right* to, if it is in its loyal functions at all in the Union. Thus the other States, in so doing, by their delegates in Congress, are assuming a superiority and a right of dictation over those States for which there is no ground or authority whatever in our National Constitution; and although the States may, for the sake of being admitted, yield to this persistency on the part of the *ex parte* Congress, that condition, those " amendments," can in reality have no binding force upon them, because not by authority of the Constitution. Thus, again, we see that no real " guaranty" can be obtained in such manner.

To present it in still another form. Those States had been wholly, constitutionally re-organized,—only wanting the Congressional members to take their seats. If, then, in this position, they are given certain conditions *perforce*, they are brought under a form of government which is not voluntarily their own, and are thus directly endued with the right of *revolution;* and may use it, the first moment they are able, to throw off this involuntary government or these statutes of the Government. Here, again, we see that no permanent guaranties can be thus obtained.

Is it possible, then, we may hear it asked, that we can have no security, no certainty whatever, against such terrible upheaving and disorder of the country as we have just been through? Must we be forever liable to the same occurrences, again and again? Reader, we beg here to pause, and look a little on our natural situation and relations.

Here we are, a great nation, composed of numerous States all on the same footing, affording no cause of rivalry or strife between them. (There *was* such cause, producing strife and rivalry, which threatened our overthrow. We were not on the same footing; but that cause, the institution of slavery, is now eliminated forever from our system, leaving us all on one and the same equal ground.) We have a Constitution large and free, as beneficent as the sun itself in its blessings; and which of itself, if we do not prove to be the most rebellious and ungrateful people in the world, must soften us into mildness, kindliness, good temper, and fraternal feeling. We have resources, the richest in the world, to occupy and interest all our people as soon as political strife may be a little allayed; and we have leisure to improve and employ ourselves in these resources. We have, it is trusted, good sense, natural intelligence, and a growing *savoir de faire* on occasions of sudden excitement or emergency. Moreover, we have now had experience,—

that true teacher of nations as well as of individuals, — and know what is to be *avoided*, and in what we are to control ourselves, civilly and politically. Above all, our national system, with its laws, has been tried, tested, and not found "wanting." Can we not trust it for the future, as it has not failed us in the past? Seeing that it has come forth so gloriously, without spot or stain, through as great a trial as any form of government ever experienced, can we not adopt it with safety, and without distrust, as our stronghold for the present, our provision for the future? All within it must and will have its influence: it forms the very atmosphere which we breathe. All nations are moulded by their institutions. We, fed and nourished formerly by our untried, *unlimited*, as we believed, liberty, have been impelled to daring deeds in one form or another: but we are learning that there are limitations even in freedom; that liberty must not become license; that the true form of any government in the world is in appropriate law and order

In these, then, let us trust. Let us leave it to the Constitution itself to right us. What that requires of us, let us maintain firmly; what it does not permit, let us depart from utterly. In this only is there a guaranty. Such course only is safe and sure, because it is the only just course. All else brings disorder, and the strife of parties. We may not be *wrecked* by these; we may come out from them as we have through other emergencies, because, we believe, the right must ultimately triumph and prevail: but, in the mean time, we are subjected to much needless suffering, — to anxiety and alarm, which must continue as long as we are not in the plain, straight road of *constitutional* freedom. Peace — that blessed peace we have looked for — cannot fully come until our car of victory is on its own smooth wheels, — the simple, easy, natural ones of the CONSTITUTION. Any others interposed to assist can but obstruct (for they are not of the character of our institutions), especially that machinery, or mode, of a part or a number of the States legislating for others *without their consent,* or with their *forced* consent, as has been adopted by the present Congress; for it must be remembered that the re-organized States were *wholly* re-organized, and were only waiting for the ceremony of admission to resume their lawful functions.

This anomaly in our country of an *ex parte* Congress is

but one of those political phenomena which have occurred from time to time. A similar one took place during the war. A party which had lifted up its voice most strenuously on this very ground of faithfulness to the Constitution against the supposed inroads upon it of the then existing administration (Mr. Lincoln's), proceeded shortly, on the strength of individual States (as Ohio, Indiana, Illinois), to pronounce and declare upon other sections (New England, &c.), that they should be forced out,— excluded from the Union. Thus they themselves, in another form, were laying violent hands upon that sacred ark, the slightest scratch upon which they had so indignantly protested against! Such a position, of course, is as untenable as was that of the Southern States; and the attempt to cast out any section or State — North, South, East, or West — would be as false and suicidal as was that of secession itself.

The truth is self-evident, that in faithfulness to the charter in which, as we have seen through the whole investigation of this work, is our sole political life and integrity, and which is all that gives us that life, we can no more shove, push, cast off, or exclude any portion of our country, than any portion can take itself off; and that, in *assuming to do this*, we are but putting ourselves on the identical ground of any other form of secession or independent State rights; namely, that of our own will and responsibility.

How, we might exclaim, are we to save ourselves from these anomalies, recurring again and again in some new form? Only, we believe, by our vast populations — men, women, and children — learning what our Constitution really is, what are its limits and restrictions; and by making the principles of government, and of our own in particular, a study in our schools and academies, that *seed-truths* may thus be sown in all our popular learning. A free people needs this well-disseminated knowledge for its own guidance, protection, and stability.

In the mean time (in the recently-uttered words of the new governor of one of the re-organized States*), "a suffering people are to be relieved, a great nation is to be saved. It will require the loftiest patriotism, and the purest devotion to principle. An enlarged and liberal charity should be exercised toward those who may differ from us in opinion. Great ends are to be accomplished,

---

* That of Texas.

not by vituperation and abuse of opponents, but by dignified appeals to reason and the nobler impulses of the heart." With these catholic sentiments, and being bound together, as we are, in an inviolable, and, we will add, providential bond (for so only could it have come about), let us, instead of any State, or any number of States, asserting or attempting this or that on the strength of its or their own wish and assumption of authority or responsibility, — thereby causing rivalry and the excitements of party spirit, and making us to be wounded and bleeding at every pore, — let us turn from these self-inflicted tortures and lacerations, and in strong and unwavering faith, dropping all minor aims and purposes, stand firmly and steadily at the HELM OF THE UNION, fixing our eyes upon that beacon-light, the Constitution, which alone, under God, can bring us to a quiet peace and rest, and, through that peace and rest, to the opening again of a happy and hopeful future; not in the weakness of dismemberment, nor even of inequality; with all the parts out of joint, but in the powerful strength and vigor of a whole united body, each member receiving power, grace, comeliness, and vitality from its union with the others, just as Providence itself has tempered them together. Then may we look for the angel that but appeared and vanished, to come and make its abiding presence with us, diffusing the blessings of a true and lasting PEACE throughout all our borders.

SECTION V.

THE GREAT ISSUES OF THE COUNTRY.

The purposes of the war just passed through have been almost fulfilled in the former seceding States having been recovered and re-organized, but not quite, inasmuch as they are not yet fully re-admitted to their position in the Union. The first issue now is, on the part of the Government, to accomplish this final step. Until this is done, the country is not wholly restored. We are not yet a Union — our former Union — of " free and equal" States. We are not therefore, as yet, a valid body for proceeding to any other purpose. We should be a valid body if those States were not yet ready; but inasmuch as they are (or some of them), and are willing to perform, and are even desirous of performing, their functions, and are not doing so, from no fault of their own, but because they are refused participation, all acts pursued without them must be nugatory and void. We have been so long accustomed (during the war) to legislate independently of those States, that our people, we believe, have in this manner forgotten or overlooked the grand, original principle of our Government, — a Federal Union of *equal* States; and that we can no longer go on, now that they are ready and able to be re-united, but *in that Union;* that the government or control of one section of the country by another was never the design or intent of our Constitution. This, then, must be the first issue of the renewed state of affairs; because we can proceed to do nothing else whatever, with any validity, until this is rightly settled: for if Congress be in a false position, and not on constitutional grounds, its every act must be invalid, as we have before said. Rather, we might say, this is the *last* issue of the war just waged, although the parties are somewhat changed. Instead of its being the Government against the seceding States, it is the same Government, or the Executive portion of it, against that party, or a portion of that party, of the people, which fought more than any other to recover those very States to the Union, but which now, instead of going on to the full consummation of that " devoutly to be wished " for event, holds back, and refuses this last step. What is *its* issue or platform; the ground upon which it thus recedes from the conflict; or delays, in homely parlance, to "clinch the nail," to "tie the knot," which would make of us again a completely restored nation?

The war, or point of issue, between the party in Congress and the Executive, which is at present agitating the country, though not with the same material weapons of powder and shot, is but a continuation of that previous one in its issues, on the part of the Executive: the Government not having yet secured the end pursued in those former long-drawn battles; namely, the complete restoration of the Southern States. In other words, it is a war, or a struggle, on the part of the Administration, for the identical principles then pursued, — the principles that the Union cannot be dissolved, and that the Constitution must not be broken. The issues of the opposing party will appear in the following examination of the

PLATFORM OF CONGRESS.

This must be allowed to be stated in the words of the party itself, and which we take from a document addressed to the " Union Republican Voters of Vermont " by the " Union Republican Committee " of that State,* — the first to enter the campaign in the coming elections, which will turn on those very issues now before the public. In the words of the address, " Nineteen States hold their annual election in the next seventy days. Vermont heads the column ; and, on the 4th of September, the Republicans of these eighteen sister States will look anxiously to see how gallantly, with what proud and resolute step, with how full ranks, she leads the line."

The issues this address takes up are these : " True to the principles of equal civil and political rights for all men, the Republicans of this State present an unbroken front. . . . The issue is now made up. . . . It declares it to be neither just nor safe to surrender all power in the insurgent States into the hands of unrepentant traitors; and it points to the atrocious butchery of Union men in New Orleans as but the faint foreshadowing of the results of this . . . policy of reconstruction. It is opposed to the unconditional admission of representatives of the rebel fraction of the Southern

---

* This address is signed "——— ———,* Chairman of Union Republican Committee."

* See note, p. 253.

communities, to equal power in the Government with those who have never deserted the flag. It appeals from an Executive, who has turned his back upon all there is in his record of which a true lover of republican government can be proud, to Andrew Johnson, hated of rebels in Tennessee, and with him holds that traitors should take back seats in the restored Union. It does not ask for confiscation or blood: it cares little for indemnity for the past; but it demands security for the future. On this rock it plants its standard; on this line it proposes to fight the battle through. . . . Republican voters of Vermont, it is for you . . . to emphasize at the polls your expression of antagonism to the policy which would at the ballot-box surrender the Government to the treason you have defeated on the battle-field; to declare again your unconquerable purpose to stand by your faith in equal rights, from whatever quarter assailed."

It is often one of the most hopeless aspects, in endeavoring to elucidate principles, to observe how little the arguments confronted have to do with *real* principles or facts; how often they are but fanciful shadows, the creation of one's own mind, opposing other fanciful shadows or " windmills," yet with the same ardor and vehemence as if they were veritable "giants." To give the full drift of the above issues presented, we must present also, from the same address, its version of the position of the opposite party, — that of the Administration. It says, "They demand the instant, unconditional surrender of all power in the insurgent States into the hands of those, who, for five years, hesitated at no atrocity in their war upon the Government. They demand the immediate, unconditional admission of representatives of unrepentant traitors to seats in Congress, and to power in the National Government."

If we rightly understand the position of the Administration, or the Executive, it is simply, that those States, having had a provisional government a sufficiently long time to assist and enable them to renew their former State governments, and having elected their representatives and senators to Congress by due form of law, are now entitled (as the final step) to have the credentials of their members examined by the proper authority, which is that of Congress; and, if these are found to be correct, that they (the members) shall be admitted to their seats.

Undoubtedly, there must be a period when this must come to pass, or we never again shall be a restored Union, unless the opposing party means to say that we are already restored, " reconstructed ;" the power to control having passed entirely, by the events of the war, into the hands of one section of the country. But was such the result for which the American people toiled through four years of war, — a war of untold fierceness, — that one section might have control of another? or was it that the *integrity* of the *Union* might be preserved? — a glorious and unbroken Union of just and equal States. It is unnecessary to say that this latter object was the one instinct which fired the American heart, or that of the great majority of the Northern people who went into the war, and was that which nerved them on the battle-field to the spilling of the last drop of their life's blood, and until the full and complete surrender of the antagonistic forces. This restoration, then, is the object. It was the prime issue of the war; and it is natural that those who most ardently sought for it through that long and anxious period should not rest until they see this end completed; should not feel that their work is done until the last finishing touch be given, the clinching nail placed, the indissoluble knot tied. The precise point at variance, we apprehend, between the Executive and Congress, is, *when* this shall be done (for we cannot presume that Congress means *never* to do it). The President had performed his part to the last minutiæ, informing Congress of the delivery of the case into their hands; that the credentials of the members to be admitted were ready for their examination. Neither his Excellency nor the re-organized States could go one step farther than this (indeed, this was the finishing of *their* duty) until the legislative branch had performed *its* function of examining these credentials, and, if all were right, to admit the States again, through their members elect, as integral portions of the community; this being the very end pursued through the long expenditures of blood and treasure, and through every preliminary since, up to this last crowning act, which was to make the Rebellion but a thing of the past, and to fairly launch us again upon a great national career, and one more splendid, we might hope, than ever before. *Then* should we be enabled to go on obtaining whatever else might be necessary, or whatever we might be capable of; *then* might we exert ourselves for the equal civil and political rights of every citizen; *then*, in our renewed state of a noble, wholly free republic, might there open to us broad vistas of an illimitable and hitherto unexampled wealth and prosperity, — all of which we have been obliged, since the cessation of arms, to forego, because we are not yet fully equipped, and launched upon the world as a single, undivided nation. Or if opponents answer, "We are already one nation," — it is one, we reply, on very different terms from those which had brought us to our former pitch of prosperity. It is not one in which the States are all on equal terms, all together pressing forward on great national topics, but one where a part of the States assume control over the others, thus exciting political strife and wrangling; producing, on the one side, discontented and rebellious feeling, and, on the other, the assumption of power and authority. So we are still diverted from what ought to be the great objects of our national life, being all unstrung, and unable to pursue them.

When, then, is that final act to be performed by which we may be able to go on in harmony and peace, and in a laborious industry for the best and highest ends? Congress deliberates. Three, six, eight months, or more, pass; and, in the mean time, those States — or, at least, the masses of their population, uncertain as to what is their condition; being now neither rebels (their arms laid down), nor yet an integral part of the community; being neither in nor out of the Union (an anomalous condition) — become restive, anxious, excited; have time to dream over their lost "independence" (which they fancied they were to have), and become more confirmed than ever in the doctrines which impelled them to rebel; for what have they had to enlighten them upon the subject, but the *force*, which was brought against, to subdue them? The mind may yield to force, but is not convinced by it: its convictions will still remain firm as ever. It is only enlightenment, persuasion, and attraction that can convert and affect the intellect and the heart. These masses, then, to be converted from the "error of their ways," must be brought into the paths of peace: by clemency, generosity, magnanimity, they must be *allured* to the right. These are the only teachers. No man yet, in the depths of his soul, was ever *driven* to be sincere and upright, much less to form correct political or any other opinions.

Which of these expedients or influences have that impoverished people, wrecked by a long and devastating war in all their fortunes and expectations, even almost to the abandoning of their faith in Divine Providence, (for who does not know how religiously many of them entered into that struggle, and with what confidence in an Almighty Ruler they looked forward to the success of their cause?) — which of these influences, during these many months of waiting, have these mistaken people had extended over them? One to calm, conciliate, soften, and pacify, and to encourage them again in the paths of loyalty and patriotism? or one to drive, alienate, exasperate, and excite them still more? Verily, we believe that in this restless, anxious, uncertain state, — not knowing what their fate was to be, — had it not been for the clemency and personal influence of the Chief Magistrate in whatever ways it could be brought to bear, we need not have been astonished to hear of other excitements and outbreaks like the recent terrible one at New Orleans. Many months * of such uncertainty must tend to demoralize any people, at the best; how much more certainly, then, one in so precarious, critical a condition, denationalized as it were, being neither part nor parcel, in a genuine sense, of the body politic!

---

* As Congress adjourned without admitting these States (except one of them), some must remain a long period in this condition.

We seem almost disposed to look for these millions, with no nation or government, as it were (for, until the national bonds are extended to them, they can hardly be said to be in national relations), to be as meek and subdued as children might be supposed to be on receiving a severe penalty from a parent. As far as the *parental* relation of our Government is concerned, we certainly do not see but that their attitude is quiet and submissive, in good faith accepting the rule meted out to them. But our relation to *each other*, as States, is but a fraternal one; and we are not to anticipate that they will lay aside, in regard to us, any of that distinctive pride which belongs to each one of us naturally, as an *equal* member of the family of States; and, if they ever come to their places in the Union, we may not expect them to have necessarily the " back seats " any more than ourselves.* The position of one State is identical with that of another. We take issue, therefore, with the address before us, on that point (and with the President himself, if that were his opinion), and also, on the same ground, with the following phrase

---

* This term cannot apply to *States;* as of course, as such, we are all on equal ground. It could only apply to individual " rebels; " but no one of any party proposes to admit *rebels*, as such, into Congress.

opposing the admission of the Southern representatives, namely, " to equal power in the Government with those who have never deserted the flag." We believe it was not with any such spirit as this that the noble defenders and supporters of our flag rallied around the standard, dreaming, when all should be over, — the country rescued and the Union restored, — that the nation would be perpetually divided, like sheep and goats, — one on the right hand, and the other on the left; or that one portion of it should be situated head and shoulders above the other. If it were to be so, we had better have been parted, nevermore to be one. No: rather, in the spirit of the father who went out to meet the prodigal son, let us exclaim, " They were dead, and are alive again; they were lost, and are found ! "

But to come a little closer to the issues of the party now presiding in Congress. The address we have quoted avers that it is neither just nor safe to deliver power in the insurgent States into the hands of unrepentant traitors. " Good heavens ! " we might hear some impatient spirit here exclaim, " is there a soul in all these States, who has given heart and hand for the last four years for the putting-down of treason wherever it might be found, that would now place an unrepentant traitor at the very head and front of the Government?"

Such, we believe, is by no means the question. Our people are not so little penetrating and discriminating, as, after the sanguinary sacrifices and cruel experiences of the long war, to put those very persons against whom they so perseveringly fought, *unrepentant*, into the seats of power.

But what would we have? Are we going to make over people in a day?—those who have been tossed on and buffeted by every wave of fortune; now beset by one government, now by another; now claimed by this party, now by that; if loyal to one rule, rejected by another; if faithful to this power, considered faithless to that; divided between the State and the confederate State rule; subject to the power of the United States and to the seceding States, all this at one and the same moment, and in the midst of the turmoils of war;* if loyal to one party, disloyal to the other; if obedient to one, called rebels and traitors by the other. If all this were not

---

* This was eminently the case with Tennessee and some other States. At one and the same time, four different governments, or ostensibly such, were claiming authority and allegiance.

enough to trouble and confuse the mind, it would be difficult to say what would be. We could hardly expect that the masses (who, in their very virtue and integrity, must, in general, be obedient to their leaders or rulers) would perfectly preserve their identity under the circumstances, or be sure that one thing was right, and the other wrong. These are the men — the millions — from whom the candidates for office are to be selected in the restored States. That they surrendered, laid down their arms in good faith, and with good faith take up the old line of march, and endeavor to fall again into the ranks of the Union, is all, it seems to us, that can be required or expected. They must have time to recover their balance, to be hereafter as devoted patriots as they have been "rebels" and "traitors."

That these representatives, however, are coming into the "seats of power," into Congress, "unrepentant," is one of those "shadows" which it is futile to fight against, inasmuch as *that depends entirely upon Congress itself.* Not one of those members elect can enter those seats until their credentials are examined; and if there be any suspicion of unworthiness, disloyalty, or aught else, *Congress has the power, and it is its duty,* — on investigation, with the suspicion proved true, — to remand those members back to their constituents. The decision as to their merit is invested in Congress alone; so that no party or power in the country can admit an "unrepentant traitor" into its halls of legislation without *its* consent.

If, then, these representatives, as we have said, should be found not constitutionally qualified, or not in good faith loyal, they must submit to rejection; and this process might be repeated for any length of time, — for years, if necessary. (Here, again, is exhibited the excellence of our Constitution in this provision of it, — the power of Congress to reject disqualified members; so that if the *virtue* of our people, in their representatives, remains proof, the Government is fortified against unworthy participants; and we may presume, that, had the constitutional forms been applied in due time in *this* case, we should have found ourselves carried as smoothly over this "emergency" of re-admission as we have been through all others.)

This, therefore, as it appears to us, is a wholly unnecessary issue to take up; and, as was said above, we may class it among the shadows, "windmills," which are being idly fought against.

It might be asked, "What is Congress dreaming about by this delay, the constitutional points of which they must understand as well as others?" Doubtless, they have ulterior views — indeed, they are avowed — of making "amendments" to the Constitution, of imposing further "conditions" upon those returning States; but which, as we have formerly seen, not being by *constitutional* authority, have no real validity, and are therefore nugatory and valueless. All this, it is plainly seen, is an assumption of power on their own "will and responsibility;" and it becomes apparent, that as the Southern States, in a time of strong temptation, had not wisdom and virtue enough to remain faithful to their constitutional obligations, so the Northern States, in *their* time of temptation, fail of the same wisdom and virtue to conduct themselves constitutionally; and it is not to be presumed that the attempt of this latter party will eventually succeed, any more than did that of the former. The former was an external war, readily discernible and appreciable by all: the latter is an *internal* one, so to say, and therefore the more insidious, and more dangerous for the populace, because not so distinctly perceived in its issues by them. But we believe that the country will emerge from this contest as it has emerged from the other. It may be a struggle of longer or shorter duration, of triumphs and defeats on either side; but the grand principle will finally be made visible and conspicuous, — that we are a system of harmonious, *equal* States; each a little nation or republic of itself, almost, in its own pursuits and interests, yet, in matters beyond, having all the unity of purpose, and grandeur, of a noble whole.

We return to the platform of Congress. Another issue of the address we have taken up is, that the Government, or Administration, demands the "instant, unconditional surrender of all power in the insurgent States into the hands of those, who, for five years, hesitated at no atrocity in their war upon the Government."

We have seen who and what the people are on whom must fall the State offices, how they were wrought upon, how worked up; but these are they, with their new oaths of office or allegiance, who must be employed, unless the party means to imply that they should still be kept in a state of tutelage. And how long should this tutelage exist? and when might we expect they would be able to be put upon their own care and responsibility? for this is not like the case of pupil and master, excepting where the Federal Government is concerned (and that maintained provisional governments so long as it was thought necessary to do so; the Chief Magistrate having the supervision and discretion in this respect). Otherwise they are States having the same experience and ability as ourselves, and are as capable of conducting their own State affairs. The sooner they could be turned over to themselves, no doubt, would be the more agreeable on all sides; saving expense, annoyances, mistrusts. This was certainly the object for which the war was pursued, — *that they might be States again;* and an energetic Administration might be presumed to endeavor to effect that object in the shortest time possible. This power is not going, however, into the hands of "*insurgent States*," as the States are no longer insurgent, having surrendered both from necessity and in "good faith."

This point of the issue, therefore, is but of "shadowy" import. Another point is, that the "instant, unconditional surrender," and the "immediate, unconditional admission of representatives," is demanded by the Executive party.

This, too, is a misrepresentation, since *conditions* were, at the very beginning, actually imposed and exacted, — namely, the declaring null and void all secession ordinances; the repudiation of the rebel debt; the assumption of the national war-debt; the ratification of the amendment of the Constitution, prohibiting slavery forever; a new oath of allegiance to the Constitution and Government. What further conditions were necessary? Were not these to be presumed to be heavy enough for those who had asserted and acted upon, even to a bloody war, the doctrine of "independent" State rights? And these were accepted in full faith and credit (as far as human relations, civil and political, can effect this), with such honor as always occurs in affairs of State. This issue, therefore, is void, and consequently but a "shadow."

The last issue is, "It demands security for the future."

What greater and further promises could be obtained than were included in the above conditions, or are embraced in an oath, we do not conceive. As to any other guaranties being secured by acts of Congress in amendments, &c., in its present situation, we saw, in the preceding section, that they could but be invalid, therefore of no obligation. This issue then, also, is of no avail, and may be fitly classed with those which have gone before. Thus, we believe, it has been plainly demonstrated that the positions of the Government against which the party in power (the party of Congress) take issue are no veritable giants, but are the fanciful creations of a mind diseased.

Diseased politically, in being inharmonious with or oblivious of the simple, actual realities of the time and the occasion.

(The position of "equal rights," which the party claims to advocate, is alluded to farther on.)

RADICAL REPUBLICANISM.

That it is time that the country should be truly enlightened as to the great questions and issues now before it, is quite evident, when we read in a daily journal of wide circulation (one which, during the war, was among the loyal in one of the most loyal and patriotic States and cities of the Union; and which paper still says, at the present date, "The voice of the people will declare, in tones not to be mistaken, that all the States of this Union shall be loyal States"), — when we read such words as the following.* In alluding to the restored States, it says " that they had to submit to our will once; that they do submit to it now; and that they will be crushed into the earth if they dare to rebel again." How does it comport with the relationship in which we stand with each other for one or any of these United States to hold such language with regard to any other State or States? Who or what has given them the power and authority thus to set themselves up one over another? And do we not know, that, if our or any section of these States should so set itself above any other section, *it* would be " crushed" by the power of the Federal Government, which holds its authority equally over all the States? the States themselves being but in a *fraternal* relation with each other. The loyalty demanded is right; but the mode and spirit with which it would be secured, wholly wrong.

That a true information and understanding of these great issues is wanting on all sides, is evident also from the extracts of a letter which we discover in the same

* Of Sept. 1, 1866.

paper, written by an honorable and a learned jurist * in one of the highest institutions of our country. It says in regard to our Chief Magistrate, " I believe that he sincerely desires the preservation of the Union; but it is only on condition that it shall contain those elements of hostility and violence and injustice which brought the country to the verge of ruin, and contain them not only unfettered, but possessing far more than their share of political power, and exasperated by a new hatred born of defeat. The atrocities of Memphis and New Orleans . . . what motives stronger than those presented by his oath, his office, and every thought and feeling of humanity, could command any human being to prevent, suppress, and punish those outbreaks of brutality? But it is charitable to say only, that nothing of *this kind* has he done; while the manner in which these murders are spoken of . . . at the South shows only too plainly whither that (his) policy tends, and what it will produce if it be sanctioned by the people."

* As the object of this work is not to continue, but to allay, party strife, the writer does not consider it necessary to communicate names of individuals quoted; but, if the authors of the citations we have made in any part of this work shall read these pages, they will themselves recognize their own words.

It is not at all the object of this work to take up party politics any further than is necessary for a clear understanding of the great issues of the present time; but we cannot resist pausing, to ask here, what may we not expect from, and what may we not fear for, our people, when one of the most (otherwise) enlarged and liberal minds among them, and occupying one of the highest positions, can thus (unintentionally, no doubt) misconceive and misrepresent the real state of the present questions? The writer is no partisan politician, and may, therefore, make bold to ask, Can any one believe that the President, with all his past splendid and glorious record, is now seeking for the preservation of the Union only *on condition*, or with the desire, that it should contain " elements of hostility, violence, and injustice"? And does not every one know that the Chief Magistrate of the nation is not able to act in a private capacity in public matters, but is bound on every side impartially, by the requirements of his office? And can we not all see, if we have any breadth of view, that those disastrous results in the South, as well as arising from the clemency of the President (if that were indeed so), must arise also from the " policy " of Congress, — tending, by so long leaving their fate undecided, to excite and exasperate still more the already sufficiently aggrieved and excited States?

The true policy in a wise ruler or rulers, it appears to us, would have been, as speedily as possible, to have got them settled and pre-occupied in their re-organized position.

This misconception, and want of largeness of view, on one side, and the spirit of arrogance manifested on another (as in the first quotation), are partly indications of a peculiar change which has come over a great portion of the loyal States since the cessation of the war; no doubt because the true issues were not then distinctly seen by some parties to be carried out to their logical results, and also because the pride of success is having, probably, but its usual effect of " lifting up the heart."

A singular anomaly, similar to that which occurred during the war (to which allusion was made in Sect. IV.), has again undoubtedly taken place, — that of a strong and popular party assuming altogether an aspect " new and strange," which accounts for and explains their present attitude and position. On that former occasion alluded to, the most conservative party in the Union suddenly burst its bounds, and swept like a flood over the country, threatening to ingulf all in destruction. That party, — the Democratic, — so intensely conservative that it could scarcely allow the rules of war to be observed, rushed into the extreme of party fanaticism, which menaced the dissolution of the Union, and so resulted in — copperheadism. Now the great Republican party, then progressive, but loyal, has joined hands with ultraists; and the result is — radicalism.

There are senses in which radicalism may be a correct principle: but, in this of party politics, it is *so* radical, that it has become oligarchy and consolidation; that is, it is so radical, that it must have *its* peculiar views carried out, at all events, at the expense of all beside. To see what this radicalism is, we have but to look at certain points on which it stands, as the advocacy of individual, *civil*, and *political* rights and equality, — for instance, that of universal suffrage, — and the following article of the "Amendment," which has been constructed as the condition of the re-admission of the Southern States; namely, "Equal civil rights shall be guaranteed to all" (in the popular version).

The adoption of these points by this party in Congress has from thence spread itself throughout the former Republican party; but the maintaining of the power of

Congress to enforce these results is the denial of the "civil rights" of the States, embracing their millions of population. It may be said that the securing political and civil rights to each individual obviates the danger there would be in taking them from the States, since every individual then would possess them. But we answer, that the States, in their own affairs, among their own people, wish to have their own way of doing things according as it pleases them, and not to be obligated to do any thing on *compulsion*. This was the very principle on which they separated from the mother-country. It is the liberty which they have always enjoyed, the very liberty which they exercised in coming into the Union; and they, as States, have just the same right to this as individuals have to their personal and private liberty. To take from them this liberty of conducting in their domestic affairs as they think proper is taking from them the first inalienable privilege of men and of States, — that of our Declaration of Independence, — the privilege of choosing their own government. Thus radicalism, in endeavoring to secure in this form the right of the individual, would deny the very right on which our Government was founded and exists.

The principles, therefore, of "universal suffrage," and of individual "civil rights," other than simple citizenship (for we are all citizens of the United States as well as of the individual States, by the very virtue of our position), it appears to us, can never be rightly adopted by Congress but by the unanimous consent of the States; as it would be changing our organic law itself, the State and Federal connection in which we have hitherto existed; transferring our internal State regulations to the central authority, which would, by this, be transformed into a consolidated Government.

(It is well, perhaps, here to state the meaning which we apply to the terms "central" and "centralizing," of which frequent use has been made. We do not design them in any manner as synonymous with "consolidation," with which they appear often to be confounded. *Centralization* is merely for simple, natural organization, making a centre to hold all things together; but *consolidation* is the concentration of authority, the power to regulate, at one point.)

"Equal protection," however, to every individual right of *person* and *property*, is clearly a legitimate subject of even the Federal or National legislation, as every human being has by *nature* a right to this; and we can now add, in our country, "equal" protection of his right of *freedom*, since this is now our national law, happily and fully coincident with the first charter of our rights, — the Declaration of Independence. Further civil and political relations are, in general, affairs of State regulation entirely, and not those of nature (since it is not essential that all people should live under precisely the same kind of government); and every one of these United States, miniature republics, or little republics in themselves, should and must have, for any freedom worthy of the name, that of forming its own internal regulations. Which of our States, for instance, would wish to have the thousands of the foreign population, who yearly land upon our shores, to be able, the hour, the day, or the month, after their arrival, to cast their vote in any of their State elections? Who would not recoil at the danger to our institutions, and the uncertainty of any *fixedness* of them, if thus subjected to the vote of an uninformed, inexperienced foreign element? What one State, in order to preserve the integrity and purity, ay, the very existence, of its institutions, would not submit to, we are not to force upon any

State in any other connection, — that of its former slave population, for example. Let them have time to regulate that matter for themselves. There is no danger but that whatever is suitable will come in time; since every State must and will, by force of circumstances, look out for its own best interests, and every citizen is privileged in his own State to struggle for whatever he may obtain of that kind.

It is this freedom and capacity of managing their own affairs that belongs to the States, that can alone preserve us as a republic. Otherwise, with all civil and political regulations transferred from them to the Central Government, we should, as was said, be but a consolidated empire. History teaches us that a consolidated government, of so extensive a territory, is never a durable one: not having the freedom of political action within itself, factions will arise to change and to destroy.

On the other hand, our system of free States, allowing to each all healthful liberty and active freedom in which to exert itself, is its own preserver; and in this alone, as has been seen, can be the preservation of our country according to the original principles of freedom which have been handed down to us. Without this, our very spirit of freedom would expire, from having nothing wherewith to occupy itself. But, with those rights reserved to the States (as they always heretofore have been), they will be occupied with their own people agitating such topics as may be demanded by their own special interests; and thus they will possess, each of them, the free, progressive, inspiring character of a whole nation in itself, as it were, instead of that of a mere province of a nation, as it would be were these powers all combined in the Federal Government.

Another article of the conditionary Amendment is the disfranchisement, until relieved by Congress, of those who, bound by an oath, had held office under the United States or *in the States*, but had joined the Rebellion. Or, in the popular language and understanding of the public press, "no man who broke his civil oath to become a traitor shall hold office, or vote for President, till relieved by Congress."

At first glance, it might seem that this was but exercising the authority granted to Congress by the Constitution for declaring the punishment of treason; and, so far as United-States or Federal officers are connected, this appears in itself perfectly justifiable. The treason to be convicted is that against the *National* Government; and we should say, as was said in another place, that the *premeditated act* must have been in the *United-States senators leaving their seats in Congress* for the purpose of carrying out secession. Whether, then, we are to go into the States, and impeach also those who were employed only in their own State governments and State affairs, appears to us to have a different bearing. The people of the States, it is true, were all engaged in the Rebellion, in "levying war against the United States;" and, in that sense, might have been held as traitors. Nevertheless, being, as it were, irresponsible (the "responsibility" having fallen upon the leaders, the highest Federal officers, the senators, who were directly, by their oath, amenable to the Government), and these masses having by their entire unconditional surrender, in "good faith," obtained, as it were, general amnesty, they are no longer "traitors," and cannot be proceeded against as such by the very circumstances of the case. Whether, then, the common State officials, having no *especial* relation to the Federal Government, should not be included in this general amnesty, being only servants, public officers, of those States as such, and whether Congress, in thus disfranchising *these* also, is not encroaching upon the " civil rights " themselves of those States (being now States restored), appear to us the questions. Or, if it is considered that these States are not " restored " until their representatives are admitted into Congress, is not this body still, towards these subordinates, declaring punishment after amnesty has been, virtually at least, rendered?

As to the representatives elect not being admitted into Congress on this very Act, Congress thus prejudging them as traitors (or *ci-devant* traitors), it appears to us to be penalty awarded before offence has been convicted; since their credentials were not received to be examined, and have been refused to be so on this very ground, — that Congress has power thus to disfranchise for the crime of treason. These men may or may not have " broken their civil oath to become traitors." Individual members may be aware, from their own personal knowledge, that such or such has been the case; but Congress, in its public character and official capacity, cannot " know " these cases until they have been tested by the proper tribunal. It has thus pronounced upon them without trial; an instance, we presume, which has never before occurred in our civil relations, since the law of our country allows to every man the right of trial before conviction. Thus radicalism, in opposition to its professed liberality, and its love for the rights of humanity, has shown itself practically not only as assuming authority, but as despotic. It might have been looked for, from the philanthropic character or reputation of the former limited "Radical" party in this country, that, on its coming to the "seats of power," that "philanthropy" would have gone forth expansively, endeavoring to recall these erring brethren by the kindly, protective influence of "moral suasion." But what do we find to be its record, on arriving at that post of great influence for good or for evil, but that of the denial of freedom in its greatest and grandest feature, — that of civil liberty of the States; a warfare against an erring and unfortunate people, who are endeavoring to return to the paths of right and loyalty; and last, but not least, in our Government of, formerly, so generous influence, a species of tyranny and usurpation, it having no warrant from the Constitution?

The original Radical party but shows itself, possibly, in its true light in this opportunity of development, since pure radicalism, or any other extreme party, cannot be comprehensive in its principles or measures; and therefore, when brought to the test, it is found wanting. But what shall we think of the great Republican party that so ably assisted in carrying the country through the perils of the war, in having allowed itself also to become merged in and subsidized by a party thus narrow in its platform, unequal to the great questions of the hour? As the party, in general, has manifestly rushed into this extreme, we can only regard it as a similar phenomenon to that of the Democracy rushing into and becoming subsidized by copperheadism.

THE THREE REBELLIONS, — SECESSION, COPPERHEADISM, RADICALISM.

Thus every section, or great party of our country, has evidently passed, or is passing, through a phase of "rebellion" peculiar to itself; providentially, perhaps, for the sake of the final good that may ensue from it. The great Southern section or party led the van in secession, which, if carried out, would, as an element of disintegration or separation, have destroyed the Union. Next followed the Democracy of the North and West, rebelling against " coercive " measures, as it was pleased to denominate the acts of the Administration ; not perceiving that war, or military rule, in its place, is as essential and as rightful as aught else. This wing of " rebellion " would have destroyed the country by the simple force of dissolution ; not allowing it power enough to stand even in its own self-defence. It would have dropped to pieces from mere inertness and inefficiency.

The " wing " of rebellion at present bringing up the rear (and may it be the last of these ghostly spectres !) is that of the North and East, which seized upon the reins of government, and is employed in turning them to its own uses. This alone has attained to the " seat of power ; " and, if it continue to triumph, will also have destroyed our republic by converting it into an oligarchy or a despotism, in which nothing but material interests will be left to the regulation of the States, — the great questions and interests, the very life-breath and vitality of civil freedom, being deposited in one vast, concentrated government, out of reach, as it were, of all practical, self-developing use and influence !

Which of these forms of rebellion might be considered preferable ? — since all are equally destructive, equally treasonable in their nature. Secession, coming visibly to sight in military force, roused at once the whole energy of the country against it: it was something to be perceived, handled as it were, managed. A long struggle was required to subdue it, for it resisted manfully; but it ended in full and complete surrender, never, we believe, to be revived.

Copperheadism was too violent, and "overshot the mark." It was too insignificant to prolong its life with any vigor, and almost died of self-suffocation.

Radicalism is now in the height of its power, to be enjoyed, possibly, for a "brief season;" but, like the others, it must sooner or later descend into the shades below. For are we to conceive for one moment that the American people, who spent its blood and treasure without stint in resisting secession, that our republic might not be broken up and destroyed by division, and who rejected and spurned from it the embraces of Copperheadism, that it might not die of inanition, is now going to fraternize with Radicalism, that it may be converted into a system of arbitrary rule? Where, then, were the history and the glorious record of our past; in the brave deeds of Lexington and Bunker Hill; in the bleeding feet and thinly-clad limbs of our army in the suffering winter at Valley Forge; in the electric thrill of triumph, after long depression, at the success of the battles of the Brandywine, Delaware, and Trenton; in the rejoicing hearts and uplifted voices of the whole people at the establishment of our independence by the surrender at Yorktown; and the sacrifices, the patience, the endurance, of those seven long years of the Revolution; and, above all, the noble names of Washington and our fathers, whose words and influence were, never to disrupt the ties of this Union and the bonds of our Constitution? No: the American people has sense, intelligence, and patriotism. During all these phases of rebellion, amidst all these mists and clouds, there have been those who still stood at the helm, looking with clear eyes and earnest hearts; who have kept the Ship of State straight on in its course; and, although it may have been rocked from side to side by the billows which have heaved against it, it has never yet, thank God! struck sail, but has ploughed the rough waves, — near rocks and reefs it may be, and seeming, just now, upon the sands; stranded, it is true; but it is not yet wrecked, neither do we believe it will be. We believe and trust in a holy Providence who has protected and helped us on thus far; and we believe that he will still do so, that he has his own high purposes to fulfil, and that he is leading us by " a way we knew not."

What good, we might say, can come out of a way like this? What need of this anxiety, this agitation, this strife? Why not let us go on in a calm and peaceful way, having contentment and satisfaction as we go along?

A hot-house plant, reared in warmth and security, withers on the least exposure to chills and frosts; but an oak in the forest becomes strong and sturdy the more that storms and tempests beat around it.

Contentment and satisfaction we soon may have, if we but improve the providences that are over us: for instance, Secession acknowledges its error, and is now " rejoicing in defeat," so says report.* Copperheadism has learned the " error of its ways," it is to be presumed, and seems now ready to come back to its duties in the Union. And Radicalism? — we believe that that, too, will, ere long, lay down its false assumptions, and take up the " onward march," and be no longer an obstruction to the wheels of progress.

* On the authority of Gen. Grant, as is asserted.

From each of these experiences, we may learn a lesson. First, that our country is not to be separated into parts; secondly, that it is to be preserved by all the efficient strength that it can lay hold of, — *constitutionally*, — for such only is permanent strength; and, thirdly, that no one portion of it is to be elevated above another by any superiority of power or position.

Thus we all stand on equal ground; each section or party having had its period of destructive antagonism, and each species of antagonism being in itself as destructive as another. In short, the whole body has been in pain, the whole heart sick, the whole head faint. To carry out the parallel a little further, we might say that Secession, with its physical force, represents the human body scarred and bruised; Copperheadism, with its shrinking and nervous excitement at the " horrors of war," might aptly picture the timid, trembling heart; and Radicalism, with its high-handed measures and lofty assumptions, is but the head carried away with ambition and success.

> " . . . ambition;
> By that sin fell the angels: how can man then,
> The image of his Maker, hope to win by't?"

So we come back to the old refrain, "All is out of joint," and is still in anxiety and misery. But the body with its wounds and sores has begun to heal; the heart is recovering to wonted vigor and strength; and may we not expect that the brain, the "head," will soon also show itself sane and sound?

Such are the great issues of the country, as they have appeared to our mind: how they will eventuate, time only can determine.

THE GOOD RESULTING.

It will probably be found that all the agitating movements of society, even if they are of adverse influence, contain in them some element, some ground-work, of truth. Shall we find such in these apparently destructive forces which have swept, and are, in fact, still sweeping, over our country, as a deluge, threatening only to destroy? We think we shall. What was it then, in secession, that could possibly give promise of good to come? We answer, it was the under ground-swell in that portion of our people, the instinct, for their due *rights*. They *felt* that they did not possess them in the Union, and they preferred to part rather than to lose that possession. This is an inalienable instinct in every American breast. We have been born, brought up, fed, and nourished with it. It has grown with our growth, and strengthened with our strength. We dwell with it at home, and carry it with us abroad. An American is known, even among foreigners, by his "independent" bearing. It is the one principle, probably, that a true-born American never will give up. He received it from the sturdy pioneers on this his native soil, and they inherited it from their far ancestral race in England. It is thus in his "bone and sinew," and may never be eradicated. Against this, then, we may not struggle with any hope of success. It is the one thing which all our States and all our people will ever, probably, maintain. The secessionists were right so far; but they were not right in their idea of an *independent* State right over and above the nation, as experience and reflection, and the fiat of the war and of Government, have proved and decided. Pass that. But we may demand every constitutional right that has been granted to us as States, as this is our inalienable privilege. Take that away, and place over us a government with civil and political conditions not of our choice, and there is instantly given us the right to *rebel*, to revolutionize. We may submit, if we feel that we have not force to resist; but the rebellion of heart and mind is there, and that under ground-swell will continue heavier and heavier until it again breaks forth in some disruptive flood. This natural and constitutional right (of choice of government) is ours by birth and education; and it must have full room to expand within our domestic limits, since we are all bound together in an indivisible band, and cannot separate to expand and enlarge elsewhere. Therefore, whatever we can do ourselves, whatever is appropriately, naturally, and constitutionally in our own power, — the power of the States, — that, for the peace, happiness, prosperity, and contentment of the nation, we may not be dispossessed of. The violent attempt of the Southern States to secede has brought visibly and prominently to light the existence of this right, the instinct of it in the people; and shows its great need and importance.

What seed of truth was there in the Copperhead outburst, that we can possibly bring to light? The whole history of the Copperhead movement shows an underlying attraction between the North and the South; the same sympathies, and likes and dislikes, in one section and the other; in short, a *fraternal* feeling which would not listen to separation. This, if exalted and ennobled by right and true action in one party and the other, is but the very element which should cement us in an indissoluble bond as *one people*, — the element of *peace* and *friendship*.

And the Radicalism that now threatens to ingulf us, — is there any thing in that that we may lay hold of for improvement and progress in the future? — we do not say for *strength*, although it is apparently now a party of consolidation. But that is not the kind of strength we are to look for, — one section holding control over another, which tends, naturally, to absolutism, tyranny, and spoliation. Our consolidation must be that which is formed by the Constitution; all parts — our State and Federal relations — harmoniously woven and interlaced one with another. This consolidation is the firmness and strength which comes from unity; but still leaving each integral part, each of the equal States, to develop itself in all healthful freedom.

The end of Radicalism is not yet come; but being

composed, as it were, of foreign elements, — foreign to our Constitution, — we do not apprehend that it can long maintain its present position. Either it will voluntarily lay itself down, — for the party contains many men of manly and honorable reputation, and who have been, we believe, unwarily caught in its folds, not seeing the true issues of the position, — or it will be forced, by the weight of public opinion, to surrender. And then what may we be able to gather up? what grains from it to plant anew in our "reconstructed" or re-organized state? what good springing out of evil? The very good that the party has sought, ostensibly, to gain, but fell wrongly upon the method, and so could not but fail, — namely, the good of the individual; but now a double good, in that, also, of the States. Indeed, it is only by securing the good, or the rights, of the States, that we can secure more entirely the rights of individuals; because, with the freedom of their State, the individuals can exert themselves in every honorable way for their own freedom; and this very exertion gives them true life and strength, and the capacity for enjoying those rights thus attained. Then only does liberty become a priceless boon, and not a common gift. In truth, each State is but an epitome of our nation: on a smaller scale, its people, with their aspirations and energies, are but the miniature, the exact copy and pattern, of the united whole.

Thus we do not quarrel with the desire of the Radical party to secure the rights of individuals, but only with the mode in which, in this case, it was proposed to be effected; believing that the only true and philosophical way — the way in which those rights would be a blessing, and not valueless — is through the Constitutions of their own States, which will leave to each citizen the freedom and opportunity of attempting to attain what he wishes.

To recapitulate: By these adversities, the equal and inviolable rights of the States will have been established, in which alone can be preserved our freedom and our Union. Peace and brotherly love, mutual kindliness and respect, — no one being able to place himself above another, — will diffuse themselves through all our borders; and the chance of individual, civil, and political rights will have free play. For, as before said, left to the States, they, in their own growth, must seek the real good of their populations. Now that slavery is eliminated, never more to be as a burning brand between us, the section once occupied by that will begin to develop more naturally, and will assume altogether another character of good. Years may elapse, perhaps, before it arrives to its best estate: but we can afford to wait; for then its growth will be but of firm character, fixed in the soil itself.

Thus we believe fully that every one of those mishaps, troubles, perplexities, and difficulties by the way, will at length, in the end, bring us round to the very results we have most desired; and we may then, perchance, be able to lift up our hearts in grateful reverence, and say, "It was well for us that we were afflicted!"

CONSERVATISM AND PROGRESS.

In the mean time, out of the great parties of the country, which will be likely to succeed? for Democracy, recovering from its overthrow into the hands of Copperheadism, will come back to its original place, doubtless, as the party of preservation, — the conservative party of the Union; and the Republicans, throwing off their disguise of radicalism, will become again, most likely, the party of progress.

These two elements we may look for in our republican government: such has been the history of all republics. But both of these parties, going to extremes in the past, have been found "wanting." Democracy, being so intensely conservative, re-acted upon itself, burst its bounds, and became the very element of destruction. So with Republicanism: going to extremes, it has but lost ground in all high influence; and, instead of being now the party of progress, — true progression, — it is falling backward to the elements of strife, oppression, discord. Evidently both, by the same process, have become distorted in delivering themselves over to ultraism. No ultraism of itself can be safe or just, because its peculiar character is to fix itself upon some one particular aim; and, in making every thing bend to that as the alone important, it either destroys all else, or takes it out of its appropriate sphere. It can never exist, we presume, without exciting heart-burnings, violence, virulence, and animosity; because its very essence is that of warfare. But, in the ways of Providence, it may have its use.

When the two great parties shall have recovered themselves to be again on their feet, sound, and of "a right mind," we may expect that they will continue to have their natural action and re-action one upon the other: the "conservative" party watching jealously to preserve the purity of our chartered rights, and the "progressive" party boldly stepping forward in whatever freedom may be allowed; thus preserving the balance in our political contests. Or, better, may they not become modified, one by the other?— Democracy perceiving that we must have progress, and Republicanism understanding that we must remain true to the Constitution; for are we not to be a progressive people? In this age, when the world is all alive, and progress is opening on every side, shall we not, too, press on to all that is good? But nevertheless, ought we, shall we, so press by assuming liberty, which thus becomes license; and by breaking law, which thus becomes lawlessness? Are we not to be guided by those broad and generous rules laid down for us in our constitutional charter, and by those alone? since, as we believe, there is no true and healthful freedom whatsoever that we are not enabled to obtain through those. We have seen what noble privileges that charter has granted us hitherto: let us trust it in every case for the future.

Then, when conservatism is able to become sufficiently progressive, and progress can keep itself sufficiently conservative, shall we not become one party of the people, all united in the general welfare or well-being of the country?

May it be that we are already approaching that happy period when there shall be but one great national party (as for a short time there was during the war), all bent upon an honest and enlightened policy, and loyalty to the nation? In this time of emergency at least, as has been in others, the impulse seems to be quickening, and the rallying-cry to go forth. Whether it will prove a party divested of all aims but those of patriotism, remains to be seen.

A VISION OF THE FUTURE.

We are unwilling to leave these pages without endeavoring to obtain some glimpse beyond the close obscurity and murkiness that now invests us. Is there not some prophecy of the future, some brightness gleaming forth, when we shall again be launched upon our path of national glory, which may nerve us for the present, and inspire us with hope to lure us on? Yea, verily: there is the vision of a land radiant with peace, smiling content, and prosperity. World-wide occupations employ its busy inhabitants; riches and trade flow in on every side; its white sails of commerce are upon every sea; and a kindly influence goes out from its shores, inviting the poor laborer or hard-pressed toiler of other lands to come and partake of its wealth and abundance, thus renewing to the world energy and life.

And our own people — will they not be trained in all the best pursuits of human life? and here, where both nature and civil government have extended a lavish hand, shall we not become a generous, large-hearted, magnanimous people; forgetting the animosities of the past, burying in oblivion the troubles, which, nevertheless, have made us *great?* Yes: these very troubles — secession itself, the civil war, and the very issues of the present parties, rightly ended — will but have brought us, we may believe, to where we should be, the very place to which we were designed, — a whole and nobly free nation, a republic in every sense of the word. We can then work out all the problems of human destiny, human freedom, and progress.

A great difficulty of our people in general — and this is especially true of the present party in power — has been to precipitate events. The radical-republicanism of to-day feels that it must at once secure every thing; that all is to be hurried up now in these few months of existence, as if they were all that we were to possess; that, if not obtained at this very moment, they were to pass from us forever.

Who can so read a great nation, just beginning, as it were, its destiny? True, it would be so, as feared, were the elements of strife, discord, and oppression, to continue. But we cannot believe that an intelligent people are thus going to lose all the healthful influences of our regenerated state. No: let us have Peace; let the white-robed, white-winged angel, so long looked for, but come, and we shall spring forward at once in a new and better career than ever before. Slavery has gone; and with it, in time, will disappear many of the prejudices and disabilities that have kept us back. The good which the radical party would have procured for the black man, — and here, we will acknowledge, we believe lies the secret motive of all their doings; honest in purpose (as far as private ends went), but mistaken in mode, as it appears to us, — this good which they would thus procure could be, at the best, but a doubtful one; for what man, black or white, ever appreciates that which he has not worked for? No: let the black man earn his manhood; let him feel that he *is* a man, with all the energies and aspirations of one. What would we ourselves or our fathers have been, had we not had to acquire our rights? Had Great Britain showered upon us even but the privileges that we entreated for, should we have been now the nation that we are, — strong, sturdy, understanding our rights because we labored for them, and *loving* them because so hardly won?

So must the negro do. He had done well, ay, splendidly, thus far, by admirable behavior at home during the Rebellion, and, in the national army, by military valor and prowess in the field; and he *earned* his freedom, — showed himself worthy of it. He is now a free man: let him use that freedom to secure himself other political rights, if he wishes to, as every white man has to secure his. This alone will make him a part of the nation, — when he feels that his honors and privileges are his by right, and not by gift merely. Let him work himself up to whatever he is fit for and capable of. The

States themselves will soon know what they must do in this respect. If the race is capable of advance, and desirous of it, no power of theirs can stop it in its upward progress : the Almighty Ruler himself arranges all that. If the negro wishes the civil franchise, he will eventually obtain it : if not, it must be from his own inefficiency, forming, as he does, so large a part of the community. Therefore, it appears to us, we need not be anxious lest he should be deprived of any right that is dear to him ; and, if ever he stands in the assembly of the people, in either house of Congress, — as one day he may, — let him feel that he can tread its floors as free and proud in his own manhood as any white man that has ever graced its halls.

SECTION VI.

THE PRESENT ASPECT OF POLITICAL PARTIES. — THE RADICAL CONVENTION.

We believed the present volume was about completed; but, as the final issues and appeals have now been made on the radical as well as on the other side, we add another section in the way of conclusion, and to keep pace with the shifting events and ideas which are passing across the scene.

The first event we have to notice is that of the late Radical Convention;[*] with which, however, as there was but little or no new discussion of principle, — it being mostly or greatly taken up in party personalities, — we have but little to do. There was one assertion, however, made, upon which we will dwell a little, and which, if true, appears to us a very remarkable revelation. That convention professed to represent, and spoke in the name

---

[*] Philadelphia, Sept. 3, 1866.

of, "eight millions" of loyal people in the Southern States. Nor was this accidental. It was repeatedly referred to, and was made especial notice of by one of the members in the following manner: —

"The assumption is this, that we have eight millions out of twelve millions of the South who are loyal. I ask this convention to note that fact. I agree with it; and I go farther, and assert, that, if you place the people of the South on the side of protection, there will be ten millions, if not eleven, out of twelve, who will be loyal to the nation, loyal to the Constitution of the United States, and loyal to the constitutional rights of the citizens of the United States."

"Where, in the name of Heaven, of all that is good and true" (we cannot but exclaim), "were these people during the convulsion of the war?" for deducting the four millions of loyal blacks, who, in their situation, might not have been counted upon, there would still be left a number equal, at least, to the remaining four millions of whites. And is not a Union loyal man at any time equal to a disunion, disloyal one, — man for man? We have been accustomed always to think that *right* produces *might;* that, other things being equal, a true man is more than a match for a false or an untrue one. Where then, we repeat, were these people during all the excitements and agitations of that time? and why, with their vast numbers, are they still demanding " protection " of the Government against their own fellow-citizens?

And why is it that Congress prefers to debar these eight or ten millions of true and loyal men from resuming their full position in the Union? Is it possible it can fear the strength of the remaining two or four millions as " rebels " and " traitors " still, over and above this vast majority of faithful, Union-loving men? Where, then, is the strength of our boasted freedom, if the twenty millions of the Union beside, with those loyal men at the South in addition as aid, shall not be able to hold ground against so insignificant a minority of " unrepentant rebels and traitors," if they so continue?

We are strongly suspicious that this — although deliberate — assertion was but in harmony with the apparent exaggerated and travestied tone of the entire utterance and proceedings of the convention; and we must confess, that in reading the reports, for the first time during the whole continuation of our troubles the thought and feeling came over us, that, if such as was there exhibited be the true character and representation of the millions of the Southern States, why, let them go. Congress has been right in keeping them out as long as possible. Once led away by secession, which we have been taught all along to believe both by friends and foes was all but universal, — and must therefore be the very element from which the present eight millions of the radical party are composed, — and now equally led astray by the similar distorting spirit of radicalism, they indeed bid fair, in accordance with their own representation, ever to continue to be, it appears to us (in the words of their "loyal appeal" *), "but opaque bodies, paling their ineffectual fires beneath the gloom of darkness, of oligarchical tyranny and oppression."

Is there, then, among the free-born millions of our States, a vast body like this who cannot stand by the force of their own principle of right (if it so be) against a disloyal and unworthy faction in their own midst? But they want the encouragement and sympathy of the Government, it is said. "God helps those who help themselves." When such a majority as that, in its proper

---

* " Appeal of the loyal men of the South to their fellow-citizens of the United States."

sphere, shall be seen standing up in its own right and might, it will, no doubt, find encouragement and sympathy sufficient.

We would not be sorry, however, to see the South become "radical." on the subject of slavery. It would be a very hopeful sign if those millions of former secessionists, — for we cannot help presuming that, as all reports hitherto had uniformly declared that the Southern people almost universally were such, these now loyal men must be the very same transformed, — if they, having endeavored formerly to depart from the Union, in the very spirit of opposition to emancipation, are now on the opposite line for its radical extirpation, were it not that the exclusive devotion to that topic — either for or against slavery — has uniformly, in all our history, closed the mind to almost all else. But in our great, constitutionally organized Republic, there are many relations to be considered, as well as the duties of the country to the black man. There are our own personal relations and duties to this Republic to be preserved in their integrity; and, if we encroach upon or over-pass our constitutional freedom, we sap, and must ultimately destroy, this free and splendid Government in its purity and virtue, not only for ourselves, but for the black man.

If the whole half of the South is thus truly radical, however, for the freedom and well-being of the former slave, we would accept it as one of the most glorious aspects of the times, and would risk its becoming accurate on all other points in the future.

But this, undoubtedly, was a great error of assertion of the convention; otherwise the Thirty-ninth Congress would have been performing a most peculiar part in its resolute and very unnecessary action — as it would be — against those who should be its own friends. Such a body of loyal people, in defiance of all opposition at home and of every interference of Government, would indubitably, in time, be able to elect its own members, — if not in the first, or even second or third trial. And it would only be necessary that those who had already been elected should be tested and proved; and if disloyal, as was confidently believed, they could only be dismissed to make way for others: for this is entirely in the power of Congress so to do; and the sooner it were done, it appears to us, the better it would be for all parties. But now, instead, there is the singular anomaly presented of those loyal millions, and not only they, but vast numbers of the millions of the Northern and other States conjoined, beseeching Congress to persevere in their part of keeping them out of the Union, in opposition to the strong and vehement pleading of the Executive, who is supposed to be against them, to have them brought in. Were ever the affairs of an unfortunate, half-dislocated republic worse confused or confounded?

Each party is conscious of this wretched, anarchical state of uncertainty and indecision, — half-life and half-death, — and each party accuses the other of being the cause of it.

POINTS OF AGREEMENT BETWEEN THE PRESIDENT AND CONGRESS.

We do not think that either party *designs* to be the cause of it, but that, on the contrary, each is quite innocent of any such intention; and each, in its more sober assertions, proclaims the views and desires of the most lofty patriotism. It is curious to observe the identical expressions, on either side, of the value and sacredness of our constitutional obligations, and the burst of indignation at any supposed encroachment upon or violation of them by the other; and one cannot surpass the other in its solemn determination to preserve to the death the precious legacy which has been bequeathed to us. What is it, then, that makes these two great parties, — for we may say that the country is now apparently resolving itself, whatever have been the efforts to form but one national party, into two distinct divisions, the one the party of the President, the other that of Congress, — what is it that causes these two to be so antagonistic, the antipodes, as it were, of each other, when formerly they were together? for there was a time when these two were agreed.

We will pass on, and let a more moderate branch of the same radical party state the former points of *agreement* between the now divided people. We say, the same radical party, as the Southern Radical Convention was indorsed by the whole press, in general, of the late Republican party, and which now itself is not displeased to adopt the name of "radical." It reminds us of the time, when, in the erratic movement of the Democratic party, its members readily themselves adopted the name of "copperhead."

The document to which we refer is styled the "Address of the National Union Committee to the American People." It is calm and serious, and designed to be conciliatory in tone ; and in this it is far in advance of the speeches and reports lately made on the radical side, and thus is an indication, apparently, of a returning of the party to a more moderate spirit. As all the antecedents and surroundings, and the personal sympathies and principles, of the writer, had been ever of the Republican party (as far as they were of a party nature at all), and so continued during all the labors and efforts of the whole war, and still so remained up to the time of the separation of Congress and the Executive, the writer is but too happy to watch any appearance of resumption of that elevated and truthful spirit which has, in general, characterized that party division of the people, not to treat in the same conciliatory manner what has thus been offered in a conciliatory mood. And we will sincerely endeavor to discover what appears to *them* the cause of difference and difficulty between the President and the people, or the party of Congress. We first quote from the address their statement of the principles on which the two parties were agreed : —

"The claim of the insurgents, that they either now re-acquired or had never fortified their Constitutional rights in the Union, including that of representation in Congress, stands in pointed antagonism alike to the requirements of Congress and to those of the acting President. It was the Executive alone, who, after the Rebellion was no more, appointed provisional governors for the non-submissive, unarmed Southern States, on the assumption that the Rebellion had been 'revolutionary,' and had deprived the people under its sway of *all* civil government; and who required the assembling of 'a convention, composed of delegates to be chosen by that portion of the people of said State who are loyal to the United States, *and no others*, for the purpose of altering and amending the Constitution of said State.' It was President Johnson, who, so late as October last, — when all shadow of overt resistance to the Union had long since disappeared, — insisted that it was not enough that a State which had revolted must recognize her ordinance of secession as null and void from the beginning, and ratify the Constitutional amendment prohibiting slavery evermore, but she must also repudiate 'every dollar of indebtedness created to aid in carrying on the Rebellion.' It was he who ordered the dispersion by military force of any legislature chosen under the Rebellion, which should assume power to make laws after that Rebellion had fallen. It was he who referred to Congress all inquiries as to the probability of representatives from the States lately in revolt being admitted to seats in either house, and suggested that they should present their credentials, not at the organization of Congress, but afterward. And, finally, it was he, and not Congress, who suggested to his Gov. Sharkey of Mississippi, that 'if you could extend the elective franchise to all persons of color who can read the Constitution of the United States in English and write their names, and to all persons of color who own real estate valued at not less than two hundred and fifty dollars and pay taxes thereon, you would completely disarm the adversary, and set an example that other States will follow.'

"If, then, there be any controversy as to the right of the loyal States to exact conditions and require guaranties of those which plunged madly into secession and rebellion, the supporters respectively of Andrew Johnson and of Congress cannot be antagonist parties to that contest, since their record places them on the same side."

Thus the distinct assertion of the Congressional party is, that they and the President were on the same ground all along,—in all the preparatory steps of the restoration. It is true, they speak of the President "alone" as doing so and so; but that was merely in virtue of his office as presiding executive officer. Some one must continue this work until the States were fully recovered,—restored from the state of rebellion; and who, under the Constitution, could do it but the "Commander-in-chief," who was the presiding executive officer during the whole war? The statement of the address does not dissent from this, but implies approval, as being on the same ground with Congress. It is now the mode with the genuine radicals (and was repeatedly adopted in all the late conventions) to retort upon the President for these former steps in regard to the military and provisional governorships, as if they were inconsistent with his present ideas, and were merely an arbitrary and unconstitutional proceeding on his part; as if those completely overturned and despoiled States — despoiled of their original organization, and still full of revolutionary elements — were to be left alone to get themselves in order as true and loyal States in the Union! Was it to be supposed that the most sudden and unexpected surrender of arms brought no surprise and consternation, but, instead, a perfect and as sudden acquiescence in their defeated state? Whoever could not see the necessity still of the "strong arm" of the Government in the immediate military governorships, and then of aid and assistance in the further provisional governorships until they should be able and reliable enough to carry on their own re-organization, is no true "republican," and merits only to be classed with those "copperheads" who would have let the very nation die from mere inefficiency and inanition. Mr. Johnson only showed himself in those measures but in the plain, simple path of a vigorous, worthy, and constitutional ruler; and his requiring the delegates composing the conventions of the States to be chosen by those who were loyal to the United States, and by *no others*, shows his determination that "*rebels*" should have no part in the renewed government. He has constantly reiterated the same assertion ever since,—that none but *loyal* representatives should be received into Congress In all his messages to that body, and in numerous speeches elsewhere, he has put forward and maintained the same idea. "*If* they were loyal," has been the constant expression; that is, if they had professedly, and in all apparent good faith, given in to the surrender of the Rebellion: for, as he properly said in a late speech, "We cannot go farther, behind the bosoms of men, and sit in judgment upon their secret thoughts." Thus the President, no more than Congress, designs to have "unrepentant rebels" brought into the "seats of power:" and he appropriately referred, as the address says, all inquiries as to the admission of representatives to that body itself, as their peculiar province; even suggesting that the presentment of the credentials should be delayed, when all else was ready, until after Congress was organized; undoubtedly that they might calmly and deliberately act upon them. This power of examining the credentials, and either receiving or rejecting the chosen representatives in consequence, as the case might be, the Executive has never attempted to usurp from that day to this; Congress being the recognized constitutional actors upon that point. He has, indeed, reminded Congress of this part of their duty, when he thought they were unreasonably delaying, which is *his* especial province as the presiding officer of the nation; the head, the supervisor, as it were, to see that all goes right. This is the very office of the President, — to see that the laws are executed, the Constitution enforced.

THE DIFFERENCE BETWEEN THE EXECUTIVE AND CONGRESSIONAL PARTY.

With all these points of agreement of the two parties remaining up to this present moment, — for the Executive, we believe, has never retracted a single one of them, and Congress certainly has not, — what room is there to consider the former as " traitorous " and " disloyal " to the nation, — any more than the latter? since they are both agreed on every one of those points, some of the most essential, certainly, which could be produced, and are entirely inconsistent with any proposition or plan to *betray* the country. *We* do not believe that either party has any designs of betraying the country, but that the great difference and disagreement between them is more as to the *mode of proceeding* than as to the principles.

Here one might be met by a cry of scorn and indignation, — that it should be presumed that all this terrible division and heart-burning, and fierceness of party strife and passion, menacing almost the very destruction of the Union, should arise merely from a difference of " mode " in regard to proceeding, and not from " principles " !

Nevertheless, to our mind, this is the great secret of the disagreement, in its outward phase; as, in law and constitutions, " mode," or the method, is vital, as well as are principles themselves. The Congressional party itself gives this explanation: continuing, in the address, from our former quotation, it says, —

"It being thus agreed that conditions of restoration, and guaranties against future rebellion, may be exacted of the States lately in revolt, the right of Congress to a voice in prescribing those conditions, and in shaping those guaranties, is plainly incontestable. Whether it take the shape of law, or of a Constitutional amendment, the action of Congress is vital. Even if they were to be settled by treaty, the ratification of the Senate by a two-thirds vote would be indispensable. There is nothing in the Federal Constitution, nor in the nature of the case, that countenances an executive monopoly of this power.

"What, then, is the ground of complaint against Congress?"

Here it is plainly evident that the opinion of Congress was, that *it* should participate in the final re-organization, and that it claimed this right; and, in this respect, the whole country will agree with it. Who can doubt that right? Is not the Legislative an equal, co-ordinate branch with the Executive in all our Government?

But did not Congress have this share, this participation, the same and equal hand with the President in those conditions presented for acceptance? Who was it that produced that immortal amendment by which slavery is prohibited forever from our statute-books, never to be re-established before our country itself shall be dissolved? Who was it but the loyal people, through their representatives assembled in the halls of legislation of Congress? What greater share could they have than this, which is the greatest of all, — the work of sober, solemn, deliberate legislation? No: not among all the conditions presented to the Southern States for their acceptance was there one so great, so extensive, so honorable and world-wide in its influence, and extending to all future generations to benefit and bless, as this of the Constitutional Amendment. Congress might well rejoice and be satisfied in itself that it had had such honor, and had accomplished this great work, — introducing this element of reconstruction; thus re-organizing, reconstructing the States on the firm and enduring basis of equal freedom, now that slavery, the great cause of inequality, was banished from our system.

Yes: so far we must and should be " reconstructed;" and the States who had borne the burden and heat of the day, by their representatives in lawful congress assembled, *had* a right to improve the providential opportunity placed in their hands, and to insist, that, when the States should again come together in re-union, it should be on this plan; and that they would not submit ever again to be subjected to the perils, controversies, and agitations arising from that cause, to which they had ever before been exposed. Those States that had remained true to the National Government, and had defended and supported it through the war, had the right, we say, to declare to those who, by the attempt at withdrawal, had forfeited the protection they had possessed on account of their system of slavery, — had the right to say to them, that they must yield to this condition, or not resume their places. It was the true and proper penalty, which they could not have expected to be released from. The President himself took this same view, coinciding with Congress; and being the presiding, executive officer, he — it was his duty — saw that this amendment, which the latter had demanded and provided, was submitted to and accepted by those States before they could begin their work of re-organization.*

There was another point which depended solely upon the agency of Congress, — one of the most, if not *the*

---

* No officer could have entered with more hearty and energetic determination to carry out the will of Congress in this condition of reconstruction than did President Johnson, as has been the constant testimony.

very most, vital of all, since it would be the sign and seal of all, — the completion of the work by which those States would be re-admitted, after, in full faith, they had given in their promise and surrender to all the conditions assigned. The Executive had already done all that was incumbent upon him; and, from that moment to this, he has done and could do no more, — excepting, as was said in occasional messages, to remind Congress, as it seemed to be delaying, that it had not yet completed *its* part of the work of restoration.

Congress, in the mean time, instead of doing this its peculiar work, was occupied in forming a *post*-constitutional amendment, to be submitted as additional conditions. Here is the precise point of difficulty and disagreement. If any other conditions were to be exacted, ought they not to have been announced at that same time before the work of restoration was commenced, instead of after the fact? But the States were allowed to go on re-establishing themselves on the strength of those requirements, in good faith, not anticipating any other. If Congress did not think of these in season, it appears to us, as in all similar private relations, they should be foregone. After a promise has been given or implied, it certainly is not customary or allowable, in common individual transactions, for either party to change the terms: how much less should this be the case where the honor of States or civil relations are concerned!

It seems to us that this mistake has arisen (for, if such were a mistake in private affairs, it must certainly be so in national and public ones; and a distinguished member of Congress in a late speech * admits that Congress " may have erred "), — the mistake has arisen, it appears to us, in Congress overlooking the great part it had already performed in the work of reconstruction, but still feeling that it ought to do *something*. And this error, it is apparent, is the one which still prevails. Appeals are constantly made to the post-constitutional amendment, as to what can be the opposition to it. " Is it not lenient, clement, even magnanimous, considering the crime — the betrayal of our country — which was designed?" are the questions asked. The document itself, from which we have copied, says, —

" Is it charged that the action of the two houses was tardy and hesitating? Consider how momentous were the questions involved, the issues depending; consider

---

* A member from Massachusetts, at a convention in Boston.

how novel and extraordinary was the situation; consider how utterly silent and blank is the Federal Constitution touching the treatment of insurgent States, whether during their flagrant hostility to the Union or after their discomfiture; consider with how many embarrassments and difficulties the problem is beset, — and you will not wonder that months were required to devise, perfect, and pass, by a two-thirds vote in either house, a just and safe plan of reconstruction.

"Yet that plan has been matured. . . .

"Are the conditions thus prescribed intolerable, or even humiliating? Are they harsh or degrading?" &c.

Thus, in perception of the real point or the main point at issue, how completely wide of the mark!

We believe it is a true maxim, When we know not what to do, do nothing. That very silence of the Constitution is an indication, we would say, that we have but little to do. One might aver that this would have applied as well to the war itself. Not so; for the Constitution expressly gives *full power* to put down insurrections: and, in all common reason, this power must continue until the former state of things is restored; *but, after that*, not one word is guaranteed for any further "reconstruction." But we have commented sufficiently on this doctrine in another section, and will now return to our first proposition, — that the original point of disagreement between the Executive and the Congressional party was more as to the *mode* of proceeding, in our opinion, than as to the principles (although some of the latter which that party adopted, we saw, in a former discussion, cannot be held as truly constitutional).

The President certainly has not denied that the Congress had a right to share in the work of reconstruction; and with eager readiness, without dispute or discussion, he adopted the amendment which they had provided, which was in special reference to this very conjuncture. *While* the States were out of their places in the Union (by their own fault), this was enacted as the plan on which we, or they, should be reconstructed when they returned. Both parties, then, were united in that simple, straightforward work of reconstruction. It seemed satisfactory to all; there was no demur at the time; it appeared quite understood, and acquiesced in. Thus all promised an easy and quick settlement of our difficulties, after hostilities themselves were over. We have already seen that the States had had imposed upon them what might seem to them, probably, severe conditions, though certainly not more so than they could have expected. They were the denial of those "ordinances" on which they had so prided themselves, making them utterly null and void; renouncing forever the payment of their — rebel — debt; assuming the burden of that which had been acquired in fighting against them; and, above all, prohibiting forever from their own States that loved and admired institution for which they had sacrificed almost all, — even life and honor. Must they not have felt these to their very hearts' core? Yet they accepted them: they felt, they knew, they must and ought. It was in good faith. They believed that the National Government was in good faith in submitting those conditions: and the implication was, that, when all this was done, it would be in effect restoration; their National or Federal functions would be resumed, and they would again be loyal States in the Union, as before.

All these preliminaries had been completed. The time had come, every thing being in readiness, to resume all their relations. But Congress then said, "There must be further conditions: you cannot come in without giving securities that you will never do this thing again. We are making an amendment to the Constitution; and it is impossible to be admitted until you have submitted to this." Who would not be taken aback with such a greeting, after all that had preceded?

Is it, then, that after an error and sin, though laid down and acknowledged, we are never again to be regarded but with fear and mistrust? The true way, we believe, to prevent any occasion of mistrust, either in private or public life, is generously to confide, which disarms an adversary if he were disposed so to continue. But, however that may be, the Executive felt that the word of the nation had in effect been falsified; that their part of the conditions — their acceptance of them — had been fulfilled, but our promise (implied) had not. That the head of the nation should be sensitive on this point is not surprising; and ought not every *truly* fraternal mind to be the same? "There is honor even among," &c.: should there not be the same, then, between our now restored people, — the people of a great undivided nation?

Thus we conceive that this mode of a new post-reconstruction adopted by Congress, when the natural, stipulated re-organization, shared in by both Congress and the Executive, had already taken place, was essentially erroneous. Not that conditions were not to be exacted, or that we had no power to exact them, but that they had already been so. These might, indeed, have been more fully elaborated, including portions of the new amendment, had they been thought of in season; but, the time passed, it appears to us that any further modifications, excepting what may hereafter occur in "full congress" of the people, are inadmissible. In social and private life, nothing is more detrimental and prejudicial to the highest and best interests than a want of the purest and most upright integrity where word and honor are involved. And is not this same morality the very soul of all public and civil relations?

"Are we then," it may be exclaimed, "to be all our lives subject to misfortunes, and to be ruled by the rebel power, just for the oversight of a single moment,—because we have missed the exact time, the precise juncture of affairs?" We are all liable to mistakes; and we must take our chances, whatever they may be: if we fall into them, we must abide by them. But the Holy Scripture somewhere pronounces a blessing upon this "abiding;" a promise to the man that sweareth, and *changeth not, though it be to his own hurt.*

We do not apprehend in this case any cause of distrust, however, even though the spirit of many of the former rebels may be still unsubdued, and a "rebel" representation from the Southern States may still occur in Congress. If the assertion of the Radical Convention be true (and this convention has been indorsed by the almost universal Republican press of the country), such vast numbers of former secessionists becoming so rapidly and radically loyal (in a moral sense), we have a very hopeful future to look forward to, and need not require of them any further guaranties, more than from any other part of the community. Or, if those "millions" were original loyal Union men, such a number, if they act at all up to the spirit of true loyalty, must inevitably, sooner or later, leaven the whole remaining portion of the population of those States, as it is the quality of *good* to spread and diffuse itself in time. At all events, we are by no means fearful that the great preponderance of our other States and millions, after having defeated secessionism with rebellion in its strongest and most plausible phase, are now going to submit to it "*on its own terms,*" or that they will fear to meet it, shorn and decapitated, even if it should " rise from its grave." Such a spectre might momentarily startle ; but to believe that it can actually come to life, conquer and subdue all these living, breathing, active forces of health, strength, and freedom, must be from a want of just confidence and faith in our people, or in the eternal principles which we profess.

THE MASSACRE AT NEW ORLEANS.

In this connection, we wish to animadvert upon the continued habit of referring to the Southern States as still insurgent and rebel. A foreigner might verily suppose from the expression of the public prints, and from our manner of speaking, that hostilities were actually yet existing. Even the address from which we have quoted, purporting to be a national document, uses the same terms in regard to those communities as if they were still, veritably, rebels confessed. " But," say some, " do not the massacres at Memphis and New Orleans proclaim this? Do not those slaughters of Union men show that they are precisely on the same ground that they were before, — warring against the loyal men of the country?"

That these people are yet at heart, perhaps the great majority of them, — notwithstanding the assertion of the radical party, of their loyal " eight millions," — wedded to their old ideas of secessionism, in our own mind we do not doubt. And who can expect but that they will remain so for a long period to come? Nevertheless, their external attitude, or that of their States, is one of surrender and submission; and this is all with which we have to do in State or civil relations: we are to keep the peace there, and not permit any overt outbreak; but we can go no further. We are not allowed to probe beneath the surface, and make inquisition upon the secrets of the heart, the views of the inner mind: for those they are responsible to their God alone. This is the doctrine which has been established by our American freedom; and by this we must abide.

In our private opinion, the massacre at New Orleans declares that the late secessionists are as determined now not to be governed by the " radicals," as they formerly were to go out of the Union: therefore, seeing no other way, they resorted to force. That this was put down by the military, and that they should be required to keep within the bounds of law, is but just and right; and this was done by the United-States troops. But that they have the right of contest within those bounds is also just as true as that our forefathers had the right of breaking away from their own government for the sake of establishing here freedom of thought and speech; and this is an inheritance for all parts of our land which we must ever retain. This is a local matter at the South, — a contest among themselves; and which, it cannot be doubted, they must be allowed to carry out (always within the bounds of law). If the radicals are right, by their great strength (according to the late convention) they ought to be able to obtain the mastery; if not immediately, they can only " bide their time."

NORTHERN AND SOUTHERN RADICALISM.

It is not for us to say what radicalism at the South may precisely mean; but if it be identical with that which has prevailed more or less at the North, with all its antecedents, we would maintain that the South are justified, no matter how lately they had themselves been on the wrong track, in not considering its partisans as safe political leaders in their reconstructed state. It is well known that the original radical (abolitionist) party of New England never stood upon any constitutional grounds whatever, but rather prided itself in going beyond, "higher" than, the Constitution. Its champion and greatest orator, who was, as it were, against every man, and every man against him, declared in a speech at the commencement of the war, that it was the first time for twenty-five years that he had ever stood under the flag of his country. Where, then, did he stand? since that flag represents our true country, our whole country, and nothing but our country. Was he alone to be exempted from its constitutional obligations? and why is now the strong cry of that party against violations, as they deem them, of this same Constitution? It did, we know, turn about, and go heart and hand for the war, not because it was a war for the Constitution, but because it would free the slave. And what but this party was it, that by its most distinguished speakers, male and female, uttered the most violent denunciations against the then President, the lamented Lincoln, and, by the continual "on-to-Richmond" cry, harassed his whole administration?

"Well, but this party had nothing to do with the present radical-republican party."

It appears to us it has every thing to do with the present party, or the present party has to do with it, having merged itself into it, to all appearances, and is moving with it heart and hand. The motto only is transformed: " abolition " being no longer necessary, it is now that of " universal suffrage." Mr. Phillips, it is true, was not permitted to be present at the Southern Radical Convention (nor was Mr. Vallandigham, the champion of copperheadism, at the " Philadelphia Convention ; " and both for the same reason, no doubt, — on account of public opinion: though we believe, in the latter case, the main body was firmly opposed to any connection with Mr. Vallandigham ; whilst this does not seem to have been the case with regard to Mr. Phillips, as was proved by an after-meeting). Nor would he be " permitted," it is presumed, to be placed on the radical ticket for Congress. Nevertheless, he is in the closest affiliation ; and in an enthusiastic popular meeting in his own city,* to welcome there those same Southern radicals, being called upon to speak, he confessed that he had no speech to

---

* At Faneuil Hall, Sept. 13, 1866.

make; that his "radicalism" had been "out-radicaled." These individuals may be allowed to have their own idiosyncrasies; and others, a large party, may yield to them, and combine with them, if they so please: we only say that they cannot be safe leaders of the people.

No one will affirm, we presume, that Mr. Phillips has made an advance, and come over to the Republican party: he still prefers, by his own showing, to be independent of any combination, and go his own way. The party, therefore, have met him on his ground; and this has plainly been effected through those members of Congress who were a tie between the two former parties, — being in close sympathy with the apostle of radicalism, but belonging professedly to the Republican organization. Those members, being a connecting link, thus carried the main party with them. We would not quarrel with this new attitude of the party, modified as it must be from the intense individualism of the original type, were it strictly reliable on true, simple, constitutional principles: for it has in it a *progressive* element which every nation needs; and, when divested of the disguise which this new partisanship has thrown over it, it will come back, we doubt not, to its former high, trustworthy position in public affairs.

There is one other point of resemblance which we wish to notice in this (radical) party, not to the original type, but to its predecessors of the opposite party at the South, — that of seeking for " protection." The former constant cry was, " protection " for slavery: now the cry is still for " protection " in another way. Is there, then, nothing for these States to do of themselves? Must they continue to seek the central power for " protection " in regard to their own State affairs? It seems to us that it would now be well for the States to learn to rely on themselves where their own interests are concerned. Now that the great cause of trouble and discussion, slavery, is terminated by the result of the war, it seems to us that we should learn a lesson, — not to bring topics which excite intense moral feeling, and on which there may be proper and lawful difference of opinion, into our national legislation; as, whichever way it might be decided, either for or against, where parties run high, the one party would always be aggrieved and dissatisfied (unless compromises were entered into; and on moral questions, or where deep feeling is concerned, these are always more or less deleterious and unreliable), and thus the country would be in constant foment.

That of universal suffrage is such a one, and has threatened to menace our peace now that slavery is over; but, as each division of the party which principally maintains it seems to have agreed to lay it aside, the crisis for the present is past, and perhaps it may never again recur to threaten to rend us in twain.

But, as was said in another section of this work, there is probably no great or excited movement of a people, without some underlying, impelling truth; and we shall, therefore, revert to this topic again, under the head of "Impartial Suffrage." At present, we design to take up the "Amendment" of Congress, to see plainly what its provisions are, and to endeavor to make good our previous proposition, — that the essential difference and misunderstanding, as we believe, between Congress and the Executive, is more, or quite as much, in regard to the *method* of proceeding, as in connection with the principles themselves.

THE CONSTITUTIONAL AMENDMENT.

We have previously referred to this in a more general way, taking it in its commonly received understanding, and noting only points of disagreement. We will now define the points of *agreement*, commencing with the lesser articles, — the repudiation of the rebel debt, and the non-compensation for emancipated slaves. With these prohibitions we heartily concur; for what has the country to do, beside the enormous debt with which it became burdened in the effort to save itself from destruction, in repaying a debt which was contracted in that very hostility against it? No: if any thing were forfeited, it appears to us it was the repayment of such a debt, created by their own voluntary action; and the repudiation of this was persistently enforced by the President himself, as one of the first steps before being allowed to re-organize.

In regard to slaves lost by the fortunes of war (and the emancipation edict itself was one of those " fortunes of war"), why should they be paid for more than any other losses? It is true, they were very great; but (in a private sense) each individual has only his share to bear. Are all to be remunerated — on either side — for the loss of property, money expended, and for blood and life given up, the dearest affections of the heart and home sacrificed? These are losses; how much more great than those of fortune merely, let the thousands of the other States answer who have thus suffered as well as the South. No: this loss of the slave-property, it appears to us, is but the natural penalty, and must be endured like any other similar infliction of the conflict; and we believe we are no more called upon in right to pay for this destruction of their institution than for any other accident or incident of the war.

The late Attorney-General, in presiding at the Radical Convention, notwithstanding that he contended for this point of the amendment, made in his speech this remark: "Although, if they will assume the vast debt which has been incurred by the Government of the United States because of their treason and rebellion, we will pay them for their slaves." We do not agree with him: it appears to us there is no "if" in the question; that all of these — the repudiation of their own debt, the loss of the slave-property, and the assumption of the national debt incurred in consequence of the very war initiated by them — are but the natural penalties, as we have said, the very ones to be looked for in the nature of things. The constantly-increasing sense of the people both at the North and the South must tell them that this was but to be expected, and we do not apprehend there will be any future difficulty in regard to this. But surely so great are these penalties, and interwoven as their institution was in all their society, we might be willing, we other States, it appears to us, to consider them sufficient; to desire no greater burdens, no further "conditions" imposed, than to be thus obliged to begin anew all their State and social edifice; broken, wasted, impoverished by the war; having to lay again the very foundation-elements; and it must needs demand long years, if ever, to recover their former prosperity and affluence. If "ever," did we say? Nay, we believe, for their encouragement, it will not take so long, on a *free basis*, to rise to a wealth and prosperity never known before; and this in itself will be a rich and high compensation, the South will themselves find, for the emancipation or loss of their slaves.

Section third (of the Amendment) relates to the disfranchisement of those who had held office under oath, both of the United States and the States, until relieved of the disability by a two-thirds vote of Congress. In reference to officers in their *Federal* relations, who can doubt but that this comes within the power of Congress, — to "declare the penalty of treason;" and that this was the least penalty that could be anticipated, — even clement, — not for life, but until Congress should remove the disability?

This, however, would not have interdicted Congress from receiving the credentials of the members elect for examination, as it had full power to reject these if not qualified; and in that case, *had* the States thus chosen ineligible members, this power (of awarding penalty) would at once have been put practically to the test, and we think the whole country would have supported Congress in the decision. Although it may have been foreknown, individually, that the members chosen were not such as should have been sent, yet Congress, in its official and simply legislative capacity, could have no right thus to *prejudge* a case, it appears to us, and therefore cannot stand on the strong and undoubted ground which the Constitution — the *Constitutional mode* — would have granted it. This "Constitutional mode," as we conceive it, was to admit these members, or their credentials, for examination, *at the time* they were presented, precisely as in any other case; because their States, under the necessary and required restrictions, participated in or approved of both by the Executive and Congress (for if the President had more of the absolute execution or enforcement of this than the legislative department, yet *it* too had, we have seen, its essential share, and the only share it could have under the circumstances, — that of legislation), had gone to work, and become re-organized to all intents and purposes, precisely in the same manner that they had been before, — to resume the *same relations and functions* in the Union; this having been the one object for which the war had been waged. And the supposition was, that, the moment this could be accomplished, — all should be completed and finished, — they would be fully *restored*, and, as such, must have the same constitutional rights and privileges as formerly (excepting those which the necessities of the war, and the change, the amendment, which the Constitution had undergone in their absence, had abrogated): otherwise, were they *not* to return in this manner, the war would completely have changed the relations of our system of States, and we should have become another kind of government from that which we had hitherto been. In this restored state, then, being precisely in all our former relations, as a system of *equal* States, the

Constitution must be in force as it ever had been before, and *from that very moment* that we were so restored; which was when the States had elected their Congressional members, and they stood waiting to be admitted. The Congressional form, *then,* was to test these members as all others were tested (or to refer them to the "Judiciary Committee," if thought necessary). If they, so tested, should be discovered to be still "unrepentant," and professedly rebels and traitors, undoubtedly the Congress had full power to reject them; and, as we have said, we believe the whole country would have sustained them in this. We believe that such is the ground which the President takes.

Another article of the Amendment is for the protection of "citizens of the United States;" and that "no State shall make or enforce any law which shall abridge the privileges or immunities of citizens of the United States; nor shall any State deprive any person of life, liberty, or property, without due process of law, nor deny to any person within its jurisdiction the equal protection of the laws." This last clause is but the *natural* law, we might say, the protection to which one is by nature entitled, and to which we may now give full force in our wholly free and happy country. The previous clause, in itself, is also one which can be applied throughout our entire country, inasmuch as we are all citizens at large, as well as citizens of the States; and this is but a just and rightful protection of a simple, general, natural citizenship, so to say. Whether that clause might mean more than this would depend upon the definition otherwise given to this "citizenship;" whether it embraced other political and civil rights which have hitherto been within the regulation of the individual States, and rightly, we think, as has elsewhere appeared. But *in itself*, its wording and phraseology, this article, certainly, to our mind, is wholly unexceptionable.

The remaining article, or section, of the Amendment, concerns the apportionment of representatives, or a change of the basis of representation. This we shall discuss under the head of

IMPARTIAL SUFFRAGE.

The Constitution as it stands apportions the representation of the States, that is, the Congressional representatives, to the number of free persons; and, in the

Southern States, adds three-fifths of the number of slaves. As the black population is now wholly free, the other two-fifths will be represented according to the constitutional apportionment; but, inasmuch as they have not at present the ability of voting, the increased political influence will proceed actually only from a part of the population, as before. The proposition of the new Amendment, in the version of the address from which we have before copied, and which we give as more explicit and readily perceived than in the original article, is, that, —

"While the States claim and exercise the right of denying the elective franchise to a part of their people, the weight of each State in the Union shall be measured by and based upon its enfranchised population. If any State shall choose, for no crime, to deny political rights to any race or caste, it must no longer count that race or caste as a basis of political power in the Union."

The effort and object of this proposition to change the basis of representation, undoubtedly, is to procure negro suffrage; that that portion of the Southern communities supposed to be loyal should have its rightful weight of political influence.

Although the States have always adjudicated their own

voting population, have pronounced who shall vote and who shall not do so, yet, as the basis of *national* representation is a subject of *national* legislation, it must be presumed that Congress has ample power to apportion this in whatever manner it is thought proper; and may base it, if it so sees fit, upon the number of actual voters, instead of upon that of the free population. This being a national topic, the same rule must be applied, however, equally to all the States; in those where the voting population has not been universal, as well as in the reconstructed States. Whether it is advisable to change the basis from the "free" to the "voting" population, would be the question, as, as it present exists, it leaves to each State the power to determine how its laws and institutions shall be guided and conducted; whether by a discriminate class, as in Massachusetts, — by those able to read and write, — or whether these shall be given into the hands of all, — the ignorant, as well as the more informed. Probably in New England, and in some of the other States where education is quite universally diffused, an objection to this, or any risk to be run, would be considered of no weight whatever; but in other States, where common intelligence is not so general, we can conceive that it would be of valid and of very important weight. We all are, or ought to be, naturally sensitive to having the purity of our republican principles and institutions despoiled by an unintelligent population. To this it may be replied, Let the States educate their own people in common learning : that they are not so educated is their own fault. It may have been their own fault in the past ; but the present fact is, that they have not been so trained. Therefore the question must arise, whether it is expedient or safe to deliver this power into their hands *until* they are better prepared for it. These remarks are applicable to any State where the suffrage has not been universal, and are also applicable to the Southern States in respect to their population of hitherto enslaved blacks. Where these blacks compose a great proportion of the population, as in South Carolina (more than half), we can imagine those States must shrink from throwing this immense political power *immediately* into their hands, — if they ever finally so do ; and we believe we have no right morally, much less politically, thus to *force* upon our States a condition so repugnant to their natural instinct of self-preservation, either in their political or physical existence. It would be taking from them their civil right, as political communities, to care for and protect themselves.

The radical-abolitionist would here say, that the blacks have as much right to rule there as the whites; and, if the control thus passes into their hands, that it is no more than perfectly *comme il faut;* that they have been subjected sufficiently long, and that now it is but proper that they should have their turn in public affairs. In our opinion, if these people are capable, if there is that in them, which, on development, will prove them to be equal or superior to the white race (as this idea has been advanced by some), no power on earth within their own States, now that they have the freedom of American citizens, can prevent their attaining eventually that position. In the mean time, we think that the Anglo-Saxon race on this continent, or in any of these individual States, is not yet prepared to subject itself to the control of the African; and that none of us, by any law human or divine, are empowered, in consequence of the misfortunes of the Southern States, — no matter how much they have been caused by their own fault, — to trample upon them in their misfortunes by *enforcing* this, without their own voluntary consent. When that

voluntary consent shall be given, it will be no longer
" enforcement;" and therefore they may have the full
privilege of being governed and controlled by the black
population if they so choose. Meanwhile we believe
that every human being, under favorable circumstances,
and every race, black or white, is capable of improvement and advancement; and, now that the negro born
on the soil has the national franchise of an American
citizen, we may expect, that, by improvement of his
opportunities, he will elevate himself sufficiently to be
able to aid and assist in the Government, in the same
manner as any other common citizen. If he does not
become the chief magistrate of thirty millions or more
of white people, or the governor of any individual
State, he may yet attain to the political privileges which
ordinary individuals enjoy, and be with them part and
parcel of the body politic. We believe that that time
must and will come, if there is the moral power in the
race equal to the occasion; that on the American soil,
surrounded by our generous institutions, if they *wish* to
attain such position, they will achieve it. But at present, altogether unused as the colored man is in the
Southern States to a condition of even personal freedom,

we would say, Let these things come gradually and naturally. Let the whole people, white and black, get settled in their new relations, and know what and where they are, and be able to discover what it is that they have, or ought to do. Then, in proper time, if the white population does not deal justly by them, the negroes themselves, with their greatness of numbers, if they are worthy of the name of citizen, will agitate the subject as far as is necessary for their own welfare. The Southerners, we believe, need not be afraid that their ambition will lead them beyond this. They have not the restless, mental ambition of the white race; but on the contrary, apparently, have the good sense and temperament to be satisfied with what is for their comfort and simple well-being. Their *ignorance* might lead them to excess, it might be said. It might, as ignorance knows no law; and, for that reason, it appears plain to us that they should be trained by degrees to their condition as citizens, and let each State keep in its own hands the power to regulate their political advancement.

"That," says the radical, "is precisely what the South wishes, and what we do not think it is safe for them to have. They are determined to have things all their own way; and, just as sure as the negro is left in their hands, they will bring him back into the depths of slavery as great as it was before. They are seeking for this, and they will never rest until they have attained it."

Who made thee a pre-judger of thy brother-man? And, if it were so, what can we do about it, except in the way of external law and order? which is the only manner in which free, political communities can act one upon another. What are we to do but to give faith and credit to solemn promises? and how do we expect to secure other solemn promises if these are of no avail? The South has already accepted the fiat of emancipation: it has given its solemn seal and pledge to the amendment of the Constitution prohibiting slavery forever in the States,— which amendment to the Constitution was a perfectly legal, valid, justifiable one (as we have before seen); and nothing more whatever can the Government do about that than to see that it is ostensibly fulfilled. It cannot create humanity in the hearts of the people (excepting by the influence of its own kindly example), and it cannot insure that the people shall have the most correct views as to their constitutional obligations,— even in the best ordered States; since, in the most generally enlightened communities, party-spirit will have its way, as is now so evident in our most prosperous and well-to-do other sections.

To come back to the question of impartial suffrage, that is, without distinction of *race* or *color*. The effort of the Congressional Amendment is, undoubtedly, to produce this; and most likely the Southern States will be forced by their own circumstances to make this choice. But let it be the growth of time and patience; and then will it be *healthful* and firm, and produce the fruits which are desired. When the Southerners get things into proper train after their terrible devastations and upheaving, let them grant the suffrage without distinction of color; and then may they limit it to whoever is prepared for such, as the free States themselves have limited their voting populations.

We have seen in a previous section that the decree of " universal " suffrage by Congress would take from the individual States their highest and dearest right, — that of regulating their own internal economy; and would transform us from a system of little republics into one vast, consolidated empire. It is not the same with " impartial " suffrage if applied simply to race and color, which would be merely granting that every man has the *natural* right or ability to vote if he be so situated as to come under the regulation; but leaves still to the States the privilege of limiting its voting population on whatever restrictions it may deem proper; for instance, those of education or property. As far as there is a natural right, one man has the same as another; as we are all born *men*, and are therefore by nature equal. But, in the civil community, this ability of suffrage may certainly be subject to regulation as well as aught else; as it is by no means necessary that one government, even if it be a republic, shall be modelled on exactly the same pattern as another. Republicanism, as we have elsewhere said, appears to consist in having a government of the people *according to their choice*. If they choose to regulate it in one way rather than in another, they are certainly at liberty so to do, or they have only the name of a republic.

It is inferred, therefore, that Congress has the power of declaring impartial suffrage, although not universal suffrage (unless, in the latter, we wish to change our whole system of government). This would not be enforcing the Southern States to give the elective franchise to the black population: they would still have the control of that in their own power, and would have *time* before them to do whatever was proper, or suitable to the circumstances. If this question should be taken up by Congress, and were not connected with the requisition of universal suffrage, we do not feel that it ought to be feared, but, on the contrary, that it would be a step to facilitate our political settlement of affairs, and to aid in the welfare and elevation of humanity, which should be the wise mission of a great, generous republic.

The above principles coincide with those of the "Constitutional Amendment," and we believe that they are those in which the Executive also concurs. Indeed, we know, from the honorable testimony contained in the very address (of the Congressional party) which we have had under consideration, that the President himself initiated the movement of impartial suffrage in the States; and we have still further testimony on this point, and on that of a change of the basis of representation (which appears to be almost identical with that of the Amendment), in a paper now before us, containing an extract from a reported conversation of the President (with Major Stearns), in which he says, —

"The apportionment is now fixed until 1872: before that time, we might change the basis of representation from population to qualified voters, North as well as South; and, in due course of time, the States, without regard to color, might extend the elective franchise to all who *possessed certain mental, moral,· or such other qualifications as might be determined by an enlightened public judgment."

And also at this very moment, since copying the above paragraph, we have still later evidence* that the President is not opposed to a change of the basis of representation, in a correspondence from Washington, purporting to contain a "revised copy" of a proposition for amendment to be submitted by him. It is as follows: —

"Representatives shall be apportioned among the several States which may be included within this Union according to the number of qualified male voters, as prescribed by each State."

Indeed, who would not approve of some such proposition, now that the whole circumstance of the Southern population is changed? There should manifestly hereafter be some equality of apportionment throughout the States. The former basis in the South was a compro-

---

* Date of Sept. 30, 1866.

mise in respect to the institution of slavery; and the inequality of the weight of political influence could not be expected to be allowed to remain after that should no longer exist. The anomaly of this, and the consequent unequal exercise of political power, was commented upon in the "Letters" of the first section of this work. We believe, then, that it has been conclusively demonstrated that truths are contained in each of the propositions of the post-Constitutional Amendment, which the Executive himself most firmly maintains, and which we believe, moreover, every true American, be he of the Presidential, Congressional, or any other party, must approve and uphold in his serious, deliberate mind.

THE CIVIL-RIGHTS AND FREEDMEN'S-BUREAU BILLS.

If, then, there is such a unison of principles, it will be demanded, Why does the President oppose this Constitutional Amendment? and why did he veto the Civil-rights Bill and that of the Freedmen's-bureau, which were also the work of Congress?

We reply, that it must already have been seen from the whole tenor of this work that we take the ground that these States are in themselves, individually, miniature republics; that is, having full and perfect power in all their internal arrangements for their own regulations; and that the Central Power, the Federal Government, is not for the purpose of divesting them of any of this ability, but is merely for general regulations, such as concern naturally and equally all the States, and for general defence, strength, and harmony. We believe that in this manner, and in this manner only (thus showing the marvellous wisdom of our predecessors who organized it, or that of an overruling Providence), can be secured the full and free development of civil governments, which should be the desire and glory of these States, and with it the highest, fullest, best, and most glorious development of the people, the populations, the individuals, of these States, through those free and individual States themselves; that, if we transfer any portion of this civil freedom (any thing but what is of general, natural right, and by the assent of all) to the Central Authority, we overburden that, and give to it a tendency to monopolize, and at length to become exacting (and the step is then short to oppression and tyranny); and by so much we lose the healthful energy, capacity, and activity of freedom, which, for our best good, should distinguish all these States. At present, where all have not attained to this highest condition, — and who can say that any one has? — these qualities are the very ones for developing their own freedom, and this best good itself to be attained is a constant impulse and incentive; whereas, if every thing is laid out for us by the Federal power, if our individualities have no room for exercise, our very powers of aspiration, which alone keep us up to a proper state, must wither and languish. We are of those who believe in the better and higher instincts of our people, and that they will never be contented with the mere prosperity of material interests, however great and ennobling that may become; but that, having been always accustomed to every species of contest for *freedom*, quickening both the mental and moral life, they will never be willing to give these up, — this freedom, and this higher life.

We believe it was on the above grounds, if we rightly apprehend President Johnson's course, — and his words have always been explicit on these points, — that he disapproved the first or any approach to this transfer of the rights which the States had always had in their own keeping; and consequently he gave his disapproval — his veto — to the Civil-rights Bill.

On reading the Freedmen's-bureau Bill before the veto of the Executive was passed on it, at least before we were aware of that action, we must say that the first thought which occurred to our mind was, what vast military enginery is here established among our civil institutions for a time of peace! And it seemed to us a precedent of evil import, an innovation upon our simple, quiet, republican system. Not that the original Freedmen's-bureau Bill was not very necessary: that was but a proper and probably essential aid in the commencement, when every thing was still "out of joint," — a half-military measure, to take the place of the full armies now to be withdrawn, — the gradual step, as it were, to full re-establishment. Its operations were to continue a length of time, which is not yet over, and will not be for six months to come,* when it might be supposed we would be in the full tide of renewed peace and prosperity. Therefore the second Bureau is not yet needed; and it seemed, at least, quite unnecessary to anticipate future need of legislation by so long an interval. Similar reasons were given by Mr. Johnson for his veto of the

* From the present date, — October, 1866.

bill, and they appeared to our mind entirely satisfactory. What is his opposition to the Constitutional Amendment will be seen under the succeeding head.

IN OR OUT OF THE UNION.

We now arrive at the final step which is to reveal to us the true and exact position, as we believe it, both of Congress and of the Executive, and the precise point of their differences. There was and is all that agreement of general and even exact principles, as we have seen, of both parties. Then why is it that the President should persist in opposing, or should oppose at all, those propositions which seem to contain so much that is perfectly, properly, and strictly true? Is not Congress thus on the right road in establishing such principles? and ought not every individual in the land to give his heart and hand until such should become the true elements, the just guides and pillars, of our country? And what is it but usurpation on the part of Mr. Johnson so to persevere in his opposition to the declared will of the people through their representatives? Is he not "setting up his own will against the will of the loyal masses?" (Such is the popular expression.) Or, now that it seems probable (as we have lately seen) that he is going to propose an "amendment," is he not inconsistent with himself, since he has always reiterated the expression that the Constitution as it was was "good enough" for him?

The amendment of the basis of representation suggested by Mr. Johnson (as is lately reported) is not one affecting at all our *organic* relations. It is simply such a change as time and circumstances may inevitably require; and to such amendments our Constitution is always open. Such a one was the late amendment prohibiting slavery. It is not to be supposed that the nation will still submit to a practical inequality in the national representation, which they had long since begun to feel, but, whilst slavery continued, could do nothing in reference to; and especially that now, since that is done away, it has become more intolerable still by the increased weight of political influence acquired by the same amount of white or voting population as before. This is precisely such a change of the Constitution, therefore, or such a *measure* (as the Constitution has it), as it is the province and duty of the President to submit. On the other side, we have maintained that any legislation which touches the rights which have always belonged to the States encroaches upon our organic law, — the very foundation-principle on which we exist, — and is therefore such a change as we have no right to attempt to make, except by the unanimous consent of the States.

The amendment which we have examined does, indeed, contain all that we have allowed and seen that it does, when *taken by itself*. But this is not all. We are forced to take it in connection with other legislation, that of the Civil-rights Bill for instance; and the article of the amendment concerning citizenship (though the latter is here taken in its simple, general meaning) must be modified by whatever that other or any similar bill might signify. It is well known that Congress had ulterior views (they were confessed), of wishing, through those, or some of those, provisions (of the amendment), to *oblige* the States, if they desired to resume their places, to alter their own internal regulations, — that, for example, of giving suffrage to the negroes. We have seen, we think, a few pages back, ample reasons why the Southerners, situated as they are, should not wish to be compelled to do this summarily; but, by obliging them so to do, we should be infringing directly those rights of internal government which belong, and ought to belong, we have maintained, to the individual States. In this manner, then, this amendment could but be considered " unconstitutional," though right in single or independent principles (had they so been).

But this is not all. This amendment was wrought out after the States had become re-organized and re-established in good faith, with the aid and encouragement of the Government, and were only waiting at the halls of Congress for admission to their accustomed places. *This was not granted;* and this exclusion, when they were ready and only waiting for this, taken in connection with Congress occupying itself at the same time in forming an amendment, when the Constitution distinctly says in reference to amendments " that no State, without its consent, shall be deprived of its equal suffrage in the Senate," in our opinion, falsifies and renders nugatory the whole proceeding, no matter how right *in themselves* may have been the principles laid down. Thus the mode, or method, in which the "Constitutional Amendment" was produced, was, according to these views, in every way exceptionable and unconstitutional; and we believe this is the precise ground which the Executive took, and on which he continues to stand.

Had the altogether-ready and waiting members been admitted, although they might have been refused to be accepted, — as this was in the power of Congress to do, — the constitutional mode, the mode in which it had always been customary to admit newly-elected members, would have been complied with as far as Congress could do it, or it was incumbent on them; and then they might have gone right on, and continued their legislation, even were those States absent (by a necessary rejection of their representatives), and might have produced whatever was thought necessary, — perhaps this very amendment itself!

Thus, we think, it has been clearly seen that the disagreement of the President with Congress was more as to their "mode" of proceeding than as to the "principles" advanced; as, with the former, there could be no accord (constitutionally), whereas, with the latter, there was some agreement.

But why be so certain, say some, that the States had

this right of admission? Had they not been out of the Union? Were not things changed on account of the war? and have we not power, by having conquered them, to bring them back in whatever way we please, on whatever terms we may think best? Is this the doctrine of the "radical" party? If so, instead of manifesting the tenderness and clemency, the expansive views, and the love of freedom in its highest and most distinguishing phase, that of States, or civil governments, which we might well expect from them, as being, in their prominent men, the leaders and "reformers" of the people, as they have generally claimed to be, and which principles the address we have made use of claims, in its closing sentence, for their proceedings, as being "based on the everlasting foundation of humanity, justice, and freedom," it appears to us that they are in practice denying all these.

A writer in a popular periodical, in referring to the conditions of the "Constitutional Amendment," uses this language,—that they "are the mildest ever exacted of *defeated enemies* by a *victorious nation*." Such may be the manner in which European or other nations may have treated and subjected their foreign, revolted *prov-*

inces; but we presume it does not often occur that their own *home* subjects in a body are thus denationalized. On the contrary, an *émeute*, or rebellion, among them, generally ends in an advance or elevation of the masses, — a concession of greater rights, — instead of being depressed or degraded as "defeated enemies." We, in our theory of the *natural* reconstruction, as it might be called, of the States, do not propose, however, to bestow on ours any additional rights. They even come back shorn of those they had forfeited by making them the cause of rebellion, — how greatly shorn, their still agitated, upturned, devastated country loudly proclaims, — and we only restore them to those which both we and they can hold, and ever have held, in common; and this, we maintain, is absolutely necessary in order to preserve and retain the true freedom, balance, and well-being of our republican system of States.

If we have not made clear through all this work the ground which we have taken, of the utter denial of the right and theory of secession, of the impossibility of any doctrine of independent States right of one or of many, and that therefore no States can be "out of the Union," we fear we should hardly be able to do so in any thing further that we might say. We will, however, recapitulate a little. We have believed and maintained that our Government was designed and constructed to be a single, united republic, composed of free and equal individual States; and that no State, nor a number of States, could of themselves, their own power or responsibility, in time of war or in time of peace, change this foundation; that it was on account of this very idea and instinct, of the perpetuity and unchangeableness of the Union, of this system of States, that the war was waged, and was persevered in to the bitter end; that we could not and would not allow that doctrine to prevail, and to maintain itself, even by force. It was on account of this doctrine — that the system of States could not, must not, be destroyed, although the people of some had risen *en masse* to endeavor to do this, to break themselves away from the Union — that Mr. Lincoln proceeded so carefully in regard to the slave question; even offering them the opportunity as still States, in their original structure, to dispose of it themselves. Emancipation became necessary as a war-measure, and he proclaimed it; but we have no reason to think that he ever changed his opinion in regard to the indissolubility of our State and Federal bonds and relations. On the contrary, we believe, that, where he stood first, he stood to the last; and we cannot think that any one would believe but that he would maintain, were he still living, the same ground still. We believe, indeed we know, that it was on the same precise ground that Mr. Johnson, our present President, stood with him during all the war; and we believe it was this idea which inspired him, when, bareheaded and barefooted (we remember to have read some such description of the scene), he fled, amid hunger and destitution, at the head of a band of refugees, — those bleeding patriots who were hunted and driven among the wilds of Tennessee by those who had declared themselves "out of the Union:" and with the same firmness with which he maintained the contrary theory then, sacrificing property, domestic life and happiness, in devotion to that idea, he now maintains it at the head of a great nation; every word and act of his since but proclaiming this continued idea

We believe that our honorable Secretary of State, who carried the country so nobly through all the *foreign* perils and struggles of the war, and who was intimately associated with Mr. Lincoln in all its plans and execution, stood with him on the same identical ground, and almost fell, like him, a martyr to the cause, under the assassin's hand; and that the very same doctrine which he maintained through all that trying period, — that the States could not and should not go out of the Union, — he never ceases to reiterate still.

The honored General of our army is not a political man, and will not allow himself in any manner to be mingled with politics; and we think he is right: but, at the same time, we cannot but believe, that he who so strenuously fought in actual arms for the *same* idea, offering his services at the commencement of the war, as against secession, — the doctrine of being " out of the Union," — and " fought it out on that line," will, if ever he thinks proper to take a political stand, or be so disposed, reveal himself as still on the same ground, and will continue to fight it out *on that line*, — our Union, our whole Union, and nothing but our Union! In the mean time, as military General-in-chief, he ought to be above and beyond all party as such; and is, therefore, justified in taking no public ground either on one side or the other: for woe be the day to our country when the military, as such, shall take rule on the stand of party politics! It is different with the soldiers, who were raised only *for the occasion,* and have been disbanded, retiring into private life: certainly they are as able to hold conventions or meetings for their own satisfaction as is any other associated body of citizens; for instance, teachers or working-men or clergymen. They are but citizens on the same ground with these; and their political opinion and influence are but of the same weight as those of any other citizens, no more or less. But the regular army, being a part of our institutions of government, should, of course, stand as firmly above all *partisan* spirit as should the executive, legislative, and judicial branches themselves. However much any of these officers or magistrates may have been elected or appointed by the triumph of " party," arrived at those posts of honor and influence, they undoubtedly should have but one instinct and aim, — that of the good of their country, their whole country. And long may our country retain the services of one so admirably adapted to his duties and sphere as is Gen. Ulysses S. Grant!

But, whatever may be personal views and preferences, these are the two platforms on which our country is now divided, — whether the States are still " in the

Union," legitimate parts and portions of our common country; or whether they are "out of the Union," on account of the event of the war. The party which maintains the former idea is that of the President, and in this we have seen that it is the direct successor of the party of Mr. Lincoln's administration. The object of the latter administration was to restore the States, as far as they attempted to "go out," in order that we might preserve our Union whole and unbroken. No one denies that they made the attempt to go out, — to break away; and, as long as the Rebellion persisted, they were in that attempt. But as the Rebellion ceased, because they were not able to succeed in this attempt at going " out," of course they are still " in." Or to express it in another way: the opposers of this theory say that the States were " practically out," — were out to all " intents and purposes." *We* say that there could be but three conditions, — either *in*, or *out*, or *between* " in " and " out ; " and that they were on this middle or half ground as long as the attempt lasted. They were neither " practically " *in* the Union, nor were they, to any " intent or purpose," *out* of it, as they never had been able to act for themselves: their whole time had been occupied in *trying* to get away, — to go "out." But as the balance turned the other way, and they could not succeed in going *out*, and as the Rebellion — the attempt — was completely overcome, so that they were no longer half-way, — on the middle ground, — they, of course, can be nowhere else but *in*.

Notwithstanding this plain and logical deduction, which coincides with the whole course and effort of the Administration (Mr. Lincoln's) and of the loyal States during the war, the opposite party, that of Congress, maintains, that, as the States rebelled to go out of the Union, that very rebellion put them out of the Union; and that, therefore, now they cannot be " in the Union," and may be treated to all intents and purposes as if they were " out." There are two ways to look at this view, which might defeat it, though we can scarcely stop so to do; but we will state one or two propositions. *If* the States got out of the Union by the Rebellion, how is it that now we have any control over them? and if, to all intents and purposes, they are still out, how is it that we have any *right* to have a control over them? since we never have conceived our country to be founded on any principle of foreign conquest. On the contrary, our republican faith and principles would not permit us so to conquer and take under arbitrary rule any foreign province or population, much less that of our own country, if it could so revolt as to succeed in getting away. But this is wasting time; and we design now only to give a slight historical outline of the party which holds this theory, as we have given that of the Administration, which has held, and continues to hold, the former one. We shall do this under the following head: —

ORIGIN OF THE CONGRESSIONAL PARTY

The views of this party, which we have just stated, were broached in Congress, even during Mr. Lincoln's administration, in the various plans and theories of the "territorial" character of the "conquered States," and of the power and necessity of treating them as such, — that they were thus by the fortunes of war surrendered into our hands, as it were, *ad libitum*. These views were not carried at that time, the party being composed of but a few individuals, probably; and Mr. Lincoln being, happily, through all the vicissitudes and experiences of the war, a *centre*, as it were, for all parties, his influence undoubtedly modified and controlled in a measure all degrees of opinion. The writer once heard in conversation a radical-abolitionist, who had returned highly pleased and satisfied from a visit to the President, say in reference to a third party, "The trouble is, Mr. Lincoln makes everybody feel that he is with *them*." Whether our lamented President would have been able to retain the same happy relations another four years, it would be vain, idle, and unnecessary for us to speculate upon. As it was, the hand of death struck him down just as new relations were to come upon the scene. Those personal influences were swept away; and that small Congressional (radical) party, now alone, or independent, as it were, began to develop its former peculiar views, when the debate came up as to *how* the returning States should be treated or regarded. Mingling in all, bold and prominent, it began to take the lead.

Congress, in general, no doubt, were endeavoring to do the best that occurred to them, feeling that it was necessary for them to do *something* in the way of reconstruction, as is now the acknowledgment; though overlooking, as it has appeared to us, the great share they had really already had in that work (as has before been recounted):

and now become increasingly radical by the influence of that originally small party, they were, no doubt, unconscious of any *incipient* dangers in the steps they might be taking; for the radical element, it is fully known, had never been accustomed to regard the niceties of our constitutional relations, or, as that party would have it, perhaps, of "constitutional etiquette." * "Etiquette," however, belongs to social and private relations: public and civil affairs must have form and law, — they are the very and only elements in which *their* life and integrity consist. They therefore proceeded to produce — nearly a year and a half before it would be needed, when it might be supposed we should be in the full tide of peace — the Freedmen's-bureau Bill, which was a half-military measure, the Civil-rights Bill, and the post-Constitutional Amendment; all of which the President opposed on grounds which have been clearly seen. This was felt as an opposition to Congress and the rights of Congress itself. Had not Congress the *right* to legislate? Was not this its own function? We do not deny the right in itself: it is the *mode* principally in which this was done which is objected to in this case, as has been seen. But,

---

* See note, p. 374.

independently of that, we know not of what advantage is the Executive, if he is not to interpose his veto, — his disapproval, — which is an express power granted to him by the Constitution for this very purpose, *when*, in his mind, it is his duty so to do. We have seen what was President Johnson's view of the States being " in the Union," and which was the view of the whole Republican party during the war, and, we may say, of the Democratic party also, since they desired peace, and cessation of hostilities, on this very ground, — that they were our brethren, our own States. With this view, backed as he was by all the former experience of the country, we know not how the Executive could have done otherwise than to have placed himself in opposition to the measures which are consistent only with the opposite theory.

That this theory is the one still held by the party in question, we have, at this very moment at which we write, the very latest evidence from its principal leader, in his own words. He says,* —

" I can never cease to regret that Congress has hesitated, by proper legislation, to assume a temporary juris-

---

* See address at the Music Hall, Boston, Oct. 2, 1866.

diction over the whole rebel region. To my mind, the power was ample and unquestionable, whether in the exercise of belligerents, or in the exercise of rights derived directly from the Constitution itself. In this way, every thing needful might have been accomplished. In the exercise of this just jurisdiction, the rebel communities might have been fashioned anew, and shaped to loyalty and virtue.* The President lost a great oppor-

---

* The party of Congress resents the charge of "usurpation;" but besides the expression here made use of, "of fashioning and shaping the States to loyalty and virtue," we have the same idea given in a still later address, also from a "member of Congress."* He says, "I am for a change in the basis of political society in those States. In place of that aristocracy which governs by force and violence and fraud, and which disregards public opinion, I want that there shall be planted a civilization not unlike that which exists in our own part of the country, which is democratic and republican in its nature." It is very true that every one may desire that the South should have the same republican simplicity and freedom that we consider ourselves to possess (though assuredly there has been, even here, of late, as great an ostracism of public opinion as that which drove the just Aristides from Athens). But how can we assume control over great bodies of States or communities to plant *our* way of thinking? Is it not the grand idea of American freedom that all opinion and action (within the bounds of law) shall be *free?* and how can we violate that principle by *forcing* any of our States to improve themselves in those respects, by taking away from them their government in order to put our own there? We believe it has never come within the category of a philosophical freedom, which, we believe, intends to be the one of our civilization, to *compel* people, *nolens volens*, to become virtuous and upright. The only possible influ-

* At Charlestown, Mass., Oct. 8, 1866.

tunity at the beginning: Congress has lost another. *But it is not too late.* If indisposed to assume this jurisdiction by an enabling act constituting provisional governments, there are many things Congress may do, acting directly or indirectly."

Thus it seems, that, at this day even, Congress, if it were so " disposed," could take these States, settled into peace, and turn them over into Territories, with provisional governments! Was ever a doctrine more monstrous instituted with regard to these States? Were such a one announced among the territories of Europe, would not the whole free and civilized world be roused in indignation against it?

One may say, ." But provisional governments were established for a time in those States." Yes; but as a remains and continuation of the necessary power to put down and finish off the Rebellion; the step, the

ence that we can see that can be used in this respect is that of example and of other prosperous freedom.

It appears to us that the "reformers" and "liberal" party are giving very little credit to the new condition of "liberty" which they have so emphatically advocated, and to the natural influences that must inevitably flow from it. For ourselves, we expect, before many years, to see the whole South entirely renewed and renovated just by this single influence of the all-ameliorating and elevating power of universal freedom, — the abolition of slavery.

necessary aid and assistance, to get the States in order to resume their own natural relations; and not for the purpose of holding them as conquered property, after the full and honorable surrender of arms. That was done; and trade, commerce, business, are revived. The peaceful occupations of life have taken the place of the agitations of war. Flourishing communities are again building up. The negro, even, is becoming educated and learned in schools and — colleges, we were about to say: but there is an approach to these in establishing seminaries for training him to become an intelligent and qualified minister of the gospel; and how many and fast others may follow, we need not say. Only the black man does not yet vote: he has not marched to the polls, and thrown his vote for members of Congress; and therefore these free and independent (in internal affairs) States of the Union, with their millions of population (the eight loyal millions, negroes and all), must be turned over into territorial possessions, to be under the sway of Congress!

And how could Congress obtain this power from the Constitution? Did the Constitution *create* these States in the beginning? or did they not come voluntarily into the system, as free and independent, — with the choice to come, or not, as they pleased? We hold them to the pledge, in that they did come; but that does not give us the power to do with them as we please. Not one hair of their head — of their populations — can we touch, except what is amenable to the Federal, and not to the State, authority. Not one article of their constitutions can we violate, excepting what may be made in contravention of that same Federal authority. And we are to create no Federal authority which shall bring the natural rights they have always possessed in contravention with *it*.

Again: the Southern communities are now querying whether, should they accept the " Constitutional Amendment," there would be any further " conditions " imposed. The general opinion of the country, undoubtedly, is, that these were to be final; that, if accepted, the States would be at once admitted. A Northern journal, in reference to this,* and that no " pledge " had been made by Congress in this respect, says, " Southern politicians . . . seem not to have considered the position in which this left affairs, in case the bitterness of renewed agitation *should incline the Northern people to more*

---

* These " more stringent demands " now occur in all the radical papers.

stringent demands;" and the leader of the Congressional party, from whose late address we have just extracted, remarks, in connection with that extract, —

"Of course, the Constitutional Amendment must be adopted. As far as it goes, it is well; *but it does not go far enough. More must be done.* Impartial suffrage must be established. A homestead must be secured to every freedman; if in no other way, through the pardoning power. If to these is added education, there will be a new order of things, with liberty of the press, liberty of speech, and liberty of travel, so that Wendell Phillips may speak freely in Charleston or Mobile. There is an old English play which goes under the name of the four 'P's.' Our present desires may be symbolized by four 'E's,' standing for *emancipation, enfranchisement, equality, and education.* Let these be secured, and all else will follow. . . . There are many things which Congress may do, acting indirectly or directly. Acting indirectly, it may insist that emancipation, enfranchisement, equality, and education shall be established *as a condition precedent to the recognition of any State whose institutions have been overthrown by rebellion.* Acting directly, it may, by constitutional amendment, or by simple legislation, fix all these forever."

Ambition, like love, " grows with what it feeds upon." We might exclaim in the words of the great dramatist, —

> " Upon what meat doth this our Cæsar feed,
> That he is grown so great?"

We would answer, politically, On the "out-of-the-Union" theory. That it has produced such travesty and distortion as we have now seen, of itself shows that it is utterly hollow, false, and base. These extracts, and the whole address from which they have been taken, show also one other thing,—that instead of our having a "One-Man-Power" President (the title of the address from which we have extracted),—though we do not well see how the President could be but one man; yet, as his theory was upheld and supported by the whole loyal country during the period of the war, with the President and all Congress at the head, and the other branches of the Government, with the army and navy beside, and has, too, many hundred thousands, at least, of present supporters,—one would have to call him, according to this idea, a Many-Million-Men-Power. Instead of this, we have had, most evidently, a One-Man-Congress. Here are the direct proofs, from the words of the speaker himself:—

"And now, to-day, I protest against any admission of ex-rebels to the great partnership of this Republic; and I renew the claim of irreversible guaranties, . . . insisting now, as I did a year ago, that it is our duty, while renouncing indemnity for the past, to obtain at least security for the future. . . . This can be only by provisions sure, fundamental, and irrepealable. . . . They must not be allowed to enter those halls which they treasonably deserted until we have every reasonable assurance of future good conduct. . . . But, while holding this ground, I desire to disclaim every sentiment of vengeance or punishment, and also every thought of delay or procrastination. . . . When, therefore, the President, in opprobrious terms, complains of Congress as interposing delay, I reply to him, 'No, sir: it is you. . . . Sir, you are the disunionist.' . . . You will ask how the President fell. . . . The part he is now playing will justify me in some details. . . . More than once, I ventured to press upon him the duty and the renown of carrying out the principles of the Declaration of Independence. . . . To this earnest appeal he replied, . . . as I sat with him alone, in words which I can never forget, 'On this question, Mr. ——, there is no difference between us. You and I are alike.' Need I say that I was touched to the heart by this annunciation, which seemed to promise a victory without a battle? . . . After expressing to him my joy and gratitude, I remarked still further, that it was important that there should be no division in the great Union party. . . . On another occasion, . . . the case of Tennessee was discussed. I expressed the hope most earnestly, that the President would use his influence directly for the establishment of impartial suffrage in that State. . . . The President replied, that, if he were at Nashville, he would see that this was accomplished. I could not help rejoining promptly, that he need not be at Nashville. . . . Let me confess that his hesitation on this occasion disturbed me; but I attributed it to an unnecessary caution rather than to any infidelity. He had been so positive with me, how could I suspect him? . . . As I was about to return home, I said that I desired, even at the risk of repetition, to make some parting suggestion on the reconstruction of the rebel States; and that, with his permission, I would proceed point by point, as was the habit of the pulpit in former days. He smiled, and said pleasantly, 'Have I not always listened to you?' I replied, 'You have, and I am grateful.' After remarking that the rebel region was still in military occupation, and that it was the plain duty of the President to use his temporary power for the establishment of correct principles, I proceeded to say, — First, See to it that no newspaper is allowed which is not thoroughly loyal, and does not speak well of the National Government and of equal rights; and here I reminded him of the saying of the Duke of Wellington, that, in a place under martial law, an unlicensed press was as impossible as on the deck of a ship of war. Secondly, Let the officers that you send as military governors or otherwise be known for their devotion to equal rights, so that their names alone will be a proclamation, while their simple presence will help educate the people; and here I mentioned Major-Gen. ——— * . . . as such a person.

* Happily, the President seems to have had more insight and judgment in regard to this nomination; as this was the gentleman referred to in a previous section, in whose speech at the emancipation-meeting in New York the slur was cast upon our "constitutional obligations." — See p. 172.

Thirdly, Encourage the population to resume the profitable labors of agriculture, commerce, and manufactures, without delay, but, for the present, to avoid politics. Fourthly, Keep the whole rebel region under these good influences; and, at the proper time, hand over the subject of reconstruction, with the great question of equal rights, to the judgment of Congress, where it belongs. All this the President received at the time with perfect kindness; and I mention this with the more readiness, because I remember to have seen in the papers a very different statement." (It is certainly well to have received from this authentic source a contradiction of *some* unfavorable newspaper report, as it countenances the probability that many others might be contradicted, relating to the *personal* bearing and manners of our Chief Magistrate.)

" Only a short time afterwards, there was a change; . . . and then ensued a strange sight. Instead of faithful Unionists, recent rebels thronged the presidential antechambers. . . . Instead of telling the ex-rebels, . . . as he should have done, that he was their friend; that he wished them well from the bottom of his heart; that he longed to see their fields yield an increase, and peace in all their borders; and that, to this end, he counselled them to devote themselves to agriculture, commerce, and manufactures, and, for the present, to say nothing about politics, — instead of this, he sent them away talking and thinking of nothing but politics. . . . Instead of designating officers of the army as military governors, which I had supposed he would do, he appointed ex-rebels. . . . This was last autumn. I was then in Boston. . . . Moved by a desire to arrest this fatal tendency, I appealed by letters to members of the cabinet, entreating them to stand firm against a 'policy' which promised nothing but disaster. As soon as the elections were over, I appealed directly to the President himself, by a telegraphic despatch, as follows: . . . 'As a faithful friend and supporter of your administration, I most respectfully petition you to suspend, for the present, your policy towards the rebel States. I should not present this prayer if I were not painfully convinced, that, thus far, it has failed to obtain any reasonable guaranties for that security in the future which is essential to peace and reconciliation;' &c. . . . On reaching Washington, Saturday evening, . . . I lost no time in seeing the President. I was with him that evening three hours. I found him changed in temper and purpose. How unlike that President who . . . had made me feel so happy in the assurance of agreement on the great question before the country! He was no longer sympathetic, or even kindly, but harsh, petulant, and unreasonable." (All this, too, after that letter was received! And this was a three-hours' visit, on Saturday evening, at the end of the weekly labors, and approaching, perhaps, to the Sunday morning, — talking of *the* one great question, as the honorable gentleman considered it; while the President, the head of a great people, must have had his mind and head and heart full of the hundred or more " great questions " of our broken and bruised nation!)

" Plainly his heart was with the ex-rebels. For the Unionist, white or black, who had borne the burden of the day, he had little feeling. Perversely, he would not see the bad spirit of the rebel States; and he insisted that the outrages there were insufficient to justify their exclusion from Congress. It was in this connection that the following dialogue ensued: *The President.* — ' Are there no murders in Massachusetts? ' *Mr. S.* — ' Unhappily, yes; sometimes.' *The President.* — ' Are there no assaults in Boston? Do not men there sometimes knock each other down, so that the police is obliged to interfere?' *Mr. S.* — ' Unhappily, yes.' *The President.* — ' Would you consent that Massachusetts, on this account, should be excluded from Congress?' *Mr. S.* — ' No, Mr. President: I would not.' And here I stopped, without remarking on the entire irrelevancy of the inquiry." (Who but an " out-of-the-Union " man would not have seen the *relevancy* and *pertinency* of the inquiry?) " I left the President that night with the painful conviction that his whole soul was set as flint against the good cause" (Mr. S——'s cause), " and that, by the assassination of Abraham Lincoln, the Rebellion had vaulted into the presidential chair. Jefferson Davis was then in the casemates of Fortress Monroe; but Andrew Johnson was doing his work. . . . From this time forward, I was not in doubt as to his ' policy,' which asserted a condition of things in the rebel region inconsistent with the terrible truth." (What, personally, could the honorable senator know of the " terrible truth," since he had been in a far different region, and had but that moment returned?) " It was, therefore, natural that I should characterize one of his messages, covering over the enormities there, as ' whitewashing.' . . . The whole rebel region is little else than a ' whited sepulchre.' . . . Meanwhile, the presidential madness has become more than ever manifest. It has shown itself in frantic efforts to defeat the Constitutional Amendment proposed by Congress for adoption by the people."

An apology, perhaps, is needed for these lengthy citations; but it appears to us, if any thing will justify the Chief Magistrate of the nation before the American people (and we might say all the world) in his misunderstanding or "quarrel" with Congress, it must certainly be this "plain, unvarnished tale." We were but sketching slightly the difficulty as it appeared to the public, and these secret confessions fell right into our hands! Not "secret," however, as they were proclaimed to a large, public, and popular audience; and therefore we, too, are entitled to make use of them. It appears to us there can be no longer a doubt or hesitation, after this plain exposition and synopsis of facts by the principal party himself (as is evident), as to what was the original difficulty, or how it occurred. It was that the One-Man-Congress had "vaulted" (to use his own expression) into the presidential chair!

Is it, then, that the President of the United States is compelled to receive unsought, outside of his own cabinet and council, an adviser, a prime-minister, a preacher, on his own special prerogatives? If the President had thus put himself upon Congress, — indeed, in any other than his official capacity, — might they not then truly have had reason to complain? But it appears to us altogether that it was Congress (this " One-Man-Congress ") that was putting itself upon the President, and not the President upon *it*. How plainly it is shown that it was this one ruler who carried all things before him, or *desired* and attempted to do the same, we certainly need not say. When *his* will, and " out-of-the-Union " theory, came in contact with the opposition of the President on his " in-the-Union " theory, after but a single interview, though lengthy it may have been, he turned about from being " a faithful friend " and " supporter " to become the most avowed denouncer, and, though we might not say it, we believe — defamer. We have no personal knowledge whatever of President Johnson; but this evidence itself, to our apprehension, goes to show, under the circumstances, a remarkable kindliness and courtesy of temper and demeanor.

We have a little more to do with this address. It would be instructive and edifying to note the promises held out, and the anticipations as to the future welfare and glory to follow the inauguration of the " out-of-the-

Union" theory, — though *when* the States are to be got "in," to enable these to be fulfilled, does not appear, since the conditions, it seems, may be indefinitely extended; and what that "One-Man-Congress," if it should continue, might propose to do after those still further conditions should be presented, cannot be foreseen, — and to compare these notes with the speeches which were made at the South, during the ascendency of secession, on this *same* "out-of-the-Union" theory. It would be only necessary, it will be seen, for those who remember those days, to alter but a few words here and there, to render the similarity of style and spirit complete. They are as follows : —

"The question at issue is one of the vastest ever presented, . . . involving the name and weal of this Republic at home and abroad. . . . It is a question of statesmanship. We are to secure by counsel what was won by war. Failure now will make the war itself a failure; surrender now will undo all our victories. Let the President prevail, and straightway the plighted faith of the Republic will be broken;" (*query*, what has become of it now, with Congress, in its additional "conditions," prevailing?) . . . "the Rebellion itself will flaunt its insulting power; the whole country, in length and breadth, will be disturbed; and the rebel region will be handed over to misrule and anarchy.* Let Congress prevail" (the "One-Man-Congress" it must be; since he was the initiator, guide, and ruler of the "territorial," out-of-the-Union idea), " and all this will be reversed; the plighted faith of the Republic will be preserved; . . . the Rebellion itself will be trampled out forever; (do we not read that even a worm, *thus* trodden upon, turns upon the foot that crushed, to sting it?) the whole country, in length and breadth, will be at peace; and the rebel region, no longer harassed by controversy and injustice, will enjoy the rich fruits of security and reconciliation. To labor for this cause may well tempt the young, and rejoice the old."

Happy days! Are we not reminded of the halcyon period predicted by the South, without their ever taking into consideration the resolute determination and fiat of the whole vast country beside?

But must not such results with certainty happen, being instituted by a "House of Representatives eminent in both ability and character," and superior to the Many-Million-Men-Power President, since he is "inferior" to it "in both respects," and it being the "House of Representatives, . . . the best that has sat since the forma-

---

* As this is the present state of things, according to Mr. Sumner's own avowal, and as the policy of Congress has been carried all this time, might we not infer that this condition is the natural consequence of that policy, the effect following cause?

tion of the Constitution"? We must look a little at the "astonishing, irrational assumption," the "usurpation," the "tyranny," protested against:—

"The evil that he has done already is on such a scale, that it is impossible to measure it, unless as you measure an arc of the globe. I doubt if in all history there is any ruler, who, in the same brief space of time, has done so much. There have been kings and emperors, proconsuls and satraps, who have exercised a tyrannical power; but the facilities of communication now lend swiftness and extension to all evil influences, so that the President has been able to do in a year what in other days would have taken a life. Nor is the evil that he has done confined to any narrow spot: it is co-extensive with the Republic. Next to Jefferson Davis stands Andrew Johnson as its worst enemy. The whole has suffered; but it is the rebel region which has suffered most. He should have sent peace: instead, he sent a sword."

And yet this man is accused of being "hand in glove" with the "rebels," and is the very head and front of his offending! "Consistency, where art thou?" we might exclaim: "thou *art* a jewel!" And it was a once "faithful friend" who has thus described a whilom bosom-friend,—apparently; he visiting him "frequently" at his "private house" and at "his office;" and his heart, overjoyed with the words of kindness which fell from his lips, swelled in "gratitude," and could "never forget" those words! *This* one, too, was the friend of Abraham Lincoln, engaged in the same high and holy cause, — the preservation or salvation of our country: for this he had sacrificed home and friends and fortune, — all but life. But now he opposes the "policy" of "One Man," or it may be Two Men, in Congress; and who, seeing it in its length and breadth, would not oppose it? And he exceeds in tyranny the worst emperors of old: "in all history there was no such ruler"! But this is not all. "Such a President dictating to such a Congress!" he says. . . . "It is 'I'" (the Many-Million-Men-Power President) " *vs.* the people of the United States in " (that identical " One-Man ") " Congress assembled." But enough of this.

We only say, further, that this speech is not the only one of the kind which has been produced by the " out-of-the-Union " party; and articles of similar import and gross exaggeration, crude and undigested in thought, disfigure, we might say disgrace, not only the pages of our journals, but those of the perhaps most popular, widely-read periodical * of the country, and are sent

* The Atlantic Monthly for September, October, and November.

abroad into the wide world as representations of the Chief Magistrate of the American Union! *O tempores! O mores!* Who does not see in this misrepresentation, misimagination, misinterpretation, the very same spirit of evil which reigned so triumphant at the South during secession, and which proves true to the very letter our former assertion (in the preceding section), — that the state of things at present prevailing at the North is but a " rebellion" similar in spirit to that which reigned in the Southern States? and who can then wonder that the Chief Executive finds or feels it as necessary to oppose himself as firmly to this state of things as he did to the former?

We will add but one more of these sad features. An eminent and popular minister of the gospel, with the kindly, genial nature which had always characterized him, and which, his life long, had been exerted for the slave and black man as well as for others, desirous of seeing our re-united country again in harmony and peace (truly the highest earthly aspiration he could possess), approves the policy of the President, of having the recovered States re-established as speedily as possible, and makes bold so to speak. Immediately on all sides resounds a cry as if he had sunk into the fathomless pit, instead of being raised a little higher towards heaven, — as he certainly was. And the journal, which, it is said, has the greatest number of readers in the country, but which, in the days at the beginning of secession, knew not but it ought to say to the South, " Sister States, go!"* (another quondam " friend " too!) now puts the name of this reverend clergyman in connection with, and as in the praises of, " every blackleg, duellist, and negro-killer . . . from the St. John to the Rio Grande ; " and his people must forego this long-loved and honored pastor, because " they have trusted too confidingly, and loved unwisely"! All this because, forsooth, he *must* have forsaken the negro!† Did ever so supreme absurdity reign triumphant over a supposed-to-be-enlightened community?

Are our citizens forever to be infected, and increasingly so, with this vice of suspicion and mistrust? — the same foul spirit of evil-surmising which blew its breath

---

* See note, p. 57.

† Mr. Beecher did not commit himself at all to *party* politics: he only desired the restoration of the States.

Of what avail, then, are virtue and principle, if their life-long practice cannot guarantee us against such dire assaults?

upon Robert Anderson at Fort Sumter, when, like the hero of a "forlorn hope," as it were, he was bearing up our flag almost alone there with his God, and which quick suspicion — on release, and coming back to the open faces of his countrymen — pierced his manly heart to the quick. The same suspicious distrust, too, which assailed Gen. Sherman after his almost "wilderness" march to the sea: "A traitor!" "A traitor!" was the cry.

And now such is resounding from almost every hill-top and in every valley of our (enlightened?) States against the men who stood by and guided the country in its darkest hours, and to whom, and such as whom, we believe it is not too much to say, that, under God, we owe it that we have a country. Those were tried years of statesmanship (in the case of Mr. Seward), which, in the annals of republicanism, has no superior, and which, to this day, has breathed no word but in the most entire consistency and harmony with the great platform of American freedom. Is it, then, that republics are destined ever to be "base and ungrateful;" that we also are to come under the rule of all others; that in advancing age, after a life-long service and experience of loyal virtue, such men are to be subjected to the partisan cry of defection, dereliction, treachery? Who, then, shall we be able to obtain for our highest officers of State, if this is the reward of unselfish and devoted patriotism? — this crucible of public obloquy, caprice, and changeableness of the people, in which, if there were room for a spark of human feeling to remain, and if we had not now the noble confession * that " he had never permitted the sun to go down on his anger, or with feelings of retaliation in his breast," and but for the sustaining consciousness of duty performed, we must believe the heart not only of their honorable Secretary of State would have been riven with anguish, but in like manner, also, the breast of the Chief Magistrate of the American people, — a President NOT " made by the hands of an assassin." The Almighty Ruler does not thŭs deliver HIS power into the hands of "assassins;" and we believe he will yet, in his own good time, further waft away the clouds, and disclose high upon the rolls of fame the name of " ANDREW JOHNSON " — the *providential President* — side by side with those of " ANDREW JACKSON " and " ABRAHAM LINCOLN," as the " con-

---

* Speech of Secretary Seward at Franklin, Ind., Sept. 11, 1866.

stitutional preservers" — we might say saviors — of their country!

It is a peculiar fact, that, whenever the one intense interest has been in relation to the black man, for him as well as against him, the same exact phenomena have taken place: all the most exciting passions, and the worst and most evil spirits of both body and mind, seem to have been aroused. But we may hope, it is to be trusted, now that the negro is free, that, when he shall have received his title to "suffrage," — as it is to be presumed we shall have no further peace until that be attained, — both he and we may be allowed to have a little of the quiet enjoyments and satisfactions of life, instead of its constant turmoils, anxieties, and alarms. But who knows? Who can foresee what earthly paradise may yet be opened, to which he must perforce be carried? Who can tell?

THE WILL OF THE PEOPLE.

Much is now said of the "will of the people." It is even become the mode, in some of our popular papers, to use the precise expression which was adopted at the

South during the reign of secession (and which establishes still further the resemblance we have instituted); namely, " bowing to the will of the people."

It becomes necessary to see what and where is this " will," so deferentially referred to. In this case, the " people " are presumed to mean the party who have followed the lead of Congress in the " plan of reconstruction; " Congress being considered as the exponent, the index, of their peculiar views.

We aver, and are supported by the whole history of the times, that the present movement of radical-republicanism did not originate with the masses, but was initiated by their representatives. That the " plan of reconstruction," which is their platform, had its origin entirely in Congress, is fully known; and the theory on which it is based had its original source also in the " resolutions " declaring the seceding States " Territories," which were introduced into Congress, during the war, by the honorable senator whose late speech we have just now so largely quoted from. Those " resolutions," or the spirit of them in some modified form, were renewed from time to time, whenever there was opportunity for a hearing. The idea embodied in those resolutions, and in that theory of the States, by war, becoming "territorial property," led, logically, to the plan of reconstruction adopted by the National Legislature. It has been, therefore, *its* special work ; with how much labor, and effort at organization, sitting with closed doors, we all know. This is now adopted and indorsed, apparently, by the people of the whole North, who, during the war. were on the other side, the " in-the-Union " theory, and, in general, opposed the movement and " resolutions " of the honorable member, although a Northern man. A change, therefore, has undoubtedly come over " the spirit of their dream."

But that they should thus follow on after their representatives we know not is more surprising than that the movement of secession was received and indorsed by the whole people of *its* States, when it was once initiated by their political leaders and representatives ; and we conceive, in the same manner, that this movement is no more expressive than was that of the *original, unbiassed* " will " of the people. In the present case, as in the former (it is human nature), the masses take a pride in following the supposed-to-be political wisdom of their leaders. It is not unnatural, therefore, and but to be expected, that the whole body of the Northern States — if they are not clearly aware of the issues — should follow on, with one general plunge, in the line which the "plan" and "policy" of Congress have marked out for them.

(The facility with which such movements take place in a time of excitement may enable us to understand more readily the general impulse of the Southern people in *their* moment of excitement; and may induce in us, perhaps, some sympathy, or some leniency at least, towards them, *in their doing what they believe to be right*.)

But we object *in toto* to the expression of necessarily "bowing to the will of the people" — right or wrong — in this or in any other case. It was the very rock on which the South split, and on which its highest and best citizens fell from a lofty pedestal of true patriotism; that patriotism which embraces our *true* country, our *whole* country, and nothing but the whole and true country. To be sure, *if* the people in a mass choose to have things so and so, we can only submit until that phase be past, and another take its place which may be more in accordance with our own, or a truer one. But to say, that, *because* the universal impulse seems to be so and so, we must fall in and go with it, is an entirely different thing, and may open but an abyss, into which we all must sink, of woe, and not of weal; of all which we have most surely had an ample practical illustration in this idea being carried out in the Southern States. Are we about to do the same thing at present because it is the " will of the people," in the popular phrase? Are we — the rest of the people — going to join in and take up that very plan of reconstruction, — the " Constitutional Amendment," — *although* proposed by Congress? which plan, it appears to us, has been clearly seen, throughout these discussions, to be not the true one. No : no one can be called upon to " bow to," that is, fall in with, and second, what, for the moment, seems to be the " will " of the people, *unless* he himself feels that it is a truly expressed one, and on the right course.

" But what is one going to do, then? We can't leave our party: would you have us rush over to the Democrats?" By no means; not where " democracy " means copperheadism. The party which could not save the country during the war is not to be trusted with it in time of peace. " What then, if neither democracy nor republicanism is allowed?" We have not objected to "republicanism;" it is only *radicalism* that we contend against: and we have refused "democracy" only where *copperheadism* was concerned.

THE ISSUE BEFORE THE PEOPLE.

But we do feel that the old-time Democrat — the vigorous, clear-minded, *constitutional* Democrat — and the genuine Republican — both of whom ably assisted to carry on the war *for the Constitution* to its honorable close — should each and all look about them, and see what is the real ground on which they do stand; and then, unitedly or singly, plant themselves on *that same side, as formerly,* of the real issue which is now before the people, — the issue of those two theories which have been discussed. This is the present pivot on which all turns, — whether we shall adopt the theory that the States are now, by virtue of the decision of the war, "in the Union," and are therefore to be held and treated as such; or whether they are "out of the Union," and may therefore be regarded as subject to our disposal, and to our alteration of their own vital State constitutions. The former theory, we have seen, is capable of a logical, and, it seems to us, of almost or even a quite mathematical demonstration. There are the two extremes, — the *out* and the *in:* the middle term, which represents the people, occupies the intervening space or time all along between. As long as they attempted to go *out*, — to go towards that direction, that extreme, — this middle term, the balance, the people, leaned, preponderated, more that way; but it happened, by the events of the war, that it never actually reached that extreme, — the *out:* on the contrary, those events gradually more and more brought the middle term — the " between " state, so to say, of the people — over to the opposite extreme, the *in*, until that middle term, mid-way state, was completely by it cancelled, and there was nothing left but the *in*.* It

---

* To be put in a more purely mathematical form, it may be stated thus: Let the people, represented by 1, be equal to O (out), and also to I (in), according to whichever should prevail; then we have —
$$1 = O,$$
$$1 = I.$$
But as, during the war, they were neither one nor the other, but in a half-way state, this may be represented by $\frac{1}{2}$; and y may represent the force of secession; and x, the force of the National Government; and as, if the former prevailed, they would be *out*, or, if the latter prevailed, they would be *in*, other equations may be stated thus: —
$$\tfrac{1}{2} + y = O,$$
$$\tfrac{1}{2} + x = I.$$

appears to us, there wants no plainer illustration than this to show that they, with us, are all fairly in the Union, with no State left out; and that, being thus *in*,

Then, as "1" also was equal to O or I, the further equations can be stated:—
$$1 = \tfrac{1}{2} + y,$$
$$1 = \tfrac{1}{2} + x.$$

These two forms thus become equal to each other (both being equal to 1); namely,—
$$\tfrac{1}{2} + y = \tfrac{1}{2} + x.$$

Cancelling the $\tfrac{1}{2}$, it would be $y = x$,— the two forces which were contending for the victory, and which, as long as the contest was undecided, might be considered equal,— of equal chance. Again: if y (the force of secession) prevailed, or if x (the Government force) prevailed, the equations would be
$$1 + y = 0,$$
$$1 + x = I.$$

Changing the terms, they become
$$1 = 0 - y,$$
$$1 = I - x;$$

that is, no more need, in the former equation (if that should prevail), of the y or secession force, because they have become completely O, *out*: and, should the latter prevail, no further need of that of x,— the Government force,— since they (the "1,"— the people) have become completely I; that is, *in*.

As the latter equation is the one which prevailed, we have only to substract x (the Government force, no longer necessary), and there is nothing left but the simple terms,
$$1 = I.$$

As it is said that "figures do not lie," it appears to us that this matter might thus, by this simple but mathematical demonstration, be settled forever.

we must be treated and treat each other as such, States in the Union, in the same precise manner as before, with the very same relations. The relations of our other States were not affected by the war: why, then, should theirs be, since the war was simply for bringing them back to the Union and to those very same relations? There was no change, excepting by the generally disturbing influence of the time; and, with them, this was greater than with us. It agitated, shook down, their institution of slavery; and, so far, they come back not as before: but this only makes them more similar to the rest of us, with a broader foundation than before of *equal* rights. On the contrary, if we do not regard and treat each other in the former " equal " manner, with the same precise relations, but adopt some other mode or way, we are changing, as far as that goes, our system of government, and of our State and Federal relations, without the form or process of law, which thus becomes usurpation, — assuming, usurping, a mode which was not ours. This opens the way to other usurpation, — the flood-gate once opened, one never knows when it may be shut, — and, if persevered in, it must end in *revolution. It is a change of government.*

If the people quietly submit and yield, it will be, for the time, a peaceable, unconscious so to say, revolution, the principles of the Government having been *insidiously* changed; but if there be a large body of the people who do not assent to this course, and are determined to resist, it might become a true and proper revolution of force, as it is in such a way that *true* revolutions arise. We do not apprehend, however, that there will be any call or cause for such revolution in our case; for, as was frequently said in former parts of this work, *our* revolutions are, or should be, by the polls, the ballot-box. It is but little time to wait from one administration, or from one term of office, to another; and, in the mean time, people have time and opportunity to change their opinion and vote on public matters and questions. Our people, as we have seen in the last few years, *do* change from one policy to another; and we need not think, because one "will" is expressed at one time, that it is to continue to remain so forever. Our populations have sense and intelligence; and we have no fear but, in the "long-run," they will come out right. Our minds may be obscured or deceived for a time, and we may make mistakes in regard to one "policy" or another; but we heartily and sincerely believe that the masses of our loyal population — formerly loyal to the *nation* — are still so in all excepting this one "plan" of Congress, which, if the ideas we have endeavored to elucidate in this volume are at all understood and are well founded, can but have been seen, it appears to us, in all its bearings, as no legitimate "republican" plan for our adoption, but, on the contrary, an innovation, an interpolation of narrow and arbitrary usage, upon our broad system of free and equal rights.

"PEACE" PROPOSALS.

But how can we desert our own representatives, — Congress, — the exponent of the people?

Congress is not *bound* by its plan, though so firmly adopted. It may reconsider it. Other policy and other tone of thought may come into play; and as Congress should but *give expression* to the will of the people, and not be its original instigator or mover, it will, of course, readily and cheerfully adopt whatever the true and genuine will of the people may demand, — even to withdrawing its own policy of reconstruction. Here alone it is, in this sense, that one may and must "bow" to the will of the people. The officers, magistrates, are but the *servants* of the people, to do as it thinks best or may require; and, be it right or wrong, these servants or officers must obey, *if they remain in office.* They can withdraw, — resign, if they so choose, — if they wish not to carry out that will; or, by some persuasive way, they may be able to lead the people to *change* its will. Thus it is that our present Chief Magistrate — although some people have seemed to believe, that, if the present state of affairs continued, he would attempt some *coup d'état* — has not, to our mind, any possible opportunity for such a thing, unless a body of the people themselves initiate a revolution, placing him at the head; but this would be false revolution, and there would be just the same rights in general, it appears to us, on one side as another, since we consider that such revolution can be never justifiable.

For this same reason, neither could Congress persist in its platform, if the will of the people should be declared in opposition; as such persistency would in itself be a *coup d'état*, — taking a position anomalous in our organization. We have no idea whatever that Congress *means* to place itself in any attitude of usurpation, or disloyalty to the nation; and it appears to us that neither of those two portions of the Government — the Executive and the Legislative — nor ourselves — the body of the people — need be anxious as to our parts, but may quietly wait for the determination of the people *at large*. — that of all the States, or the constitutional majority. Whatever that decision be, though it may now be hasty and precipitate, we must peaceably yield for the time, and, if we think it erroneous, make every proper effort to have that decision reversed another time. In the course of this volume, we have made many appeals for our whole country, our *true* country, as we believe it to be. For this present decision that is now about to be made, we will present one more; a summary, as it were, of those that have gone before.

The line is now drawn more distinctly and decidedly than usual between two great divisions of the people. What does this line, this division of the people, indicate? or on what is it actually founded? Principally, as has appeared in the preceding pages, in a difference of opinion as to *method of proceeding* in regard to the Southern, late rebel States, and not so much as to the principles professed by either party. Both divisions undoubtedly desire and intend that the Union shall be finally one, whole and undivided. The Democratic party, which strongly supports the President, are, without question, on the very ground where they have always stood, — for the perpetuity of the Union; and the Republican — even the radical portion of it, if they are true Americans at all, notwithstanding the severity of their language as to the forfeiture of all rights, in the Union, of the late rebel States — must undoubtedly, at heart, desire to see us again a glorious nation, unshorn of any portion or prestige of our noble number of undivided, equal States, or little republics as they are. Without this, that splendid career of a wholly great and free nation to which we had all so ardently looked forward for long years, as *some time* to be our privilege, would be defeated. We might be free from African slavery indeed; but a portion of our own white population, our native-born free American citizens, nearly a third part of our country and States, would be despoiled of the priceless liberty which was bequeathed to us by the blood and sacrifices of our Revolutionary forefathers. We should become in time, in our relations to each other, a part of the nation set up on high, the other trampled to the dust; for whenever such epoch shall have once commenced, by changing our former natural and constitutional relations with one another, — one part controlling another in their vital relations, or functions, no matter in how incipient a degree, — there can be no political guaranty whatever, of avail, against these two divergent extremes. It is the nature of prosperity and success to go on increasing and aggrandizing itself; and it is just as much the nature or tendency of a depressed or despoiled state to go on to a deeper and deeper state of depression and spoliation. It does not answer in public and political affairs to trust to the good feeling or good sense of the populace, the masses. Only *law* is of abiding and effectual influence ; and only a perfect, constitutional *political equality* of the States can preserve for the long future the integrity of every portion of our country, and secure our yet divided sections from falling into these two unequal conditions. We may say also that this alone can preserve the many stars on our nation's flag from becoming, any of them. more or less dim and obscured. No matter how some of them have been extinguished, as it were, for a time : we would have them all now happily restored, glowing forever hereafter in equal lustre ; a glorious picture, and example to the world, of true "liberty, fraternity, equality."

That any honest, honorable-minded man of any party would wish to have our country shorn of this, its noble prestige, we do not believe; and the only question is, or should be, how to recover or regain this happy, primitive, natural state, — which of the two policies now before the country will most rightly and truly insure this. They have both here — that of the President and that of Congress — been fully, and we think fairly, discussed; and this discussion, it is trusted, will afford some aid to our citizens in forming their decision for the present and future welfare of our country.

It is true, party spirit has run high, and misconceptions and misunderstandings have arisen; but we believe they must and will pass away. They ought so to do; for can these States afford to lose the priceless blessings which an undisturbed harmonious government, in all its parts, would now secure to them? — blessings of which we have never yet known the full value, because we have never yet possessed them in their fulness. Mistakes we undoubtedly have made, and shall still make from time to time until the whole and true theory of our institutions shall be by experience developed; but these can never be fatal, if, with an honorable and true candor and sincerity, they are rectified when perceived. We believe that *all* sections have been wrong, more or less; and that all parties, at times, have been more or less under the influence of party passion and excitement. This we can, in a measure, but expect. When great matters and principles are to be wrought out, there will be earnestness, haste, and eagerness, on one side and another; over-stepping in some places, coming short in others.

But we must have patience, — the meek-eyed, heavenly *patience*, — which is the triumpher over every ill; and, as far as possible, peace and quiet. In " QUIETNESS shall be your STRENGTH," says the Book of books.

Above all, it should be remembered that the power of our Government, by the will of the people, does not exist in one branch of it more than in another. Every part belongs to us, — the executive, the legislative, the judicial, the forces of the army and navy; and we are not to take the part of one of these, as especially belonging to us — the exponent of our will — more than another. The legislative is not more for us than the executive, and *vice versâ*. Each is essential in its sphere, but only in its sphere: if one mingles and interferes with another in its functions, but confusion and disorder are introduced.

These are connected, and have their mutual relations; but their organic functions are separate and distinct. Indeed, it seems to us that no system could be more admirably and perfectly arranged and adjusted in all its parts than is ours; and the true question before the people to-day — above all party strife and excitement — is, Shall they change this system, or allow it to be changed, either voluntarily, or by any accidental or informal means?

We suspect, if this were put thus distinctly and openly to our Northern people at this moment, the answer would be this: "We have no idea of changing our Government. It is 'good enough' for us; we never could have a 'better:' in fact, it is the 'best in the world.' But we don't want to have 'rebels' ruling over us." Some would add, "copperheads;" and others, "radicals."

On the main question, we may take it, then, all are agreed. In regard to the "rebels," *ci-devant* rebels, we suspect, if they could get quietly into the Union, into their old places (for, notwithstanding all we have said about their being *in* the Union, we have meant that such was the true theory: they can no doubt be pushed, driven out, excluded, as well as they could have drawn themselves out, *had there been no opposition to this;* and the knot is not yet tied, the clinching nail driven, as we have elsewhere said, until they be in their full, State and Federal, functions and relations), we should hear very little, we suspect, about " wishing to control" one part of the country or another, excepting what was their own natural province. They will surely have enough to do there, it would seem, to occupy them for some time to come. (On this very account, — for their own occupation, — it appears to us, it would be well for the radicals to leave the question of suffrage, &c., to themselves.) The cry that they are coming in, " dictating their own terms," is one of those Quixotic giants — windmills, as we have before spoken of — which always will appear when party spirit runs high. How are they dictating terms, if they come in *precisely* as they *were*, as we all are, — all *equal*, none more, none less? — excepting, indeed, that they have been shorn of some *unequal* rights and privileges which they had; and, if any of these are remaining, — that of increased political influence for example, — it should and ought to be one of the first duties of the restored state of affairs to *equalize* this. On the ground of " equal" rights of the States, there is now no political, and therefore just reason, that this should not be done.

As to "copperheads," as long as they remain such, we trust they will never be received into the partnership of the Government. But we presume their day is past, or fast passing away; as the object for which they became so, the re-union of the States, — being willing to sacrifice all else, even principle, for this, — is accomplished, or being accomplished, in the process of time.

And the "radicals"? The great point of the radicals is that of negro-suffrage. If this is secured, we presume they would be ready to give in to all else; they ought, at least, in all reason; and then the *purely* radical element would be eliminated from among us, or perchance would turn itself to less universally agitating topics. We see no reason, as has been formerly said, why *impartial* suffrage — the *ability* of the negro to vote — should not be carried by Congress; and then let the States have their own voluntary restrictions and qualifications. It is known that the Executive himself is not opposed to the suffrage, *in itself*, of the black man. If such might be a *peace* proposition, it appears to us that all, on one side and another, could and should give in to it, Southerners as well as Northerners. Any thing so simply equable and justifiable as this, it appears to us, might be a means of recon-

ciling the whole country, and re-establishing harmony.
The radicals might still say that such a decree would
secure nothing; that the colored man would still be left
to the exclusion and injustice of the whites. We do not
think so, but that the national franchise, so far, would
remove the prejudice of color; and, probably sooner
than we think, an example practically would be set in
actual suffrage, which would continue to be followed.

POWERS OF THE GOVERNMENT.

We have expressed the impossibility, in our opinion,
of a *coup d'état* taking place in either branch of our
Government; such being, as we conceive it, a sudden
and extraordinary mode of action, or an assumption of
power on one's own authority and responsibility. We
have inferred, therefore, that such would be impossible
in our case, unless all respect to our law and institutions
were abandoned: whereas, in other governments whose
restrictions and limits are not so specifically defined,
such always have at times occurred, and still continue
to occur, — though we may believe that they are much
less frequent, as governments become more constitu-

tional; that is, of a mode more clearly defined and established.

It would be interesting, however, to discuss a little the real powers of our Federal Government, and discover distinctly what these may be, or whether they might be brought into any peculiar use; as undoubtedly there has been occasionally some vague, undefined idea among the people, that something startling may possibly occur in the present situation of affairs.

In regard to military force (and that is all which we intend here to designate), the law of the Constitution is, that Congress has power to raise and support armies (of course, in the service of the nation); to provide for calling forth the militia to execute the laws of the Union, suppress insurrections, and repel invasions; to provide for organizing, arming, and disciplining the militia, and for governing such part of them as may be employed in the service of the United States (this " governing" can only mean a *general* ordering, as the President is made commander of the militia, as well as of other forces, in time of actual war); and that the President shall be commander-in-chief of the army and navy, and of the militia of the several States when called into the actual service of the United States.

Thus we perceive that the control of the military force is equally divided between the two branches of the Government, the legislative and the executive. And we know also, that, in the secession war, it was readily seen what was to be done. The States, by adopting force against the National Government, showed themselves plainly to be in a state of insurrection; and for this there was a plain law laid down in the Constitution: the insurrection was to be quelled; Congress was to provide the forces for this; the Executive was to take the command. Thus, by the two branches unitedly, the war was carried on to its proper and successful termination. But in the present case, where the contest would be between these two branches of the Government themselves (should such a one occur), how could one or the other make use of full military power, without *assuming* what has not been constitutionally granted to it? If Congress, for instance, should raise and equip armies, and appoint its *own* commander-in-chief, this would be direct usurpation of power, and would, of course, be treason against the Constitution and the United States; and should the President attempt to employ military force, even though it were but the regular army and navy (which, of course, are supported by Congress), without the coincident aid of Congress in the "raising and supporting" them, this too, in the same manner, would be treason against the Constitution and the United States.

Such action then, in either case, could but be resolved into a simple *coup d'état*, which, we have just seen, is a power which could not be exercised by either party, without violating or destroying the principles, the laws, of our institutions. It would be simply *revolution* without justifiable cause, as was before said.*

Were there, however, in either of these branches of the Government, openly and plainly, a case of defiant wrong and treason, then, undoubtedly, a common instinct and judgment would come to the rescue, and disclose at once what should be done: for example, should Congress attempt armed force, thus "levying war" in or against, as it were, our own country, undoubtedly the President, as commander-in-chief, might and should quell this disturbance, or insurrection, as well as any other. Or should the President thus institute action, "levying war," on his own account, it seems plain that he might be impeached.

* The subjects of "revolution" and our "right" of it, if such may ever occur, are more fully treated in another volume of this work, — "Light out of Darkness."

But as neither of these is the case, and as no provision has been made in the Constitution, applicable to the present contest, or opposition, of the two branches of the Government, any more than there was for the peculiar doctrine of secession in itself, or for that of reconstruction, — in any other than its simple, natural form, — we can but wait, it appears, for the simple unravelling of *time;* either side, meanwhile, maintaining, if it think proper, its own principles and protest against the other. Congress on its part has submitted the case to the people; and, according to present appearances, the people may decide in *its* favor. It is not necessary, however, that such decision, in this moment of high excitement, should be deemed as of itself correct or unrepealable; and then we could but wait, it seems to us, for a still further " decision " or reconsideration of the subject. Manifestly, the Executive, supposing him to be on the true ground, could do nothing with a strong majority of the people against him, — excepting in the way of *protest,* as was said above, against such decision, or as to the principles implied; and, if he believed these erroneous, he certainly ought to maintain that protest. Besides this, he would have nothing, it seems to us, to do, but to *wait.*

There has been some talk from time to time, in the Congressional party, of impeachment of the Président, on account of his opposition to their "plan;" but we do not perceive how this could be instituted without more plain evidence of treason, or constitutional "misdemeanor." "Investigation," however, might be had, as is now suggested by a member of Congress,* in reference to the course of the President; and as principles are deeply concerned, — the opposition of the President being grounded on a *different view* of our constitutional relations from that adopted by Congress, — it should be, as this member rightly says, not " in heat or in excitement, or from a feeling of disappointment, or from the influence of passion or revenge." If, then, "nothing," as he elsewhere says, "shall be done for party-purposes, nothing with malice, but all in the spirit of justice," the whole country must agree with the honorable representative in these following conclusions: " If upon a proper, and in its nature inquisitorial, but nevertheless in the spirit of a judicial proceeding, it shall be found that this public officer is guilty of any violation of his constitutional duties, then, for one, I should feel that I was false to my

---

* At a radical meeting at Faneuil Hall, Oct. 10, 1866.

trust, to my constituents, to my country, if I hesitated to do what was in my power to cause him to be arraigned, tried, and, if found guilty, condemned. . . . Congress will find it to be its duty to inquire into these proceedings. I interpret the voice of those four great States yesterday* as not only authority, but a command, to the representatives of the people, to inquire into all these things. Justice must be done in all these matters. If the President has performed his duty as he should have performed it, then he is not only acquitted in his conscience, but he will be acquitted by the constituted authorities of the land."

Such a proceeding, fairly and justly conducted, were it either in investigation of the course of the Executive, or of that of Congress (if such were possible), must essentially embrace a thorough discussion of and examination into all the great underlying principles of our Government, and system of States, similar to that which we have patiently gone through with in these pages. So only, we believe, could the course of his Excellency, or that of Congress, be put to the test, and be rightly understood and embraced; and then in the

* The elections of Pennsylvania, Ohio, Indiana, and Iowa.

decision, whatever it might be, the whole country, it appears to us, should cordially and quietly assent.

OUR REPUBLICAN FAITH AND PRINCIPLES.

The following, from the same speech from which we have just quoted, expresses the last issue which we shall notice between the two great parties: —

"The Republican party claim that those men, who, in the field and in the council, organized success, are the men who are to be clothed with the authority to restore the Union to its fair proportions; and that the rebels of the South, and sympathizers with the rebels at the North, shall consent — or, if they will not consent, that they shall be forced — to be excluded from active participation in the Government until the questions at issue between the loyal people and the rebels have been finally adjudged and settled to the satisfaction of the loyal people of the country."

The two prominent points here expressed are precisely those on which the whole discussion and difference between the two great parties turns, — that of restoring our country to its "fair proportions" (whether there can be any "fair proportions" but those of our original relations, and which are still the relations of the other

States); and the *forcing* consent; in other words, adopting arbitrary rule.

Before proceeding further, we wish to clear away one *small* matter, apparently, but which pervades the above extract, as well as almost all discussions on this subject,— the use of the word "rebels." It is an acknowledged fact with one at all familiar with mental operations, that thought itself, and clearness of thought, are intimately associated with and dependent upon the expressions used; so that, if we desire to be accurate in our own perceptions, or commonly correct, we must also be so, as far as possible, in the words which express them. We object, therefore, to the continued use of the term "rebels." Undoubtedly almost our whole general population conceives, from the constant application of this term, that the entire Southern States are about in the same relation towards the Federal Government that they were during the war; whereas, as a political fact, "rebels" no longer exist after their full and final surrender of hostilities: and in all honor, and common brotherhood, and common truth, the term should now be dropped in public and political discussion, as wholly erroneous and misleading. There may be individual "rebels" in spirit still (undoubtedly there are large numbers of them); but, in politics and State affairs, we have only to do with great external questions and issues, and not with individual idiosyncrasies (for, if they retain that spirit after all the public action upon the question, it is certainly an *idiosyncrasy*, and nothing else). There is no question of admitting "rebels" into partnership of the Government. No one, or no party, designs to do any such thing; and if Congress does its duty in testing members elect in its simple, constitutional right, none *can* be admitted there and to a share in legislation.

The only question is, or should be, whether the States shall be re-admitted just as they were before the war, excepting the great and necessary changes which have already and naturally, so to say, taken place; or whether they shall be still subjected to other changes imposed upon them by ourselves, and which implies necessarily a change from our simple, republican system of *equal rights* of the States; since, if they are *in the Union* (and we think we have seen even by mathematical demonstration that they are so), they must be on the *same ground* that they and we all were before the war in all their *organic relations*, or else our system is changed. And we would now put the serious question to our people, whether they are prepared, calmly, coolly, and deliberately, to take this responsibility of change; or whether they prefer to retain our system in its State and Federal relations, as it has been handed down to us from the wisdom and "inspiration" of our fathers, and in its strong (as it is now proved to be), just, equable, and liberal character, as we have heretofore experienced it. We believe, without hesitation, that, in their cooler and better judgment, they would pronounce unhesitatingly for the latter; and that they are only inclined now to adopt the other mode from a *fear* that those, who, by their action, had once almost destroyed the Union, may yet obtain undue influence, and control us again, to our sorrow and detriment, if not destruction.

It is true, we cannot be too cautious and guarded where *principles* are concerned. Secession has been defeated outwardly; but it must also in theory be banished from our midst. And we think that this will just as surely be effected in time as that any other errors become discarded through trial of their falsity. Instead of that, its opposite truth, of the close adherence and intimate union of the States, is advancing, and must advance with time, to its full and firm strength and ascendency. That is the doctrine, we believe, which Providence has destined for us; and therefore it will be in vain for any party or section to endeavor to overthrow it. With the unanimous voice of two-thirds of the Union for this doctrine (unless, indeed, they may now be committed still to a secession, out-of-the-Union theory in another form), one need not fear, it appears to us, the *waning* strength, on their own point, of the other third. If they have not succeeded thus far in the actual attempt, they will never be able to succeed further, we believe, in establishing the idea of secession by discussion or otherwise.

As to other policy, now that slavery is out of the way, what could there be of detrimental that we need fear to meet fully, face to face? Have we not confidence enough in the principles we profess of a true liberty, fraternity, and equality, to feel their *strength*, and to know that these must prevail here with every favorable surrounding (if we do not ourselves obstruct them), over and above all efforts to the contrary? and cannot we deliver ourselves to frank, manly, open argument, without anxiety, let come what opposition there will? Truth of itself is power, and the only real power; and if we have it, although it may have been pressed down and covered over for a time, it will ultimately rise, prevail, and shine forth. It would be but poor praise and commendation of the high and holy principles in which we have been fostered from our birth, if we now distrust their power to aid and strengthen in any battle for the Right.

For all such and similar reasons, we feel that we need not fear the *immediate* admission of the Southern States. They, too, have had their lesson in their time of trial and disturbance, — a lesson which will lead them, as it does all, to "better" things; and — shall we say it? — if they are able now, despoiled as they have been, to obtain the mastery and control over these vast States, it will and must either be from our own weakness of virtue and principle, or that they, in truth, have the right, and therefore *ought* to prevail. Shall we be afraid to meet them, then, on the open, simple ground of *equal opportunity*, with the advantage on our part of a long training in the highest republican principles our country professes, whilst they, in some respects, have to begin at the beginning, as it were?

This timid anxiety and alarm are unworthy of us, but have proceeded, we believe, only from *misapprehension*. Let us, then, be like men, demanding only our fair and equal chance; and, if there be any sectional rivalry or feeling hereafter, may it be in diffusing the broad, republican faith, that all are entitled, our States as well as individuals, to the same and equal share of open, free discussion!

THE "PERIL OF THE HOUR."

Since writing the preceding, and before closing, we have the opportunity of noticing other significant addresses,[*] the title of one of which we have made our present heading. These afford food for thought, and reveal more distinctly still the real perils which actually surround at this moment every true lover of his country, not only in the Northern States, but throughout the entire Union. We do not consider the author of this address as the exact representative of the party now pre-

[*] Delivered in Boston Oct. 18 and Nov. 6, 1866.

vailing in the Northern communities, as few members, we presume, are as yet bold enough to come up to the length of the measures here proposed. Nevertheless, as this distinguished prototype of that party has met with the gratifying success of finding himself in open and public league with the popular heart and sentiment of the radical organization, there can be no guaranty from his well-known influence and eloquence, but that the ideas now broached by him may become diffused to an indefinite and alarming extent. It is proper, therefore, to view them as sentiments of that portion of the people which is now attempting to obtain full control of the Government and of the destinies of the nation, and see where they will lead, that they and we may know the true nature of the ground on which we stand. Or, where they are not fully indorsed by them, we must remember that it is but the first step which costs, — *le premier coup qui coute;* that a thought, once aroused and given utterance to, seldom ceases until it has wrought itself out in some marked, expressive, and effective manner.

We have but the abstract of the speech, reported for the public press; but the few ideas here compressed contain germs of danger sufficient to rouse every genuine republican to the true "perils of the hour," — not those which may lie in the imagined future, or may come from distant States, but those which are at this very moment in the midst of the Northern people, by their very doors, at their own homes and firesides, conceived in the thoughts and expressions of their own fellow-citizens. The speech (or abstract of it) says, —

"He (the speaker) would say to 'The New-York Tribune,' the National-Republican Committee, and Congress itself, Go back, and sit down in the House of Representatives, and govern the Republic; and, for the first act in that government, impeach the President. He would have the House of Representatives impeach the President, place the President of the Senate in his office; and then the people would run the machine. The great trouble of our Government was, that the pivotal man of the Republic can have his policy unchanged for four years."

How long is it, we might ask in passing, since "The New-York Tribune," the National-Republican Committee, or Congress *of itself*, — as all these are severally appealed to, — have been instituted as our "Government"?

We will go on, however, to the measure recommended to the — newly-instituted — government by this "one-man-power;" as, undoubtedly in the same manner that we have had a "one-man-congress," we have in this instance, it appears to us, a one-man-*people*, who himself desires to lay down the law for every one of these more than thirty millions of — formerly — independent freemen who compose our country, as to what they should do or think. The measure recommended, not to these thirty millions, but to "The New-York Tribune," the National-Republican Committee, and to Congress itself (as apparently an independent power), is to impeach the Executive Head of these thirty millions. In the later address (which we do not yet take up), the speaker says, "There are to-day in the North a million and a half of people indorsing the effort of the South to regain power, against two millions opposing that effort." These "two millions," then, represent the political voters of the now successful party in the Northern States. Are the rest of the twenty millions, leaving out the ten or twelve of the South, as they may be supposed to have no President, — the old men and young, the women and children, — to have their legally and constitutionally appointed Chief Magistrate made thus, in the moment of party excitement, the buffet and sport — to be placed or displaced — of these two millions of politicians; or, more properly, by the authority of Congress, — independently, — and of the National-Republican Committee, and of "The New-York Tribune"?

"Startling discoveries" (in party abuse) may indeed be invented to impose upon the public, which "out-Herod Herod;" but it will be unfortunate if any one of these — to be — impeachers of the Executive shall ever so have forgotten the "dignity" of his character as to have conspired with such spirit of slander and low ribaldry; as in that case, probably, the great and best heart of those two millions of "politicians," and the remainder of the twenty millions of the States besides, would consider him unworthy of the office of "judge" on the part of the nation, and he might, therefore, be deposed from that office of impeacher of its President.

But to look at this proposition in a more reflective manner, as it seems now to be distinctly entertained, at least by the most radical members of the party.

Common intelligence would inform us that there could be no just impeachment of a public officer without some overt act having been committed by him; and, as Mr. Johnson has not yet committed that act, an impeachment at present would be direct usurpation of power (since we must presume that the Constitution, in conferring that authority on Congress, never designed the power of arraignment to be employed but on the most plausible at least, if not direct, evidence of culpability). In the present circumstances, therefore, to impeach the President for what he might *in future* do would be following the precise course which the Southern States pursued. For *fear* lest the then elected President (Mr. Lincoln) should do something *unconstitutional*, they themselves committed one of the most unconstitutional acts possible.

Thus to impeach this public functionary, without due warrant of actual crime on his part, would be ourselves committing the very act — treason to the Government — for which he, by anticipation, would be condemned.

Or in another view: The Executive branch in our Government is equal to and co-ordinate with the Legislative; and for the Legislative, without any further call (by some overt act) than at present exists, to denounce the Executive Head, would be usurping authority, and committing itself to a *coup d'état;* thus introducing one of those *false* revolutions (having no justifiable cause) which we have before alluded to. Yet the proposal of this *coup d'état* is now deliberately and publicly made by the foremost man of the party which is at present seeking to control the sentiment of the Northern States.

Again: "His theory, Mr. Phillips said, was that there is no President. He is a deserter. The legislative power is the only power left. . . . He wanted Congress to commence its next session as a perpetual one. Every moment that it was not in session, the South was ruling the Government; and he would have the next Congress enact that they should re-assemble in March, 1867, and be themselves the Government."

Here also is a plain, direct, open proposition, that Congress shall assume the reins of Government, deposing the President, and making itself the dictator of the nation, — this not for crime on the part of the Executive, but because *his* theory and policy are different from ours; and that we cannot wait for the natural, constitutional termination of his now short term, but must summarily end it by our own commission of crime! And this — a greater violation, in idea, of our whole principles and Constitution than ever before appeared in our history — was received from the speaker with applause! Spirit of Republicanism! dost thou not hang thy head for shame? or hast thou but thy shadow left in this our boasted Republic, or in that boasted party of "true freedom," "progress," and "*equal rights*"?

However much it may be Mr. Phillips's *theory* that the President has deserted the chair of state, we certainly have constant and indubitable evidence that he is still the same active, living, official power that he has ever been. As a matter of fact, then, it is against him, in his organic functions, that this proposal is directed. Congress is to depose the Executive branch, and make itself perpetual! If this be not treason, we know not what is, and treason far more perilous than that of secession: because that was but an attempt to withdraw *from* the Government, still leaving it for those who preferred; but this would be an attempt, by usurpation, to revolutionize the very form of our Government itself.

In the later address, the same speaker discloses still further the kind of government which he would have Congress institute for our hitherto broad-principled, free, generous Republic. He says, —

"What do our senators and representatives go to Washington for? To do their duty; to make the governmental machine work." (Is our system a "*machine*," to be turned by the crank, as it were, of any political party?). . . . " One man made New Orleans safe to live in. Could not Congress make the South so? You have but to extend New Orleans until it covers ten States, and the problem is solved. Cannot Congress take example from one of their successful agents? There is no secret about the problem. . . . If the white men at the South have their lives spared, then the Government must hold that territory by the iron arm of military despotism for some years to come. Just exactly as Butler governed New Orleans is the South to be governed in the next five or seven years. Hang a traitor as an example, and keep the rest in order by the example."

And *why* should we adopt this rule?

Because, as the speaker averred, " the nation was now endeavoring to establish a system at variance with the laws of God;" that is, it has not given (yet, though, as soon as it can have a breathing moment for the purpose after its great perturbations, it may give) the negro the right to vote. We grant that the nation ought to care for the best good of the negro, as well as for that of the rest of its citizens; but, for this, must we necessarily despoil and destroy that blessed, magnificent Constitution, which the same God, in his divine providence, gave us? and must we falsify the word of the nation, casting it away as it were an unholy thing, and forget, abolish, and abandon all those eternal principles of political fraternity, liberty, and *equality*, with which we, as a people, were so gloriously born and brought up?

We cannot believe that God requires us, in order to obtain one good, to destroy all others. Unison and harmony with his " laws " cannot demand of us to violate any of those which are the very principles of his nature. On the contrary, we believe that this " iron rule of military despotism " has belonged only to those ages and histories of the world which have denied God in his best attributes; which knew not the loving-kindness of the All-Father, who is kind even to the unthankful and the evil, and who sendeth rain upon the just and on the unjust.

It is a violent transition; but we must refer to the gentleman alluded to, who carried out the same sentiments in a recent speech, while addressing a crowd which was noisily, it must be said, — rudely, — opposing itself to him. " If there was any thing," said the speaker, " that could be argued in favor of a despotism, and against the rule of the minority by the majority, it was such a scene as that before him. It would take but a few demonstrations of a like character to make the *Republican party* become *disgusted* with the *free elective franchise.*"

So, because the mob (in this very free country) will at times, when it is not disposed to listen to an out-and-out radical citizen, burst all bounds of civil decorum and restraint, the commonalty, that which makes the warp and woof, the strength and sinew, of a country, may expect, after a few more such exhibitions of freedom, to be deprived of its " free, elective franchise."

Upon whom the *Radical*, we will not say " Republican party," may see fit to bestow it, does not yet appear; though formerly the name " Radical " was supposed to be a synonyme with the greatest and most entire freedom of action as well as speech : why not, then, for the crowd to express their sentiments in their way, since they cannot stand upon a platform and make a polished speech? " Poor fools ! " (to use the expression of the speaker,) they will stand but a small chance, we fear, in that iron rule of despotism which is to be established. " I have faced your superiors in Baltimore and New Orleans ! " continued he. " I have hung your betters ! If you do not behave yourselves, I shall have the pleasure of seeing you hung!" "What!" we may hear it exclaimed, "is that rule to be established here — in New York — and our cities of the North, as well as at the South?" Of course: otherwise we shall not be a country of *equal* blessings, privileges, and rights. What is established in one part of the country, whatever of Federal authority, must be so in all or every part, or we shall be inconsistent with our fundamental doctrine of *equality*, and for which we went to war, and fought almost to the very death.

The first act of this change of government (to the rule of "despotism," as the radical speaker himself called it), or rather the second act, — since we conceive, as will have been seen by all that has gone before, that the post-Constitutional Amendment was the first, — the second act of this change is, undoubtedly, to be the imposing and impressive scene of the impeachment of our highest functionary of State. As the gentleman referred to, having (it is presumed) high legal abilities, has already a long list of articles, or counts, elaborately and minutely drawn up for that purpose (see papers of the day *), he will, undoubtedly, be on the bench

---

* The "indictment" which goes by his name appears to have been written out by another person, although taken down from the speeches, and submitted to the correction, of Gen. Butler himself.

with his compeers in that proceeding. We rather regret this, however, for fear that *exact* justice may not be done. (But why should we look for "justice" in the reign of *despotism?* We cannot help feeling, however, that there may be a little *show* at least of justice left in our country, even when that reign shall have become quite inaugurated by this ceremony.) We have reason for fear, since this gentleman is known not always to have discriminated between what is due to a just *freedom of opinion* and to overt guilt; as in the memorable instance of the clergyman who was sentenced to the galleys for maintaining the *same ideas*, in their essential features (and with a heroism worthy of a *truer* faith, as we believe it, and, we must say, of a less ignoble penalty), that were maintained, as was seen in the first half of this work, by a clergyman of the party of the most "advanced thought" of the country, even in enlightened New England itself.*

* The proceeding referred to occurred early in 1864, during the military rule of the gentleman at Fortress Monroe. The whole examination, the questions and answers of which were given in the papers at the time, show the entire "inquisitorial" nature of it, and that the condemnation was peculiarly on account of the *belief* in secession. This was the impression produced; but, the documents not being now accessible, if the statement is erroneous in any particular, the author would be most happy to see it corrected.

In returning to the former speaker, we have but little more to say of him, and the subject, the "peril of the hour;" but that little, we believe, is important.

This orator is very fond of denouncing others as traitors; and not content with the old expression, "We have a traitor in the White House, who calls himself an humble individual," (it would be excellently well for our country, it appears to us, had we many "humble" individuals!) he now, in this address, adopts a new one, and takes up the present idol of the people, initiating against him the same denunciatory cry;* which is, no doubt (if Mr. Phillips should continue to prevail in the counsels of the people), but an opening to the same fiery crucible into which his contemporaries and fellow-patriots have already passed,— with no more reason, to our apprehension, in the one case than in the other. And this, we believe, will be the future verdict of the American people.

"Ah! but Mr. Phillips is peculiar; he is an exceptional person; we must not mind what he says and

---

* The expression in the report is, "If he [Gen. Grant] does not want to do his duty, then denounce him as a traitor." Is Mr. Wendell Phillips to be the umpire of what is the "duty" of all the different officers and departments of our Government?

does," say some: "his opinion and influence are of no weight whatever."

On this plea, he has long passed scathless; but, as he is now in open and public affiliation with the successful party of the country, it should be no longer of avail. And the true and most important question for our Northern States to-day is, Are they going, in their sober sense, to submit to such leadership, such influence, such dictation? Do they consider it *safe?* Or, with all the weight and responsibility upon them of a hitherto genuine Republic to preserve, not only for themselves and their children, but for the good of the world at large, will they now go weakly and basely, in such manner, to yield to its betrayal?

Rather will they not rise in their majesty, and declare *what* is the "treason," and *where* is the "traitor," and awake, and see for themselves the true "peril of the hour,"—that the real traitor and his uttered treason are now in their very midst?

THE RIGHT OF PETITION.

The great elections have taken place; and the verdict of the Northern people, in the popular understanding, has been given, as was anticipated from the peculiar situation of parties, for the "Constitutional Amendment." Whether this has been a correct verdict, or whether the true and exact issues have been embraced by the public mind, is another question, and which time will answer. In the mean time, what are those to do who do not believe in the Constitutional Amendment; that is, as a condition precedent to the admission of the Southern States? Of these, thousands, tens and hundreds of thousands, no doubt, of former genuine Republicans, have voted on the present popular *Radical* platform, because they knew not what else to do, or felt a necessity of going with their party (as was of late strongly argued by a popular speaker*), or because *everybody else* seemed to be going that way, and therefore they fell in with the tide.

Are they willing, however, to submit to the essential change which the final and permanent adoption of this platform must inevitably bring in all our institutions? We do not believe it. If they were ever simple, genuine, constitutional Republicans, we believe that, *at heart*, they are so still, and must deprecate any such change. The

* On "The Issues of the Hour," Brooklyn. Oct. 15, 1866.

matter, for the present, as far as votes can go, has been *constitutionally* decided. They cannot go to war against this decision — as we have elsewhere upheld — for the maintenance of *their* theory of the Constitution, even with the most entire belief of its being the true one. But are they to sit down, and be able to do nothing to preserve their country from an informal and insidious alteration of its system of government? When that is to be done, it should be with the plain and direct issue placed before the public. The late balloting was not such in its open bearings. We believe there were far other and different issues embraced in the popular mind; that, to the common apprehension, it was virtually an indorsement and a renewed expression of the sentiment which roused the whole Northern people at the commencement of the war, — that nothing but *loyalty to the nation* was to be tolerated. With this, every true patriot must agree; and we believe that the Southerners themselves will now cordially fall in with the *propriety* of such verdict. So far as it is *such* a decision, therefore, it is well. Henceforth, on *that* issue, there should be but one party, North or South.

But the more direct issue of the adoption of the Constitutional Amendment — which adoption, as appears from all the examination we have been able to make in these pages, would be but a yielding (undoubtedly to many, if not to most minds, an *unconscious* yielding) to the insidious change we have spoken of — is yet to take place in the more calm, deliberate action, or what should so be, of the constitutional assemblies. There, even the minority can use all proper influence in respect to such decision; or if they have no place, voice, or influence in legislation, they have the *right of petition.*

This, and not a resort to arms, we believe, is the true power to be made use of in such cases, as was said in the earlier part of these pages. A minority may wait patiently for other opportunities, but, in the mean time, can be exerting itself in this constitutional manner. The right of petition is an acknowledged one, and is a power which may be wielded not only by politicians, but by the entire masses of a nation, — men, women, and youth (of discretionary age). Thus used, it may be a power more potent than the ballot itself. It was by this that England secured the abolition of the slave-trade; and the use heretofore, however limited, of this right and power, in our own history, has always stirred the public consciousness to its depths.

Whoever desires to enter his protest against the passing of the amendment in the State Legislatures, or its final seal and ratification by Congress, has this method of appeal, — the right of petition; and, even if ineffectual, it would stand permanently on the records of the country, for future use, if necessary. The Southerners themselves, although debarred from national legislation, have this power of petition, which is the right of even the guiltiest, if so be, and most unfortunate of individuals or of peoples. *This* is not derogatory. It has been employed in the highest of causes, and is simply a constitutional right, because a *natural* one, and is alone consistent with our republican professions.

Members of *all* parties and sections, if they desire to meet *this* issue of the Constitutional Amendment, — that is, to protest against it for its unconstitutional form, which, it appears to us, has been plainly proved as a condition of the admission of the Southern States, — have thus, if they please, a simple platform on which to stand; so forming a *really* national party (which seems hitherto in vain to have been attempted); and might make, it seems to us, the *true* voice of the country, upon this point, to be heard as powerfully as in the balloting which has just taken place. In this manner could the best heart of the nation be brought into play, instead of its finer instincts and deep yearnings for renewed peace and union, happiness and prosperity, being smothered, and its destinies held principally at the sway and mercy of political leaders and rulers.

May such — by petition, if in no other manner * — be the next great, overwhelming verdict of the popular voice, and of the generous *national* mind and heart! Even *conquerors* can yield gracefully to prayer and entreaty.

THE CITIZEN-PRESIDENT.

We have but one more point on which to touch. There have been much public passion and obloquy displayed. Perhaps the spirit of party never ran so high (unless in the days of secession) as now. But we have to remember how much most of this is due to mere party excitement and rancor; and the very instance explained by the senator from Massachusetts, in his late speech (which we copied), shows what is due to misprint, misrepresentation. If we could fathom to the bottom all such instances, we should probably find a

* We know not why petitions to Congress, by the thousands and millions of names, should not be poured in for the direct admission of the Southern States.

very different state of things from what appears on the surface. Then, instead of being wounded, outraged, and indignant, we might often be called to change our feelings to those of commendation, sympathy, and praise.

The late presidential tour called forth in many quarters much animadversion and censure, not only for "indecorums," as they were considered, of the occasion, but from the fact itself, apparently, of the Chief Magistrate of the nation continually addressing the people on public questions. A late speaker even went so far as to say that the American people were made "to bow their heads in shame and sorrow." We do not, certainly, design to justify or excuse any personal discourtesy on one side or the other (though, unhesitatingly, much that was so pronounced upon was but the result of misconstruction and perversion); but there seems to us a misapprehension.

We know not how it may appear to others, but to our mind there is no more beautiful or noble feature of our institutions than that of the *citizen-President;* that our highest officer can lay aside the "dignity" of his high office, and come face to face with the people, and be in the crowd with them, — a *citizen*. What crowned head in Europe has so noble opportunity of knowing those whom he governs? of being able, by the quick electricity of voice and speech, and as man to man, to discover their thoughts, their opinions, their feelings? and of impressing also, in the same living manner, his own ideas of the aims and views to be brought about? This must be a privilege which we should suppose every true ruler in the world would wish to possess; and must be especially prized by one in the position of chief ruler here, where topics of vital interest so often come upon the scene.

No qualification was more general, and we might say essential, in the magistracy of the ancient Roman, the model republic, than that of eloquence, — the power of addressing the people; and none was made more constant use of, as long as Rome continued to be free. With us it is not so essential, as intelligence is more commonly and readily diffused. But, in this crisis of our country's fate, — for it is a crisis, however calmly we may have treated it, — the most serious principles are to be decided, which may bear their fruit for all time to come. In such a crisis, it appears to us that our

Chief Executive has shown himself but the example and precedent of what the genuine citizen-President should be, — a WORKING man; that his office is no cynosure for his own pleasure, ease, and self-indulgence, but one for laboring in devotion to his country. And it appears to us that it should be but with pride and honor that we should behold him now not only as able so to do, but as throwing himself into the breach, as he considers it; not in the cabinet alone, but in the forum, although it be but one of the wayside and stopping-places of a public journey; and that there, with a noble simplicity (because elevated by the greatness of the cause) and with a generous self-forgetfulness, spending and being spent, in season and out of season, through good report and evil report, he has never been weary, or ceased to reiterate, though it were for the thousandth time, this true, or what should be the true, American sentiment: * —

"Let the Constitution be our guide and platform. This is our league. It is not one of the leagues extending over the country for revolutionary purposes. It is unnecessary to form other leagues for the preservation of this Government. It is unnecessary to have any other or higher

---

* Spoken at Indianapolis, Sept. 10. The sentences were frequently interrupted and broken by the cheering and applauses of the crowd.

league than the Constitution of the United States. I want no higher constitutional league than that was. The Constitution is my league: I belong to the constitutional league of my country. I had hoped the time had come when we all could rally round the Constitution, and lift ourselves above party, to preserve our country one and united. Fellow-citizens, . . . I do now proclaim that none of the States have a right to go out of the Union. Though they may revolt or rebel, they have no constitutional right to go out of the Union. Whether this doctrine is assailed South or North, I plant my feet firmly against it. I come here to-day with the flag of my country, containing thirty-six stars, with the Union of the States unbroken; I come with the Constitution of the United States; and I place them in your hands, where, I believe, they will be protected and defended."

Shall they so be? We believe they — eventually — will.

It will have been seen throughout this book, that the author has taken no party stand, *as* such: the only desire has been to ascertain, as far as possible, what may be the real truth, and so to be a means to assist and facilitate the conciliation and harmony of all parties and sections of our vast country. With this purpose of pouring "oil upon the troubled waters" (though this may appear sometimes to have failed), what can be so suitable with which to conclude as these words of Holy Writ? —

"Wherefore, putting away lying, speak every man truth with his neighbor; for we are members one of another. Be ye angry, and sin not: let not the sun go down upon your wrath. . . . Let all bitterness and wrath and anger and clamor and evil-speaking be put away from you, with all malice; and be ye kind one to another, tender-hearted, forgiving one another, even as God for Christ's sake hath forgiven you."

THE END.

From the Cornhill Press of Geo. C. Rand & Avery.

Deacidified using the Bookkeeper proc
Neutralizing Agent: Magnesium Oxide
Treatment Date: OCT 199

PRESERVATION TECHNOLOGIES,
111 Thomson Park Drive
Cranberry Twp., PA 16066
(412) 779-2111

LIBRARY OF CONGRESS

0 012 026 619 6

www.ingramcontent.com/pod-product-compliance
Lightning Source LLC
Chambersburg PA
CBHW022148300426
44115CB00006B/394